THE DEMONIC IMAGINATION

THE DEMONIC
IMAGINATION

Style and Theme in French Romantic Poetry

JOHN PORTER HOUSTON

Louisiana State University Press   BATON ROUGE

Copyright © 1969 by
LOUISIANA STATE UNIVERSITY PRESS
Library of Congress Catalog Card Number 69–15051
Manufactured in the United States of America
by THOS. J. MORAN'S SONS, INC.

CARISSIMAE UXORI
Je t'apporte l'enfant d'une nuit d'Idumée!

PREFACE

Most accounts of French literature from 1800 to 1860 center on its emotive content. Taking over from Chateaubriand and Musset, critics have tended to define French romanticism as a state of mind compounded of melancholy, nostalgia, and impatience with established institutions, Rousseau being its creator. This has led to some strange predicaments. For example, when scholars began to investigate eighteenth-century literature in detail, they found that much of it resembles in sensibility and ideas that of the early nineteenth century. Daniel Mornet declared that "almost everything the romantics believed to have originated had already been discovered in the eighteenth century." [1] Thus the word "pre-romanticism" was coined—one of the strangest terms in literary history, since it implies that the eighteenth and nineteenth centuries were the same but different. It is quite possible that sensibility did not greatly alter between the two centuries, but literature is something more than feeling.

It has also been customary to discuss French romanticism in a sociological manner since the movement coincided with a series of upheavals in French politics and manners. Ferdinand Brunetière announced that it was a social phenomenon with "individualism" at its roots,[2] but a reading of Tallemant or Saint-Simon might convince one that the seventeenth century was unequalled in personal eccentricity; care must be taken not to identify imaginative literature with life completely. However, in one form or another, Brunetière's view persisted for decades, and in the early twentieth century, discussions of romanticism largely turned into Rightist vituperations against the revolutionary mentality and the decline of

[1] Daniel Mornet, *La Pensée française au dix-huitième siècle* (Paris, 1947), 73.
[2] Ferdinand Brunetière, *Evolution de la poésie lyrique en France au dix-neuvième siècle* (Paris, 1895), I, 178.

France. These polemics obscured the fact that while romanticism can, if one wishes, be described as a social movement, the word designated primarily a literary one.

It seems to me that too exclusive a preoccupation with literature as a social phenomenon has obscured the esthetic importance of French romanticism and has encouraged the mistaken notion that its interest as art is secondary. Even Maurice Souriau, who, in 1927, after the great period of polemics against romanticism, attempted to sum up and dismiss them as extra-literary preoccupations, could not say anything more enlightening about early nineteenth-century literature than that it was the opposite of classicism,[3] a notion that hardly takes us very far into the complexities of this period. Movements in French poetry between 1800 and 1860 have especially been neglected, and one may legitimately doubt that many critics in France or elsewhere realize their significance. Nothing of any scope has been written on the subject in France for a good many years, and, as nearly as I can ascertain, there has never been in English a broad treatment of French romantic poetry. In fact, Anglo-Saxon insularity seems, in this matter, to have been almost complete, although not without justification. Those Americans who have been exposed to French romantic verse in the course of their schooling probably feel it to consist, by and large, of insipid Victorian pieces, unworthy of much attention; if one glances through anthologies, the dominant impression is of old-fashioned themes and styles, for anthologists of French verse seldom attempt to make their choices according to the canons of modern taste. Small wonder, then, that in this age of renewed studies in romanticism, French poets of the early and mid-nineteenth century receive little acclaim except, of course, for Baudelaire and Nerval, whose production is so compact as to be easily digested.

Our initial task in this volume has been to sift through the huge poetic production of the first decades of the nineteenth century and to determine what in it seems valuable by present-day standards. (Of course, it has been necessary to omit detailed discussion of works in prose, even, regretfully, prose-poems.) Next, we analyze the dominant characteristics of French romantic verse, its presiding themes and symbols. While keeping in mind recent attempts to give a coherent description of romanticism,[4] in the following chapters I have chosen to focus on certain kinds of

[3]See Maurice Souriau, *Histoire du romantisme en France* (Paris, 1927), I, liii.
[4]An especially important attempt, along with a critical survey of others, can be found in René Wellek, *Concepts of Criticism* (New Haven, 1963), 128–221.

symbolism and thematic content, which, if they do not give a total account of French romantic poetry, seem in any case to be a striking feature of it. There is an obvious *parti-pris* in this study. Countless works on French romanticism have emphasized the ideas of pantheism and social progress, which indeed play a noticeable role in the thought of the period. I have not, however, chosen to stress demonic symbolism in order merely to contradict my predecessors: it seems to me, in most of the important poets at least, that a preoccupation with the theology of evil far surpasses any "romantic optimism" on their part. In the case of two poets, Hugo and Vigny, there is an elusive dialectic of optimism and pessimism in which the latter seems ultimately to prevail, at least in regard to the height of poetic expression it receives. Demonic symbolism essentially constitutes an attempt to express the intuition that God or nature is an evil force, whose victim is mankind.[5] There are, as we shall see, various patterns of thought which inspire demonic themes, and they do not exclude the parallel conception of a benevolent deity. Above all, the romantic preoccupation with the sinister must not be confused with the Satanism or worship of evil described by Huysmans in *Là-bas*. On the contrary, the demonic themes of romantic verse reflect the fear that no proper object of worship exists or that true godhead has been eclipsed.

The demonic imagination especially deserves inquiry in regard to French literature, for it probably held greater sway in nineteenth-century France than elsewhere. Exceptions like Coleridge, Poe, Melville, or Novalis come to mind, but other literatures show other characteristic preoccupations. Hellenic themes, for example, inform some of the greatest nineteenth-century German and English poetry, but in France they are more the concern of minor poets. Why French writers should have been so richly inspired by the forces of darkness cannot, of course, be readily determined; various speculations suggest themselves, but they are probably idle.

In the course of our inquiry we examine the increase and nature of demonic themes against the larger background of the evolution of prosody and poetic language from the end of the eighteenth century to the 1850's. In this way we shall not artificially separate themes from the poetic forms which support them. Symbols are difficult to discuss outside the general context of imagery, while considerations of imagery lead to the problem

---

[5]For a more general theory of the demonic in literature see Northrop Frye, *Anatomy of Criticism* (Princeton, 1957), 147–50.

of poetic diction. And even versification is relevant to the shape and patterns of romantic poetry. It cannot always be shown, of course, that theme and prosody correspond; indeed, there are cases such as Vigny's poems where versification (and metaphor) lag behind thematic inventiveness. However, this gap itself deserves some attention. Therefore, in order for the reader better to understand the background of romantic poetry, Chapter I deals not at all with demonic themes but with the poetic materials inherited by the romantics from the eighteenth century—a matter which has seen few serious attempts to understand it. Likewise, Chapter II is only a prelude to our main subject in that it traces the conflict between neoclassical and "modern" diction in the work of Hugo and Musset from 1820 to 1850. With Chapter III the study of the demonic proper begins: here we examine the development of the *genre romantique* as well as the mood and images characteristic of several minor poets—Sainte-Beuve, Gautier, Philothée O'Neddy, and Petrus Borel. The later chapters are concerned with the principal romantic poets, their verse forms, their dominant symbols, and the patterns of thought and feeling which determine their particular use of demonic themes. While Vigny, Baudelaire, Nerval, and Hugo are very different poets, I think it will be possible to demonstrate an essential relation between theological preoccupations and certain types of imagery they share.

The concept of literary history, once maligned by those who insisted on the importance of close reading, has been changing in recent years to the point that now we may conceive of a new way of examining literature in chronological perspective: this method centers on textual analysis, the filiation of genres and styles, while social, psychological, and philosophical influences on individual writers are peripheral, if indispensable. Obviously, this approach to literary history is in theory unwieldy by its vastness, but it comes closer, I feel, to tracing the actual conditions of literary creation than does any previous method. No one has yet, to my knowledge, produced a broad study of a period of literature which actually takes adequate account of the work of art both in itself and as a product of historical factors, but the ideal is there and is one toward which we should work.

This study is offered as a modest sketch of what a truly art-focused history of French romantic poetry might be like. Its scope is primarily esthetic; its main concern, the development of styles in a chronological perspective. Certain considerations about the poet's place in society will arise, for it is impossible to ignore the problem of his audience, but they are subordinated to matters of language: ideally perhaps, we should be able to infer the sociology of literature from the analysis of style. No technical history of French verse exists as yet, and, although the present book cannot pretend to be exhaustive, it will, I hope, suggest useful ways of looking at romantic poetry.

The degree of emphasis placed on individual writers is determined necessarily by our guiding theme; however, in certain instances I have tried, by the choice of passages discussed, to make a kind of anthology of fine but generally unknown romantic verse. Whereas the work of Vigny, Baudelaire, and Nerval is largely familiar, poets like Gautier, Petrus Borel, or Hugo are but little or partially read. The case of Hugo demands particular comment: few people know more than a small fraction of his immense poetic output, and the pieces they are familiar with tend to be the anodyne sort of thing judged suitable for school recitation. However, there is an immense amount of verse by Hugo which, in tone and style, appeals more to the twentieth century than to his own; this is especially true of the posthumous *Dieu* and *La Fin de Satan*. These are, at least in part, really modern poems discovered and appreciated only in the last few decades.

Since there are few textual problems which arise in connection with French romantic poetry and since a number of good editions exist for most of the poets, I mention here only a few important sources for texts: *Feu et flamme* by Philothée O'Neddy (Théophile Dondey) was properly edited by Marcel Hervier (Paris, 1926); the only serious modern edition of Gautier's *Poésies complètes* is that of René Jasinski (Paris, 1932); and Sainte-Beuve's *Vie, Poésies et Pensées de Joseph Delorme* has finally been carefully edited by Gérald Antoine (Paris, 1957). The editorial problems concerning Hugo's *Dieu* are discussed in their place. All translations of French into English which appear in this volume are the author's.

CONTENTS

THE DEMONIC IMAGINATION

I

THE WANING OF NEOCLASSICISM

The French romantic poets wished, by and large, to be considered revolutionaries, at least in literary matters. In a sense they invented the concept of modernity which informed the arts in nineteenth-century France, although the term *modernisme* became common only toward the end of the century.[1] One of the characteristics of modernists and revolutionaries is to claim to represent a new beginning and to deny any origins in the past. Since it was also a romantic convention for the poet to stress the personal character of his genius, the French poets of the 1830's succeeded in convincing the public that their art had come suddenly into being without the mediation of any poetic tradition.[2] No view could be more congenial to the nineteenth-century mind, with its fondness for attributing events and things to the afflatus of the inspired. The romantics succeeded so well in diffusing their attitudes, in confounding their enemies, and in discrediting their immediate predecessors that the usual conceptions of French literary history are still distorted by their polemics. In particular, their scorn for the eighteenth-century and Empire poets banished them from much serious consideration, and witticisms like "poésie sans poésie" were substituted for any real investigation of the subject. Yet without some acquaintance with the late neoclassical poets it is impossible to understand the peculiar development of French romanticism.

The main fact about the history of French poetry which romantic attacks on the *classiques* managed to obliterate was the great poetic revi-

[1]But Wilhem Ténint, Hugo's pupil in versification, entitled his treatise *Prosodie de l'école moderne* (Paris, 1844), and Baudelaire spoke of things "modern" in the 1840's and 1850's.

[2]See A. Richard Oliver, *Charles Nodier: Pilot of Romanticism* (Syracuse, 1964), 145–88.

val of the late eighteenth century. Far from being one uniform wasteland, the development of non-dramatic French verse between 1660 and
1820 is a varied matter and includes styles of different quality. To begin
with, it appears that after the great flowering of baroque poetry in
France, less and less lyric verse was written. The "Discours prélimi-
naire" to Delille's translation of the *Georgics* (1770), an extremely lucid
essay on the contemporary situation of French poetry, remarks that
"our authors" have an exclusive passion for verse-drama and an "unjust
disdain" for any other genre. "The English," he notes, "more reason-
able than ourselves, encourage all poetic genres; hence they have pleas-
ing poems on all kinds of subjects and an infinitely more varied literature
than our own," while "our language, confined to [tragedy and comedy],
has remained timid and poverty-stricken." [3] Aside from minor genres
such as the epistle and epigram, France had no sustained tradition of
non-dramatic verse. The eighteenth-century feeling for linguistic purity
was so offended by what seemed the exuberance and archaism of the
great renaissance and baroque poets, that they could in no way serve as
models. Thus French literature was deprived of the continuity of lyric
and epic inspiration which we find in eighteenth-century England, where
imitations of Spenser and Milton lead from the beginning of the century
right up to the romantics. But despite the lack of a native vein of serious
non-dramatic poetry, Delille felt that somehow, by translation, French
verse could be invigorated and nourished, and he presents his rendering
of the *Georgics* toward this end.[4] Although it would be rash to affirm
that Delille's efforts, by themselves, had any decisive effect, it is nevertheless certain that by the end of the eighteenth century there was more
well-received poetry in more genres and that the public was better prepared to absorb the gigantic poetic production of the nineteenth century.
But before examining French verse on the eve of romanticism, we must
first trace certain earlier developments within the neoclassical tradition.

The influence of neoclassicism on French has no parallel among the
other major European languages, for only French received its definitive
modern form under that impact. The spirit of neoclassicism tended to
be selective and eliminatory, and its effect on the French language is
most noticeable in regard to vocabulary. The intense dislike of neologisms, archaisms, and even Latinisms, which French writers came to feel,

[3]Jacques Delille, *Oeuvres* (Paris, 1824), II, xv, xvi.
[4]*Ibid.*, xxxviii.

is one of the most curious phenomena to be found in the history of literature. Nor was the neoclassical impetus spent by the end of the seventeenth century; its demise lies closer to 1850. Contrary to what one might expect, the principal romantic poets claimed to be narrow, almost academic purists in linguistic matters, and therefore we cannot point to a sudden theoretical break with neoclassical conceptions of style. However, we can better understand the romantics' point of departure, if we examine those changes which neoclassicism itself had undergone after the Age of Louis XIV.

For most people, French neoclassical verse means the plays of Racine and Corneille, and the obvious characteristics of their diction are familiar: a circumscribed and abstract vocabulary, the coincidence of sentence forms with the alexandrine distich, and subdued imagery. But although Racine's influence was to be pervasive, the neoclassical dramatic styles are far less important for the development of other poetic genres than one might imagine. The reason for this is that neoclassicism established a close relation between style and genre, a much closer one than we can readily feel today, and that only isolated devices of the playwrights were relevant to the conventions of other poetic forms. One has only to compare Racine's lyric poetry with his plays to see how separate the genres remain: his occasional lyric pieces were written throughout his career, and yet they seem to reflect none of the progressive exploration of style which we can trace from *Andromaque* through *Bérénice* to *Phèdre* and *Athalie*. The lyrics simply belong to another kind of writing with its own conventions.

Since we had best ignore Racine *fils*, the poet with whom to begin an account of eighteenth-century poetry would seem to be Jean-Baptiste Rousseau (1671–1741), one of those men who seem vaguely presumptuous because of the existence of a more famous homonym. It would be a mistake, however, to take too lightly the role that Rousseau played in the development of French poetry: although they may not have admitted it, more than one nineteenth-century poet owed a great deal to Rousseau, for, from Hugo to Verlaine, they studied him in school as a model for writing French verse.[5] Through the Second Empire it was customary to place on the official *lycée* and *collège* reading program only writers of

[5]See Gérard Venzac, *Les Premiers Maîtres de Victor Hugo* (Paris, 1955), 333–35; Georges Zayed, *La Formation littéraire de Verlaine* (Paris, 1962), 24; and Henry A. Grubbs, "The Vogue of Jean-Baptiste Rousseau," *PMLA*, LV (March, 1940), 139–66.

the seventeenth and eighteenth centuries;[6] of these, Jean-Baptiste Rousseau served most conveniently as a model for the various French lyric forms, which were the object of an exercise like Latin verse composition. In fact, the definitive modern study of French stanzaic forms praises him for his prosodic skill.[7]

The four books of Rousseau's *Odes*, his most famous work, are conceived in the Malherbean tradition of strophic cohesion and ornamented style: the point of departure is frequently a commonplace, following classical tradition, which is then developed in often lengthy stanzas. A major source of themes and images is Psalms, ("no work so merits the title of Odes . . ." [8]), and it is curious to see how different the impact of biblical style was in French from its influence on English poetry: the solemnity of tone remains, but little of the crabbed, obscure imagery passes through the Vulgate into French; instead a flood of "noble" terms provides stylistic problems of a different nature. Here is a stanza from an Ode based on the proposition that hypocrisy is bad, and "drawn" from Psalm 58 in the King James numbering:

> L'hypocrite, en fraudes fertile,
> Dès l'enfance est pétri de fard :
> Il sait colorer avec art
> Le fiel que sa bouche distille,
> Et la morsure du serpent
> Est moins aigüe et moins subtile
> Que le venin caché que sa langue répand.
> (Book I, Ode IV)

A typically biblical image is eliminated: "they are like the deaf adder that stoppeth her ear," *sicut aspidis surdae et obturantis aures suas.* The specific snake becomes merely a general one, which serves the purpose of introducing a relatively lengthy simile, for the elaborate comparison was considered a distinguishing property of the ode and the epic.[9] On the other hand, the imagery which is added to the biblical text is significant: it provides a perfect example of the "ritual imagery" [10] of neoclassicism. "Pétri de fard" must be understood as a translation into noble terms of some such expression as "full of deceit." While *pétri* and

---

[6]In *Rhétorique* the teacher was free to introduce whatever he thought fitting.

[7]See Philippe Martinon, *Les Strophes* (Paris, 1911), 66.

[8]Jean-Baptiste Rousseau, *Oeuvres* (Paris, 1824) I, xxx.

[9]See Emmanuel Barat, *Le Style poétique et la révolution romantique* (Paris, 1904), 17.

[10]René Wellek and Austin Warren, *Theory of Literature* (New York, 1956), 186.

fard were both used metaphorically, this juxtaposition reminds one of the literal sense of both words, which is not felt, however, to be objectionable. Nor is the poet hindered by the fact that the literal meaning of *pétri* (kneaded) suggests a far from noble activity. The neoclassical sensibility characteristically refused to take notice of the interplay between literal and figurative meanings; our whole sense of "imagery" was not shared by eighteenth-century French poets,[11] and properly speaking we should not use that notion in regard to their verse. Metonymy is the correct word for the process at work here. Each idea is expressed by a term which must be judged for its own metaphoric elegance, rather than understood in a context of imagery. Thus the hypocrite can "cleverly color bile" which comes out of his own mouth. This conception of ornamented language could lead to rather strange effects at times. It has been observed that in a line like "La toile est animée et le marbre respire," *toile* (canvas) means picture and *marbre* (marble) designates a statue; however, if the poet had really wanted to speak of canvas or marble, he would not have used those words but would have said *tissu* and *albâtre*.[12] The end point of this process was inevitably the compilation of treatises in which the "noble" equivalents for words were given,[13] and inevitably purists found that Racine himself had lapsed occasionally into *la bassesse*.[14] An eminent historian of the French language has summed up the neoclassical state of mind as a "horror of the *mot juste*." [15]

Despite criticism, the "ornate language" of the ode, with its penchant for metonymy and periphrasis was never banished from nineteenth-century poetry, and we shall often have occasion to allude to Jean-Baptiste Rousseau's esthetic in discussing nineteenth-century poets. Especially since Mallarmé renovated many of the old rhetorical devices,[16] it has been possible to perceive a certain charm in the neoclassical manipulation of literal and figurative meanings. Unquestionably

[11]See Charles Bruneau, *Histoire de la langue française* (Paris, 1948), XII, Pt. 1, p. 34.

[12]*Ibid.*, 40.

[13]See Yves Le Hir, *Rhétorique et stylistique de la Pléiade au Parnasse* (Paris, 1960), 157–58, and also Charles Bruneau, *Petite Histoire de la langue française* (Paris, 1955), II, 39.

[14]See Alexis François, *Histoire de la langue française cultivée* (Geneva, 1959), II, 91.

[15]Bruneau, *Histoire de la langue française*, XII, Pt. 1, p. 40.

[16]See Barat, *Le Style poétique*, 307. This critic, nourished on nineteenth-century conceptions of poetry as pure emotion and sincerity, found a suspiciously close relation between Mallarmé and the neoclassical "poésie de style."

there is charm in the Latin models for the device: an expression like Virgil's "infidum remis impellere marmor" (*Georgics* I, 254) has only gained in beauty since the sea has ceased to be called marble in a familiar system of poetic diction.

Jean-Baptiste Rousseau was in most respects an *attardé*, preoccupied with developing conventions established in the seventeenth century. The other eighteenth-century poets we shall now examine were, on the other hand, conscious of attempting something new. The great discredit into which eighteenth-century poetry has fallen has generally concealed the fact that some pleasant if minor verse was written then and that the characteristics of this poetry are proper to it and not imitated from any seventeenth-century model.[17] A *geistesgeschichtlich* exploration of the "rococo" age has attempted to clarify our understanding of eighteenth-century sensibility by studying the interplay of neoclassical convention and contemporary taste in Delille.[18] It is likely that a minute study would reveal all manner of discrepancies between late eighteenth-century styles and the high period of neoclassicism; the contemporaries of Delille and his fellow poets certainly did not feel that their verse was merely a pastiche of earlier writers. If the differences which distinguish poetic styles between 1660 and 1880 are not immediately evident to us, it is because we are incapable of perceiving subtle shifts in taste within the framework of neoclassical convention. It has long been established, in any case, that patterns of sensibility had greatly altered by the late eighteenth century, and the word *pré-romantique* is often applied to the period.[19] I dislike, however, the irritating and fallacious assumption that eighteenth-century writers were "preparing" romanticism; they were simply trying as best they could to satisfy their own taste in literature.

Jacques Delille (1738–1813) is unquestionably the dominant figure in the history of late eighteenth-century poetry. Chénier, one might claim, was a better poet, but the circumstances of his work's publication pre-

[17]A fine selection of eighteenth–century French verse, as well as a perceptive introduction to it, can be found in A. J. Steele, *Three Centuries of French Verse, 1511–1819* (Edinburgh, 1956).

[18]Victor Klemperer, *Delilles "Gärten": ein Mosaikbild des 18. Jahrhunderts*, Sitzungsberichte der deutschen Akademie der Wissenschaften zu Berlin (Berlin, 1954).

[19]Of the many studies by Mornet, Van Tieghem, Baldensperger, and others, perhaps the most convenient remains Daniel Mornet's *Le Romantisme en France au XVIIIe siècle* (Paris, 1912).

vented him from exercising the same kind of authority as did Delille. The latter's translation of the *Georgics* was a school text for Victor Hugo,[20] and his funeral assumed the character of a national event—another curious link between him and Hugo. His avowed aim was to enrich French poetic diction, but he aimed at this goal only within certain limits. He realized that the French conception of levels of style was unique in literature: neither Greek, Latin, English, German, nor any other language had established so rigid and elaborate a distinction between high, middle, and low diction. He also understood that French verse suffered from this limitation. (The contemporary critic La Harpe estimated that less than a third of the vocabulary of the language could decently be used in poetry.[21]) But Delille, theoretically at least, did not feel that the French poetic lexicon could or should be transformed. In his opinion the very structure of French was inseparable from neoclassical conventions, which is a perfect demonstration of how inextricably bound together were the notions of language and literature. (The neoclassical mentality is almost comparable to that of the Carolingian period, when one spoke some obscure dialect but one wrote in Latin.) Instead of radical change, Delille proposed, by dint of translation, to increase the possible combinations of words within the set bounds of traditional vocabulary.

By and large, the poems that Delille translated or imitated have in common an attention to descriptive detail that was a considerable challenge to the abstract character of French poetic vocabulary. The problems the *Georgics* present are obvious, but Delille did not confine himself to Latin and showed both courage and sophistication when he set out to imitate contemporary English poetry. One of the dominant aspects of eighteenth-century English poetry was descriptiveness. Even Pope, whom we do not tend to associate with this fashion, wrote a sylvan *Heloise and Abelard*, which was to be a French favorite in translation.[22] Thomson's *Seasons* are perhaps the high point (or low point, as one wishes) of the descriptive school, which was supported by the revival of interest in Spenser. A whole psychological-esthetic theory grew up about description, which to justify itself took, out of context, the Horatian motto "ut pictura poesis." Addison's *Spectator* papers "On

[20]See Venzac, *Premiers Maîtres*, 333–35.

[21]See Bruneau, *Histoire de la langue française*, XII, Pt. 1, pp. 49–55.

[22]Or imitation. See Henri Potez, *L'Elégie en France avant le romantisme* (Paris, 1897), 37–41.

the Imagination" advise the poet to take walks and look at nature so that his verse will be properly rich in tableaux.[23] Delille himself later devoted a lengthy poem (*De l'Imagination*, 1788) to these notions, but first he attempted a Thomson-like work on gardens.

Les Jardins (1782) is at once a bold and timid poem. Certainly Delille did not reinvent poetic language nor violate the canons of neoclassicism; on the other hand we find in it an insistent use of a whole vocabulary, which, while not "low," had not been much used in previous decades:

> Remarquez-les surtout lorsque le pâle automne,
> Près de la voir flétrir, embellit sa couronne.
> Que de variété! que de pompe et d'éclat!
> Le pourpre, l'orangé, l'opale, l'incarnat
> De leurs riches couleurs étalent l'abondance.
>   (Chant II)

The casual, colloquial use of the imperative and the delicate choice of color adjectives stand out amid the weary, common abstract words. Even when the vocabulary is far from new, the mood of Delille's poetry can strike one as refreshingly different from the traditional sublime style:

> Ils sont passés, les jours d'ivresse et de folie :
> Viens, je me livre à toi, tendre Mélancolie.
> Viens, non le front chargé des nuages affreux
> Dont marche enveloppé le chagrin ténébreux,
> Mais l'oeil demi-voilé, mais telle qu'en automne
> A travers des vapeurs un jour plus doux rayonne.
> Viens, le regard pensif, le front calme, et les yeux
> Tout prêts à s'humecter de pleurs délicieux ...
>   (Chant II)

Here the numerous adjectives, though commonplace, are disposed so as to qualify and enrich one another; the mixed mood of delectation and sadness is nicely reflected in the changing, ambiguous autumn landscape, and the repeated imperative adds a suitably lulling note. Perhaps even

---

[23]For the theory of descriptive poetry in France, see Margaret Cameron, *L'Influence des Saisons de Thomson sur la poésie descriptive en France, 1759–1810* (Paris, 1927), 153–75. For English influences on the theory of the imagination, see Margaret Gilman, *The Idea of Poetry in France from Houdar de la Motte to Baudelaire* (Cambridge, Mass., 1958), 25–27.

more important for the history of French poetry is the rhythm of the last two lines: the strong pauses after *viens*, *pensif*, and *calme* are coupled with enjambment in a way that breaks up the traditional pattern of sentence movement within the alexandrine distich. Normally enjambment was used in a limited, specified way,[24] and pauses within a line of alexandrine verse were not numerous, save at the customary caesura after the sixth syllable.[25] Delille, like many of his contemporaries, thought that the alexandrine lacked rhythmic variety and set about remedying this state of affairs, with results that some found shocking. In his verse a strong stress or pause can fall anywhere in the alexandrine, and the ostentatiousness of the traditional caesura is diminished. It has been claimed that, aside from exploiting the 4 / 4 / 4 alexandrine, Victor Hugo added nothing to the alexandrine distich and merely echoed Delille's innovations.[26]

The abbé Delille altered the syntactical character of French verse in still another way than by enjambment. In Racine's alexandrines the principal parts of speech are the subject, verb, and object, while adjectives are relatively sparse, with the result that clauses are not freighted with slow-moving epithets. In Delille's syntax, however, the adjectives and participles used as adjectives have come to equal finite verb forms in their frequency: the sentence patterns are "phrasal" rather than "clausal." [27] This phenomenon is all the more remarkable in that literary French had always been poor in adjectives, and Josephine Miles's categories work all the more decisively in French, because French avoids adjective-plus-noun in favor of noun-plus-*de*-plus-noun phrases. When

[24]In Racine we principally find enjambment (1), when two lines form a complete sentence (2), when one word of a sentence alone runs over into the following line, a device consecrated by the rhetorical tradition under the name of aposiopesis, and (3), for some vivid and singular effect (e.g. *Bajazet*, 657–58). See Walther Suchier, *Französische Verslehre auf historischer Grundlage* (Tübingen, 1952), 111.

[25]Unfortunately there is no adequate evidence for determining the patterns of pause and stress with which alexandrines were recited in the seventeenth century. We do know, at least, that by the eighteenth century it was generally thought that the alexandrine had a monotonously regular stress at the caesura. See Daniel Mornet, *L'Alexandrin français dans la deuxième moitié du dix-huitième siècle* (Toulouse, 1907), 11–18.

[26]*Ibid.*, 91–95.

[27]I am alluding to the important theory of Josephine Miles (see *Eras and Modes in English Poetry*, Berkeley, 1957) which classifies styles according to the dominance of finite verbs ("clausal") or to that of participles and adjectives ("phrasal"). This syntactic distinction implies a rhythmic one: a clausal style permits a more rapid flow of thoughts and feelings.

an English poem has a predominance of adjectives and participles over verbs, that is less striking than when a French one attains the same percentage, since French, for etymological reasons, cannot transform simply any noun into an adjective, and in general can tolerate only widely accepted adjectival formations from nouns (on the model of, say, *peur-peureux*). "The azure heights" and "les hauteurs d'azur" exemplify this difference between the two languages. We do not want to assimilate English noun-plus-noun to French noun-plus-*de*-plus-noun, because the latter construction is usually not repeated in the same line or at close proximity, in order to avoid accumulations of the preposition. Although there are patches of Delille's verse where many finite verbs are used in sequence for vivid description of movement, by and large he prefers the somewhat more sluggish rhythm created by heavy adjectivation and by the substitution of participles for relative clauses. The static effect is further increased by the abundant use of forms of *être* and the passive mode. The way in which Delille upset the Racinian proportions in sentence patterns and parts of speech helps to differentiate his verse from the earlier, more famous neoclassical styles and to characterize it as part of a poetic movement proper to the second half of the eighteenth century.

Delille's genuine gifts are easy to illustrate, and more than once his work has been culled for charming passages.[28] The prevailing insipidness of his language, however, becomes disagreeably evident when we turn to his translation of *Paradise Lost* (1805), which, in the 1824 edition of his *Oeuvres complètes*, is printed facing the English text. It is astonishing that a poet who could read and enjoy Milton should not have utterly despaired at French neoclassical conventions after trying to render a few lines of the original. Delille's vocabulary is minuscule, and he must constantly translate words of some force and inventiveness into the *grisaille* of the *style noble*. Even worse, the translation is always gasping in its attempt to catch up with the English text on the opposite page, which contains huge blanks while the French runs on both wordily and vaguely. An attempt at rendering the even more concise language of a passage from *Othello* proved much more disastrous: the French is *twice* as long as the English.[29]

[28]See Robert de Souza, "Un Préparateur de la poésie romantique," *Mercure de France*, CCLXXXV (July, 1938), 298–327, and Pierre Guégan, "Florilège de l'Abbé Delille," *Mercure de France*, CCCXXV (November, 1955), 448–75.
[29]Delille, *Oeuvres*, I, 112–17.

But if his translations incline one to meditate on the element of genuine folly that was implicit in the neoclassical esthetic, a certain amount of Delille's work displays the solemn beauty that highly rhetorical writing can have and which should not be deprecated. One of his "fugitive" poems, about his grave, inspires a quality of admiration similar to that which we feel before Mallarmé's neoclassicizing *Tombeau* for Gautier. Delille is instructing his wife to have some of his own verse put on his tombstone:

> Tu n'y pourras graver ces titres solennels
> Qui survivent aux morts, et qu'au sein des ténèbres
> Emporte dans l'horreur de ses caveaux funèbres
> L'incorrigible orgueil des fragiles mortels :
> Au lieu de ces honneurs suprêmes,
> Du néant vaniteux emphatiques emblèmes,
> Place sur mon tombeau quelqu 'un de ces écrits
> Que ton goût apprécie et que ton coeur inspire,
> Que tu venges par un souris
> Des insultes de la satire.
> ("Epître à Madame Delille" [30])

The odd interplay of abstract and concrete meanings is in the finest neo-classical tradition; the periphrases add gravity and elegance. The balance of epithets is also masterful: lines four and six in particular embody formulas—a line consisting of two nouns preceded by two long adjectives or the same elements arranged in chiasma—which are to be encountered in certain nineteenth-century poets and which seem invariably to create impressive effects.[31] The real difference between seventeenth-century neoclassicism and that of Delille's age can perhaps best be summed up in a few lines from *Les Jardins* where the rhetorician criticizes rhetoric:

> Mais l'esprit aisément se lasse d'admirer.
> J'applaudis l'orateur dont les nobles pensées
> Roulent pompeusement, avec soin cadencées :
> Mais ce plaisir est court. Je quitte l'orateur
> Pour chercher un ami qui me parle du coeur.
> (Chant I)

[30]Printed with *De l'Imagination* in *Oeuvres*, VIII, 6.
[31]Alliteration also seems inherent in such lines: "Et l'avare silence et la massive nuit" (Mallarmé). Sometimes the grammatical elements are altered but the pattern remains quadripartite: "Ton amour taciturne et toujours menacé" (Vigny); "L'immense majesté de vos douleurs de veuve" (Baudelaire). Ténint comments on the importance of such lines (*Prosodie*, 138–41).

The poet has been contemplating the formal gardens of Versailles and becomes bored by them. The term *admirer* is important, for we must remember that Corneille made of *admiratio* a fundamental esthetic principal. And what one admires is oration, the very basis of neoclassical literary method. Ironically enough, the last line of this quotation is borrowed from Racine, the master rhetorician, who, in *Bérénice*, created almost a prototype of Delille's sensibility: the inner sadness and detachment beneath the noble, sustained exterior is what separates the Queen of Palestine from Racine's other heroines. There is, in these lines, a kind of self-questioning, a sense of inability to express oneself as one would like to, which, despite his careful workmanship, is at the bottom of Delille's esthetic predicament.

The role of André Chénier in the development of French poetic styles complements that of Delille and Jean-Baptiste Rousseau. The latter were the romantics' inevitable first models, for it was under their influence that *lycée* students were trained in the art of verse composition. Chénier, on the other hand, being virtually unknown until the publication of his works in 1819, was a poet that the first romantic generation really chose to admire and imitate. His particular vein of neoclassicism, coming at a time when the words *classique* and *romantique* had as yet no stylistic meaning,[32] simply reinforced the traditional conventions.

Chénier's importance transcends the mere fact that he used periphrases, "noble" words, and the customary poetic baggage of the period;[33] his theory of radical pastiche was to nourish the romantic fondness for the *faux ancien* which crops up in Vigny, in Banville, here and there in Parnassian poetry, and even in *La Légende des siècles*. Chénier was the first of the erudite philologist-poets, such as Racine and Milton, who wished to force poetry as completely as possible into ancient molds: his spirit was that of the antiquarian. However, his pastiches labor under the same difficulties as Delille's translations. Read in an edition annotated with Greek and Latin sources, Chénier's pastiches seem hardly to render the flavor of the originals. A few poems such as "La Jeune Tarentine" actually succeed in suggesting the charm of Hellenistic verse, but, by and large, there is something equivocal and uneasy in his neo-antique style. More satisfying, ultimately, are the pieces he composed in prison in 1794. It is

---

[32]See Bruneau, *Histoire de la langue française*, XII, Pt. 1, p. 21.
[33]See Jean Fabre, *André Chénier, l'homme et l'oeuvre* (Paris, 1955), 140–49.

not that autobiography adds any value to them; the fact is simply that
the complicated, nightmarish experience of the Revolution was a far
richer matter for poetic exploration than the already perfected elegance
of the Greek Anthology. One of the best-known of the "Iambes" is
especially striking:

> Quand au mouton bêlant la sombre boucherie
> Ouvre ses cavernes de mort,
> Pâtre, chiens et moutons, toute la bergerie
> Ne s'informe plus de son sort.
> Les enfants qui suivaient ses ébats dans la plaine,
> Les vierges aux belles couleurs
> Qui le baisaient en foule, et sur sa blanche laine
> Entrelaçaient rubans et fleurs,
> Sans plus penser à lui, le mangent s'il est tendre.

The beribboned sheep and gushy virgins have nothing to do with ancient
pastoral: this is the rococo bucolic of Marie-Antoinette at the Petit Tria-
non, and the slaughterhouse is all too accurate an image for the Reign of
Terror. This grotesque juxtaposition is possible only because the poem
is conceived in the tradition of invective, and, in the course of the nineteenth century, through Hugo to Rimbaud, vituperative verse in particular will bring about a leveling of styles and freedom of imagery. Roman
poetry had been, of course, frequently at its most inventive in satire and
abuse. It is therefore not surprising that in the midst of events that an-
gered and horrified him, Chénier's language should have increased in
power.

It is not unjust, I think, to consider Jean-Baptiste Rousseau, Delille,
and Chénier as the most gifted of the eighteenth-century poets. All three
were learned, painstaking craftsmen, whose work had a noticeable influence on French poetry. But aside from these three figures, there are
several poets, interesting perhaps most of all as *Zeitstimmen*, whose
names should not go unrecorded. Their work tends toward the facile,
the sentimental, and the autobiographical. Elegy was their preferred
mood—the similarity or contrast between the cycles of life or love and
that of nature—and if a revival of lyric emotion is to be attributed to anyone in French literature, it must surely be ascribed to them. These are the
poets from whom Lamartine first learned his métier; these are the writers
who finally distilled *sensibilité* into verse. Parny, Fontanes, and Millevoye

are perhaps the best known to posterity; Parny and Millevoye are re-membered especially as elegiac poets, Fontanes for his association with Chateaubriand. The following lines by Parny are perhaps too serene and too pagan to be typical of these ennui- and autumn-ridden souls, but they have an unusual rhythmic grace:

> Viens, la nuit est obscure et le ciel sans nuages :
> D'un éternel adieu saluons ce rivage,
> Où par toi seule encor mes pas sont retenus.
> Je vois à l'horizon l'étoile de Vénus :
> Vénus dirigera notre course incertaine.
> Eole exprès pour nous vient d'enchaîner les vents;
> Sur les flots aplanis, Zéphire souffle à peine;
> Viens : l'amour jusqu'au port conduira deux amants.
>
> (*Elégies*, vol. I [34])

This *embarquement pour Cythère* suggests the narrow range of the eighteenth-century elegiacs as well as their pallid charm. Time has in-vested them with a certain attractiveness, since we read them with eyes trained by Verlaine's and other nineteenth-century writers' fondness for *ancien régime* taste, but we cannot claim much for the originality of this verse: the sentiments derive from Hellenistic tradition, and the vocabu-lary is Racine's. At most, there is a certain erotic intimacy in these lines which contrasts charmingly with their conventional form.

In the way of technical innovations on the eve of the romantic move-ment, two are worth noting and both are associated with the name of Millevoye. One concerns vocabulary: the slowly growing interest which the eighteenth century had felt for the "Gothic" ages suddenly found a literary embodiment in France, the *genre troubadour*. This forgotten literary fad consisted of verse narratives more or less medieval in subject and written in an astonishing combination of the periphrastic *style noble* with archaisms (like the omission of a subject pronoun) and terms per-taining to medieval art and life (*créneaux, ogive, astragales*, etc).[35] The *genre troubadour* represents the very worst in late eighteenth- and nineteenth-century attempts to recapture the mood and spirit of some earlier literature, and it would not be worth mentioning save for what it means linguistically: sudden bizarre additions had been made to the vo-cabulary and syntax of verse which would have been unthinkable not

---

[34]Quoted in Potez, *Elégie*, 145.
[35]See Fernand Baldensberger, *Etudes d'historie littéraire* (Paris, 1907), Chapter 3.

many decades before. One might almost characterize it as Keats's sole-cisms without his genius. Some years in advance of the romantic polem-ics over poetic language, the *genre troubadour* signified that the reading public had largely lost the genuine neoclassical sensitivity to style. The chaotic, almost meaningless way in which the adjectives *classique* and *romantique* were hurled about in the 1820's also demonstrated how badly readers and writers understood what was the basic issue of the period in poetry: the possibility of expanding its vocabulary. With the creation of the *genre troubadour* a real revolution in poetic diction was beginning, although contemporaries, lost in labyrinthine polemics colored by per-sonal, religious, and political issues, did not seem to realize it.[36]

The second innovation in verse that Millevoye elaborated was the use of refrain, which was to be connected with the romantic *ballade*. Refrain, of course, is a medieval device exemplified in the fifteenth-century *bal-lade* and *rondeau*, but these genres had ceased to be practiced,[37] and Millevoye's use of refrain is essentially new in its conception. In his narra-tive *ballades* (this new sense of the term is derived from English or Ger-man) the refrain may recur in a free, irregular way, for dramatic effect; this is the model followed by Vigny in "Moïse." Even when the refrain regularly terminates every stanza, it still constituted an innovation: the introduction of a device of song into recited verse. There are few impor-tant nineteenth-century poets who did not try their hand at refrains, and Millevoye's otherwise rather slim talent deserves some attention for this reason.[38]

That the character of poetic inspiration had definitely altered by the turn of the century can be seen from the titles of some of the poems of the period: Fontanes wrote "Le Jour des Morts dans une campagne" and "Le Cri de mon coeur"; Millevoye is best known for "La Chute des feuilles" and "Le Poète mourant." Seen in this perspective it is clear that Lamartine's first volume, *Méditations poétiques,* is the culmination of an elegiac tradition rather than the expression of a new movement in poetry. When Gustave Lanson invented the customary notions of French liter-ary history in the closing decade of the nineteenth century, he chose to

[36]The confused quarrels of the first decades of the nineteenth century are résuméd in Bruneau, *Histoire de la langue française,* XII, Pt. 1.

[37]See Steele, *Three Centuries of French Verse,* xxviii.

[38]The taste for refrain was subsequently reinforced by Banville's influential, if minor, work.

minimize Lamartine's similarity to previous poets and to present him as the first authentic poet of the romantic movement. Lanson, like his essentially romantic readers, could not distinguish between Lamartine's glamorous personal figure and the uneven merits of his rather minor verse. By now, Lamartine's vast reputation has declined, and we may see his achievement in a less distorted way. The *Méditation* appears to be a gifted, if conventional, *summa* of late eighteenth-century and Empire elegy. Their character is less personal and autobiographical than was once thought,[39] their craftsmanship more evident. "The lyrical poet, concerned with expressing certain feelings or emotions in the lyrical conventions of his day often takes a similar attitude, because it is natural for him to identify his conventional literary emotions with his 'real' personal emotions." [40] What is most clear to us is that Lamartine's first collection of verse both exemplifies and surpasses the melancholic strain running through his predecessors' verse:

> Que ne puis-je, porté sur le char de l'aurore,
> Vague objet de mes voeux, m'élancer jusqu'à toi!
> Sur la terre d'exil pourquoi resté-je encore?
> Il n'est rien de commun entre la terre et moi.
>
> Quand la feuille des bois tombe dans la prairie,
> Le vent du soir s'élève et l'arrache aux vallons;
> Et moi, je suis semblable à la feuille flétrie :
> Emportez-moi comme elle, orageux aquilons!
> ("L'Isolement")

The key word here is "vague." The Racinian *objet*, designating the loved one, is already rather abstract but the epithet stresses the generalized vagueness of emotion which makes the poet aware of the landscape without his being really interested in it; "la terre d'exil" (the expression belongs to a favorite category of neoclassical poetic diction) is foreign to him at the same time that it reflects his feelings. A similar ambiguity exists between description and metaphor: dawn's chariot, the dead leaves, and the possibility of the poet's being borne off in a storm are all introduced as equally present and real. The debris of neoclassical periphrasis, mingled with descriptive elements, produces an odd feeling of haziness,

---

[39]See Alphonse de Lamartine, *Poésies choisies*, ed. J. L. André Barbier (Manchester, 1925), lii.

[40]Northrop Frye, "The Road of Excess," in Bernice Slote (ed.), *Myth and Symbol: Critical Approaches and Applications* (Lincoln, 1963), 9.

which is increased by the soporifically regular alexandrines. Lamartine early showed his distaste for enjambment or unexpected pauses within a line of verse: the sentence form coincides with the line or distich. Rimbaud remarked that Lamartine's verse was "strangled" by an outmoded form; certainly his alexandrine was conservative even by late eighteenth-century standards.

The only sound way of evaluating Lamartine's early verse is, I think, to compare it with lines by Leopardi in which the themes and images are similar. Leopardi is the only major European poet who, around 1820, was still writing in the "pre-romantic" or late eighteenth-century conventions, but these conventions, though the same as those of "L'Isolement," produce in the Italian poet incomparably finer measures. This comparison will, I think, demonstrate some important facts about neoclassical French poetic language which will not be lost on English-speaking readers. The essential picture in the two poems is that of a lonely man on a wooded hill overlooking a valley and the distant horizon:

> Sempre caro mi fu quest'ermo colle,
> e questa siepe, che da tanta parte
> dell'ultimo orizzonte il guardo esclude.
> Ma sedendo e mirando, interminati
> spazi di là da quella, e sovrumani
> silenzi, e profondissima quiete
> io nel pensier mi fingo . . .
> ("L'Infinito")

> Souvent sur la montagne, à l'ombre du vieux chêne,
> Au coucher du soleil, tristement je m'assieds;
> Je promène au hasard mes regards sur la plaine,
> Dont le tableau changeant se déroule à mes pieds.
> . . . .
> Au sommet de ces monts couronnés de bois sombres,
> Le crépuscule encor jette un dernier rayon,
> Et le char vaporeux de la reine des ombres
> Monte, et blanchit déjà les bords de l'horizon.
> ("L'Isolement")

Lamartine's description is at once more detailed and more colorless than Leopardi's; the latter mentions only the hill and the hedge, yet the landscape is made vivid by the unusual adjective *ermo*, with its rich etymological associations (*erêmitês*, hermit). No such means are at the disposal of Lamartine, who, for heightened effect, has only a conventional periphrasis. (He might have done better to say "moon"; a comparison with Leopardi's "Alla Luna" suggests itself.) But the greatest difference between the two poets is one of syntax: Lamartine cannot upset the basic core of the sentence with its inevitable subject-verb-object order; nor can he risk the polysyndeton ("and . . . and . . . and"), which imparts such a dreamy movement to "L'Infinito." In short, it is not so much the conventional themes of eternity, sadness, and sunset which limit Lamartine as lexical and syntactic poverty.

It is not usually realized that Lamartine's style was the object of careful thought on the poet's part and that it evolved considerably in the course of the years. He preferred the reputation of being an aristocrat and statesman to that of a man of letters, and completely concealed from his contemporaries the care he took in working out and revising his poems. Nineteenth-century readers were content to believe that poets whipped off their verse in moments of inspiration and sent it on directly to the printer. Poets did not undeceive their readers, and only the patient work of scholars has permitted us to suspect how much more complex was the behavior of the most famous verse-writers. By the mid-1830's Lamartine, after a wary glance at the work of younger poets, had eliminated much of the neoclassical diction from his vocabulary, and he had acquired a more precise, *nuancé* technique of description. But the change in Lamartine's style—which did not, incidentally, increase his reputation as a poet— is due not only to the influence of Hugo and others; it comes also from the fact that in *Jocelyn* (1835) he was no longer writing elegies, no longer working in an eighteenth-century tradition of poetry. The relation between poetic style and poetic genre must be understood if we are to trace the development of French romantic poetry, and we shall now turn to the interplay of these two elements in the work of Hugo and Musset.

II

STYLE AND GENRE:
THE EXAMPLES OF HUGO AND MUSSET

We are accustomed to thinking of the modern poet's work as an evolution; the end point is a fuller vision, and in the process we may distinguish more than one phase, such as juvenilia, the mature style, the late manner, and so forth. The assumptions behind this way of thinking are the supremacy and autonomy of the imagination and the organic, biological nature of the *oeuvre*. Neoclassical thought, on the other hand, divided a poet's work not by period, but by genres and sub-genres. Thus Virgil's style did not evolve; he merely elected first the low style, next the middle, and finally the high one, as the poet was supposed to have explained.[1] A close relation was assumed to exist between subject matter, genre, and style. Various hierarchies of styles and genres were proposed both in antiquity and afterward; let us recall French neoclassical attitudes toward this question: the ode and epic were to be written in the *langue ornée;* the tragedy, which shared their eminence, had merely *style noble,* while genres like the elegy and pastoral belonged to an ill-defined middle range. Comedy might be classed as low or middle, as one saw fit. The possible variations and usual vagueness present in these theories did not, however, prevent them from exercising a genuine influence upon literary sensibility.

Beginning with the romantics the old distinctions of genre became by and large useless, but certain writers still felt them. Wordsworth's sense of genre has been pointed out,[2] and Victor Hugo's early poetry cannot be understood without reference to genre theory. Even after 1850 we

---

[1]See the apocryphal lines placed at the beginning of the *Aeneid* in some manuscripts (editors commonly include them in the apparatus) and the genuine ones at the end of the *Georgics.*

[2]See René Wellek and Austin Warren, *Theory of Literature* (New York, 1956), 170–71.

still find in his work the Virgilian topos which announces a change of
genre: *ego qui quondam illa ceceni nunc cano* ....[3] One might argue that
any shift in subject matter will involve some change in style, but I think
it is possible to observe in Hugo's poetry certain clear-cut distinctions of
genre which can only be ascribed to the persistence of neoclassical sensibility.

Hugo's first collections of poems are the five books of his *Odes* (1822–
28), whose content, for the most part, has well-defined social, political,
and historical reference;[4] formal panegyric, the genre most foreign to
modern poetry, dominates, and one almost feels oneself in the presence
of a court poet of the seventeenth century—a feeling one does not experience with any other major poet in European romanticism. France
had been the true *foyer* of neoclassicism, and French literature shook off
its conventions far more slowly than English or German letters. Hugo
is a particularly illustrative writer in this respect; he was the only French
romantic poet whose career is partially comparable to that of someone
like Racine:[5] he pursued a *cursus honorum* which began with a pension
from Louis XVIII, included the French Academy, and reached its climax
with his appointment to the *pairie* under Louis-Philippe. Much of his
writing up to 1851, the date of his exile from France, must be understood
in terms of patronage, personal influence, and social position. Thus we
can explain Hugo's preponderant interest in the theater during the
1830's: the stage provides the most direct communication between author
and public. Thus we can account for the occasional or ceremonial
character of much of his non-dramatic verse until the exile.

The title of *Odes*, the first of Hugo's volumes of verse, does not, any
more than later ones like *Les Voix intérieures* or *Les Rayons et les ombres*, give us a satisfactory idea of the various kinds of poems contained
in the work. The earliest ones tend to be lengthy patriotic eulogies in the
Malherbean tradition. Indeed, the first book of the *Odes* (1822) contains
little else; it established Hugo's reputation as a royalist. The style is suf-
ficiently ornate as to require prose translations' being appended to certain poems in order to explain the periphrases,[6] and the strophic forms
are frequently elaborate enough to look like Greek odes in their typo-

[3]See the first of the *Chansons des rues et des bois*.
[4]A group of "personal" odes will be discussed later.
[5]See Raymond Picard, *La Carrière de Jean Racine* (Paris, 1956).
[6]See Emmanuel Barat, *Le Style poétique et la révolution romantique* (Paris,
1904), 118.

graphical disposition.[7] But Hugo already had several cords to his lyre, and subsequent volumes of the *Odes* display other traditions of poetry. The late eighteenth-century elegiac and descriptive genre is not absent, witness these lines on ruins:

> Je vous aime, ô débris! et surtout quand l'automne
> Prolonge en vos échos sa plainte monotone.
> Sous vos abris croulants je voudrais habiter,
> Vieilles tours, que le temps l'une vers l'autre incline,
> Et qui semblez de loin sur la haute colline,
> Deux noirs géants prêts à lutter.
> ("Aux Ruines de Montfort-L'Amaury")

Except for the final simile, which betrays Hugo's growing taste for enormity, and monstrosity, this stanza could well be from the pen of Delille or his contemporaries.

In the last book of the *Odes* a number of poems are addressed to Hugo's wife, but their language is not very different in style from that of the solemn political odes. Here we encounter what is the greatest failure of neoclassical style in its last phases: the language fails to adapt itself to the subject matter; the same gravity of tone used for the anointing of a God-sent king applies to the selection of a shawl:

> Ceins le voile de gaze aux pudiques couleurs,
> Où ta féconde aiguille a semé tant de fleurs!
> Viens respirer sous les platanes;
> Couvre-toi du tissu, trésor de Cachemir,
> Qui peut-être a caché le poignard d'un émir,
> Ou le sein jaloux des sultanes.
> ("Promenade")

Later, Mallarmé was to exploit the weighty periphrasis consciously and for ironic aims, but in Hugo's earliest work, despite an inventiveness which is perceptible even at our remove in time, this ornament simply reflects a wrongheaded esthetic. In short, the *Odes*, despite variety in subject matter, of which we shall have more to say later, represent a curiously petrified form of neoclassical diction in which the middle and low styles have been forgotten and only the noble tone survives, forcing all subjects into its mold. The low or trivial is not *avoided*, as in the

[7]The neoclassical attempt to build up elaborate stanzas derives perhaps from the desire to imitate the complicated look of Greek choral measures.

seventeenth century, but *ennobled* by means of epithet or periphrasis.[8] That Hugo, who was to be one of the most varied poets of the nineteenth century, should have begun writing in such a rigid manner is especially surprising.[9]

Inappropriateness in language did not vanish all at once in Hugo's work, and traces of it remain even in *Les Orientales* (1829), which are generally considered to mark a fresh departure in style for him. There is a particularly arresting example in one of the first of his many poems on Napoleon, which begins:

> Toujours lui! Lui partout! — ou brûlante ou glacée,
> Son image sans cesse ébranle ma pensée.
>
> ("Lui")

What is disturbing here is that the vocabulary is that of Phaedra dreaming of Hippolytus. Poetic style was clearly out of joint. As a contemporary wrote about Delille: "One can easily understand that it is impossible for a style composed of a careful combination of so many other styles to be distinctive, and that when it is applied to essentially varied subjects, the result is a contrast, painful for the reader, between the basic ideas and the stylistic effects." [10] The ill had been diagnosed well before it was remedied.

What first led Hugo to invent another kind of style and genre was a subject matter that he felt to be genuinely new: the picturesque life of the contemporary Ottoman Empire. Although Racine's *Bajazet* and numerous eighteenth-century novels had pretended to deal with the Near East, the Greek War of Independence gave the description of Turkish life a certain *actualité*. Rather than an exercise within an accepted tradition, *Les Orientales* represents a convergence of distinctive topics of interest in the 1820's.[11] A new genre and a new word were born, and, although Hugo did not completely abandon conventional diction, one feels that, at his best, he had discovered a fresh vein:

---

[8]See Victor Hugo, *La Préface de Cromwell*, ed. Maurice Souriau (Paris, n.d.), 269–77.

[9]A comparison with Lamartine is instructive: the latter inclines far less toward periphrasis, perhaps because he is using the less ornamented, middle style of elegy.

[10]Jacques Delille, *Oeuvres* (Paris, 1824), I, lv.

[11]See the introduction and notes to the critical edition of *Les Orientales* by Elisabeth Barineau (Paris, 1954).

Oh! laissez-moi! c'est l'heure où l'horizon qui fume
Cache un front inégal sous un cercle de brume,
L'heure où l'astre géant rougit et disparaît
Le grand bois jaunissant dore seul la colline.
On dirait qu'en ces jours où l'automne décline,
Le soleil et la pluie ont rouillé la forêt.

Oh! qui fera surgir soudain, qui fera naître,
Là-bas, — tandis que seul je rêve à la fenêtre
Et que l'ombre s'amasse au fond du corridor, —
Quelque ville mauresque, éclatante, inouïe,
Qui, comme la fusée en gerbe épanouie,
Déchire ce brouillard avec ses flèches d'or!

Qu'elle vienne inspirer, ranimer, ô génies,
Mes chansons, comme un ciel d'automne rembrunies,
Et jeter dans mes yeux son magique reflet,
Et longtemps, s'éteignant en rumeurs étouffées,
Avec les mille tours de ses palais de fées,
Brumeuse, denteler l'horizon violet!

("Rêverie")

The preface to *Les Orientales*, as that of *Les Feuilles d'automne*, talks of "pure poetry," and I think "Rêverie" gives us some feeling of what Hugo meant by the term. There is no clearly stated initial topos or theme: of the six main verbs only two are declarative, the others being imperative, conditional, interrogative, or optative. The richness of verbal modes represents a tendency toward implication as opposed to explicitness. The movement of the poem has an agreeably unexpected character: the opening imperative is not followed by another second-person reference; the richly elaborated syntax contains many parallelisms and parenthetical elements suggestive of the devious patterns of thought; and the sentence structures are so varied that one has not the slightest feeling of confronting a conventional development. The emphatic positions of *longtemps* and *brumeuse* seem to be a *trouvaille* rather than a formula. As for vocabulary the commonplace poetic language like *front* or *astre géant* is balanced by the "low" terms *rouillé* and *corridor*, while the rich descriptive language reflects the discussion over local color in the late 1820's.[12] Indeed the poem functions primarily as a visual evocation. The versification

---

[12]The locus classicus of this theory is the fifteenth and sixteenth *pensées* in Sainte-Beuve's *Vie, Poésies et Pensées de Joseph Delorme* (Paris, 1829).

also deserves comment: the composition of *Les Orientales* marks Hugo's abandon of such extensive stanzas as the *dizain*, and he was from now on to prefer the quatrain and *sixain*.

If "Rêverie" seems like the starting point of a truly new kind of poetry, reflective, intimate, addressed to oneself rather than to a formal audience, and free from well-worked commonplaces, the other *Orientales* do not, by and large, have the same degree of promise. The theory of "local color" which they exemplify is in itself only partially contradictory to neoclassical principles: the neoclassicists, it is true, preferred somewhat abstract epithets, but the very idea of inventing a theory for choosing colorful epithets smacks of codification and rules. If in *Les Orientales* Hugo has given up epic similes, he has not as yet greatly expanded his range of metaphor.[13] One feels that, like the *genre troubadour*, this work is a curious byway in the history of poetic taste. If one wishes to, however, it is possible to discover in *Les Orientales* certain adumbrations of the peculiar spatial imagination of Hugo's later years. He *saw* from high altitudes or distant vantage points as we are accustomed to doing today, and as we shall be more and more accustomed to do, as our technology advances. But such considerations belong to the history of Hugo's mind rather than to that of French literature. Everything that is genuinely important in *Les Orientales* we shall find again in discussing the work of the older Hugo.

In Hugo's volumes of the 1830's we can finally see exactly how close the correspondence between genre and style was to remain for him. Certain neoclassical devices he had discarded on principle: hyperbaton and periphrasis have become uncommon; the substantial Malherbean stanza has, as we have seen, given way to short stanzas or alexandrine couplets arranged in verse-paragraphs. And yet when he writes a solemn commemorative poem on a public theme, his style tends toward the old, ornate of writing. Many examples of rather insipid neoclassical style (for example, frequent metaphors involving *nefs* and *nochers* and the continual mention of *chars*) can be found from *Les Feuilles d'automne* to *Les Rayons et les ombres*, but I prefer to take as a sampling a really elegant passage of verse, in which metonymy, periphrasis, and personification do not seem outmoded or misplaced:

[13]See Barat, *Le Style poétique*, 198–99.

Et moi je ne veux pas, harpe qu'il a connue,
Qu'on mette mon roi mort dans une bière nue!
Tandis qu'au loin la foule emplit l'air de ses cris,
L'auguste piété, servante des proscrits,
Qui les ensevelit dans sa plus blanche toile,
N'aura pas, dans la nuit que son regard étoile,
Demandé vainement à ma pensée en deuil
Un lambeau de velours pour couvrir ce cercueil!
("Sunt Lacrymae Rerum," III)

The death of Charles X called forth these lines, and Hugo was inspired to a rhetorical gravity by the event. At times Hugo still echoes Malherbe (see, for example, "A Olympio" in *Les Voix intérieures*); on other occasions he builds up poems by series of commonplaces introduced by *quand* or *puisque* ("A Villequier" in *Les Contemplations* is the most famous example); these pieces are frankly conceived in the ornate tradition of the ode. There seems to be a close relationship between neoclassical rhetoric and the poet's public function. Whenever he addresses an audience that can be clearly defined as Frenchmen of the 1830's, his voice strives for formal, oratorical cadences. This is not the Hugo of verbal experiments, the author of historic *drames*, or the later exile speaking to a public of whose nature he is not at all certain. From the very beginning of his career Hugo had been conscious of poetry as an act of address,[14] and it is notable how great a proportion of his verse of the 1820's and 1830's is dedicated to and directed toward a specific person or body of people. Occasional genres like the epistle, the compliment, and the *discours en vers* abound in these volumes,[15] as well as a certain tendency to digress, to moralize, and to generalize. Indeed, Hugo is so conscious of his audience that when he speaks specifically to a friend, relative, or enemy, the modern reader is sometimes at a loss to determine exactly what is the point of departure for the poem's development.[16] This is a poetry to which maxims and assertions are essential; in a sense, it is basi-

[14]See the first preface to the *Odes*.
[15]These poems are not, of course, called by their traditional genre terms; like Lamartine in the *Méditations* and Vigny in his *Poèmes*, Hugo often presents rather conventional material under a new label. The romantics disliked old-fashioned genre tags such as *élégies* or *poésies sacrées*, even though the genres survived.
[16]For example, "A l'homme qui a livré une femme" (*Les Chants du crépuscule*), "A un riche" (*Les Voix intérieures*), or "Sur un homme populaire" (*Les Rayons et les ombres*).

cally rather anti-lyrical, and its fundamentally traditional character may well have been a factor in its success with the poet's contemporaries.

That Hugo in the 1830's was simultaneously pursuing several conceptions of poetry—by no means related—is quite apparent when we turn from his poems of declaration and address to certain briefer pieces which appear to have been written solely as studies in imagery. The ending of "Nuits de juin" is a pertinent example:

> Les astres sont plus purs, l'ombre paraît meilleure;
> Un vague demi-jour teint le dôme éternel;
> Et l'aube douce et pâle, en attendant son heure,
> Semble toute la nuit errer au bas du ciel.

Hugo has not discarded *vieilleries* like the "dôme éternel," which probably has more charm for the modern reader than it did for someone of Gautier's generation, but he has, on the other hand, caught one of those marvelous impressions in which sight, illusion, and intellectual awareness fuse together. Summer nights can be curiously bright, and one is uncertain, on thinking about it, whether the phenomenon is a projection of mood or a fact of astronomy. Best of all, the poem seems to have an autonomous existence, free from contingencies of speaker or hearer.

More so even than "Nuits de juin," many of Hugo's studies in imagery turn on conceits of various sorts. These were by no means the aspect of Hugo's work which the nineteenth century preferred by and large: one critic even went so far as to condemn them as an absurd and distasteful outgrowth of the neoclassical taste for sheer "verbal" effect.[17] The famous "Tristesse d'Olympio" is, in a sense, one long-spun conceit about nature's indifference: Musset, who knew that the poem was conventional and had little precise autobiographical meaning, spoke of it in "Souvenir" as "empty" and "frivolous." Nineteenth-century readers felt they could distinguish between Hugo's "sincere" or autobiographical poetry and his purely verbal pyrotechnics, but they failed to see that Hugo's attempts at intimate, familiar verse were far more conventional, far more mechanical than the extravagant accumulations of imagery which they felt to be mere rhetoric. Hugo's poems about the sweetness of children or God's presence in nature do not show anything more than a banal nineteenth-century sensibility, while his stronger flights of imagination presage the

[17]See Barat, *Le Style poétique*, 299–300.

very free creative processes of his later style. The following lines, which describe a night impression, illustrate the element of *fantaisie*, as it has been called,[18] in his early work:

> Souvent alors j'ai cru que ces soleils de flamme
> Dans ce monde endormi n'échauffaient que mon âme;
> Qu'à les comprendre seul j'étais prédestiné;
> Que j'étais, moi, vaine ombre obscure et taciturne,
> Le roi mystérieux de la pompe nocturne;
> Que le ciel pour moi seul s'était illuminé!
>
> (*Les Feuilles d'automne*, XXI)

At times, Hugo goes even further, and in what seem to be almost meaningless, fragmentary poems anticipates, perhaps a bit crudely, the visions that were to haunt him during his exile:

> Puits de l'Inde! tombeaux! monuments constellés!
> Vous dont l'intérieur n'offre aux regards troublés
> Qu'un amas tournoyant de marches et de rampes,
> Froids cachots, corridors où rayonnent des lampes,
> Poutres où l'araignée a tendu ses longs fils,
> Blocs ébauchant partout de sinistres profils,
> Toits de granit, troués comme une frêle toile,
> Par où l'oeil voit briller quelque profonde étoile,
> Et des chaos de murs, de chambres, de paliers,
> Où s'écroule au hasard un groupe d'escaliers!
>
> (*Les Rayons et les ombres*, XIII)

As yet Hugo himself hardly appears to know what the significance of this vision is; the poem terminates with a mechanical comparison between the vision and destiny, which does not justify the fullness of the development. Shifting, sinister architecture will later symbolize the universe and will neither need nor tolerate any simple, abstract gloss. Hugo was only gradually to find the patterns in his obsessive images. "La Pente de la rêverie" is the most famous of these adumbrations of his later style, but it, like the others, seems abortive, and unsustained by any informing philosophy.

None of Hugo's volumes of the 1830's are planned with the care of the *Odes*, *Ballades*, and *Orientales*. They appear to be nothing more than casual collections of recent works of varying inspiration. I think we may

---

[18]See Jean-Bertrand Barrère, *La Fantaisie de Victor Hugo* (Paris, 1949), I.

explain this by recalling how large a place his plays occupied in his concerns at that time; more so than on his lyrics, which were almost a by-product of his imagination, he was counting on the theater to establish his fame. We need hardly be surprised that the drama was considered so necessary a genre to master; the old hegemony of the play in French literature, which Delille had complained about in vain, persisted through the nineteenth century, and certain writers whom we associate only with fiction and verse—Gautier and Nerval, for example—were in fact quite active in the theater. Nor should we forget how direly the stage tempted Balzac and Flaubert. With these facts in mind we may try to examine what the importance of Hugo's verse plays was for his general poetic practice.

Most of Hugo's rare preserved remarks on poetic style were made with regard to the *drame* in verse.[19] It was not from lyric poetry that he proposed to banish epithets, "noble" terms, periphrasis, and hyperbaton; too much of his production consisted of essentially traditional genres like the panegyric odes or *discours en vers* for him to think of proscribing neoclassical diction in this realm. After the *orientale*, the *drame* was the most conspicuous new genre that he adopted, and it is there primarily that he saw fit to remake poetic style.

The intrinsic interest of Hugo's earlier verse dramas has always been overshadowed for literary historians by the publicity, polemics, and censorship they excited, and it is difficult for a modern reader, confronted merely with the text of one of them, to imagine how it could ever have been the object of such notoriety. Much of their fame was certainly manufactured and artificially maintained,[20] but at the same time, some attentive reading can reveal why they are essential to the history of French verse. At first one notices that the style, while hardly representing Hugo at his most inventive, has the negative originality of avoiding really fossilized diction. Hugo's initial effort in the theater was to replace the *langue noble* by direct, less periphrastic language and a more clausal style. The result is not really in itself a great gain for poetry; not until *Ruy Blas* did Hugo succeed in introducing a noteworthy range of meta-

[19]In the preface to *Cromwell*, "Réponse à un acte d'accusation," and "Suite," the latter two in *Les Contemplations*.

[20]It must be remembered that *Hernani* caused an uproar because it was presented at the Comédie française; in another theater the situation would have been different. See Maurice Descotes, *Le Public de théâtre et son histoire* (Paris, 1964), 245–71.

phor and imaginative diction into the *drame*. Nevertheless, the technical, prosodic problems and solutions he came upon in trying to create a viable verse language for the stage were to have considerable repercussions. We cannot hope generally to feel the startling lowness and bluntness Hugo's *drames* must have had for contemporaries, but an example chosen from an insignificant passage of *Ruy Blas* can teach us something about Hugo's innovations. Indeed, these lines can perhaps indicate better the direction of our inquiry than a well-known tirade. Ruy Blas and Don Salluste are speaking:

DON SALLUSTE   Personne, en ce cas, au château
                        Ne vous a vu porter cette livrée encore?
RUY BLAS   Ni personne à Madrid.
DON SALLUSTE   *(désignant du doigt la porte par où est sorti Don César)*
                                                C'est fort bien. Allez clore
                        Cette porte. Quittez cet habit.
(Ruy Blas dépouille son surtout de livrée et le jette sur un fauteuil.)
                                                Vous avez
                        Une belle écriture, il me semble. — Ecrivez.
                                                (11. 462–66)

Something very strange has happened to the seventeenth-century alexandrine here: it no longer has any relation to sentence forms. Here the sentences, which are mostly brief, colloquial in syntax and vocabulary (except for the verb *clore*), begin where they will, run on from one line to another, and generally function apart from the prosodic form. The pause which marks a sentence's end corresponds only once to the customary caesura after the sixth syllable. Otherwise we note that pauses at the end of sentences obscure the caesura, that enjambment destroys any pause at the end of a line, and that the second line cannot be read with a pronounced caesura. That two characters are speaking further disguises the fact that the verse form is the traditional alexandrine couplet: lines keep getting split up in an irregular fashion. Even the stage directions, apparently involving pauses in speech, contribute to the break-up of the couplet. Finally, Don Salluste's first two lines do not rime, and in the second two that he speaks, which do rime, an enjambment and a sentence pause conceal somewhat the consonance of *avez* and *ecrivez*.

To establish a standard, a point of comparison, for the handling of alexandrine *distiques* or couplets in drama, let us summarize Racine's usage. The seventeenth-century dramatic poets conceived of the distich as the container and informer of syntax. It was the basic unit of verse discourse in regard to both sound and sense. Poets tried to reduce speech to one sentence filling two lines or to two sentences of twelve syllables each, and we can find many such simple patterns in Racine: "Voilà sur quoi je veux que Bajazet prononce. / Sa perte ou son salut dépend de sa réponse" (*Bajazet* I, 3). "Quoiqu'il vous reste à peine une faible lumière, / Mon âme chez les morts descendra la première" (*Phèdre* I, 3). These are Racine's basic formulas, and their underlying principle is that a sentence, a unit of sense, should end at the rime, and, if it is a long sentence, should end on the second rime-word. Exceptions can be found, but they are distinctly unusual. In Bérénice's last words to Antiochus there is a curious sequence:

> Prince, après cet adieu, vous jugez bien vous-même
> Que je ne consens pas de quitter ce que j'aime,
> Pour aller loin de Rome écouter d'autres voeux.
>
> (*Bérénice* V, 7)

The line riming with the passage just quoted is a complete syntactical unit, but seems neither to belong entirely to the preceding sentence, nor to be the point of departure for a new, lengthy rhetorical development: "Vivez, et faites-vous un effort généreux." This verse is at once a conclusion and a transition, and the shift of mode from declarative to imperative underscores its dramatic value. The three-line-plus-one pattern is extremely uncommon in Racine (and in the other classical dramatists), for summing up is usually assigned to still another couplet. Normally, when obliged to fit a one-line sentence and a three-line sentence into two distichs, Racine places the short sentence first, so that the more elaborate grammatical structure will have the conclusive cadence of rime:

> Votre présence, Abner, est ici nécessaire.
> Laissons là de Joad l'audace téméraire,
> Et tout ce vain amas de superstitions
> Qui ferment votre temple aux autres nations.
>
> (*Athalie* II, 4)

Here, the one-line sentence is a muted and neutral statement, which by rime alone leads to a more syntactically complex and more rhetorically persuasive structure.

In Racine's esthetic, the very purpose of rime would vanish if it did not serve as a mold for syntax, despite whatever small departures he might make from the complete correspondence of sentence and distich. When concerns of eloquence or variety oblige Racine to write very long verse sentences, he constructs them within the tight framework of two, three, or even four distichs, avoiding uneven numbers of lines. This lovely passage from *Bérénice* is typical:

> Si l'espoir de régner et de vivre en mon coeur
> Peut de son infortune adoucir la rigueur,
> Ah! Prince, jurez-lui que toujours trop fidèle,
> Gémissant dans ma cour, et plus exilé qu'elle,
> Portant jusqu'au tombeau le nom de son amant,
> Mon règne ne sera qu'un long banissement,
> Si le ciel, non content de me l'avoir ravie,
> Veut encor m'affliger par une longue vie.
>
> (III, 1)

Each of the three clauses in this sentence corresponds exactly to one or two distichs.

It becomes clear, I think, that Hugo had deeply modified the whole conception of French dramatic prosody by 1840. His use of run-on lines and of the alexandrine trimeter (4 / 4 / 4) are generally mentioned in textbooks as his great contributions to French versification, but we have seen that Delille had already employed frequent enjambment and some examples of trimeter can be found in earlier poetry. Hugo's rejection of the traditional esthetic of the couplet had far greater consequences for the history of French poetry—especially since Hugo greatly extended the use of the alexandrine distich. Sainte-Beuve, Vigny, and others before Hugo had written relatively short poems in alexandrine distichs rather than in stanzas, but Hugo was to do far more than any preceding poet in drawing attention to the lyric possibilities of this form. As he experimented with the alexandrine distich in his dramas from *Cromwell* (1827) on, he also exploited it in his collections of verse. In *Les Orientales* (1829) there is only one poem cast in this mold; by the time of *Les Chants du crépuscule* (1835) half the poems are written in it.[21] What Hugo was doing resulted in giving French poetry a relatively supple form like English blank pentameter. The extension of the alexandrine

---

[21]See Philippe Martinon, *Les Strophes* (Paris, 1911), 75.

distich from plays to short poems is a decisive step in the breaking up of neoclassical genre theory, which ideally would have assigned a set verse form to each subject matter as well as a set vocabulary. This is the decisive point where the neoclassical ode and the theory behind it are banished from lyric poetry.[22]

While Hugo's prosodic innovations and stylistic finds are of considerable importance for the development of French poetry, there is no parallel enrichment in subject matter—or at least not a very consistent one. Here and there we find some of the characteristics of his late work, odd spatial imagery or paratactic sequences of metaphor, but in his volumes of the 1830's Hugo does not seem to be moving in any particular direction. In that respect they constitute almost a regression compared with *Les Orientales*. Indeed, one sometimes wonders whether most of Hugo's work up to 1850—so overshadowed by his far larger and greater production during exile—should not be considered an exercise in style, a patient attempt to invent an instrument capable of giving out new harmonies. Some of his contemporaries were in fact disconcerted by an apparent disparity between Hugo's virtuosity and the frequent mediocrity of his inspiration. Vigny, close to him in age and lacking high capacities for verbal invention, noted in irritation that the content of Hugo's verse was constantly inferior to its style.[23] Baudelaire, whose prosodic inventfulness was slight but whose precocious maturity of taste led him to spot a certain uneasy quality in Hugo's earlier work, remarked, in his *Salon de 1846*, that Hugo is "the composer of a period of decadence or transition, who uses his tools with a truly strange and wonderful dexterity." [24] By "decadence" and "transition" I believe that Baudelaire was trying to express the feeling of disparateness, of miscellaneousness, that one has on reading Hugo's verse collections of the 1830's. Musset was even sharper in his criticism. Handicapped by an esthetic of spontaneity and sincerity which was not adequate to account even for his own verse, he complete-

[22]Wilhem Ténint, *Prosodie de l'école moderne* (Paris, 1844), 153–58, maintains that the ode must be stanzaic: thus Hugo was avoiding more and more the traditional conception of high lyricism. But Ténint also claims, somewhat conservatively, that the *alexandrin brisé* should be confined to drama and light verse (p. 56). Needless to say, his stricture was not followed.

[23]See Alfred de Vigny, *Journal d'un poète*, ed. Fernand Baldensperger (Paris, 1935), 157.

[24]*Oeuvres complètes*, Pléiade edition (Paris, 1951), 612.

ly mistrusted so fecund, so skilled, and yet so routinely inspired a poet
as Hugo. We have already quoted his remark on "Tristesse d'Olympio"
in "Souvenir"; he considers Hugo to lack the seriousness essential to
lyricism. Toward the end of his own poetic career, Musset rather meanly
contrasted Hugo with Leopardi in these words:

> Il peut tant qu'il voudra rimer à tour de bras,
> Ravauder l'oripeau qu'on appelle antithèse,
> Et s'en aller ainsi jusqu'au Père-Lachaise,
> Traînant à ses talons tous les sots d'ici-bas;
> Grand homme, si l'on veut; mais poète, non pas.
>
> ("Après une lecture" XV)

In the light of Musset's opinion of Hugo, it will be of some interest to
observe in his work the vanishing of the relation between genre and style
that characterized the verse of the older poet. Musset began to write in
very different circumstances from Hugo; he was born late enough to
have come directly under the influence of newer kinds of poetry, and
was the first important nineteenth-century French poet to have begun
his career other than in the neoclassical tradition.[25] The new genre that
he cultivated most relentlessly was the Byronic verse tale: Musset was
virtually possessed by the author of *Don Juan*. Imitation of the English
poet's affectation of doggerel, improvisation, and general insouciance led
Musset to some startling effects in French prosody. Besides radical enjambment and use of the trimeter alexandrine he introduced an alexandrine divided 7 / 5, which is normally considered an invention of Verlaine's:[26]

> Ayant donc débarqué, notre héros fit mettre
> Sa voiture en un lieu sûr, qu'il pût reconnaître . . .
>
> (*Mardoche*, XXII)

The style is willfully prosaic. Elsewhere Musset indulges in a favorite
comic device of juxtaposing "noble" and familiar words,[27] the shock
effect of which has largely vanished for the modern reader. Yet at the
same time Musset was an accomplished pasticheur of neoclassical style

[25]See Barat, *Le Style poétique*, 247.
[26]Ténint, *Prosodie de l'école moderne*, 66, 70, calls this alexandrine "rather rare"
but gives examples of it from La Fontaine, Molière, and Hugo.
[27]See Charles Bruneau, *Histoire de la langue française* (Paris, 1948), XII, Pt.
1, p. 253.

(the very use of *rimes mêlées* in the first of the following two examples establishes a filiation with La Fontaine[28]):

> Regrettez-vous le temps où le ciel sur la terre
> Marchait et respirait dans un peuple de dieux;
> Où Vénus Astarté, fille de l'onde amère,
> Secouait, vierge encor, les larmes de sa mère,
> Et fécondait le monde en tordant ses cheveux?
>
> ("Rolla")

> Depuis que le soleil, dans l'horizon immense,
> A franchi le Cancer sur son axe enflammé . . .
>
> ("La Nuit d'août")

Musset did not avoid neoclassical style; on the contrary he *mixed* styles in a way that seems to me the characteristic trait of his verse. The once famous "Nuits" are a particularly relevant example: in them he asks his Muse—a personification characteristic of old-fashioned high rhetoric—to sit by the hearth and sing with him, a situation belonging to the low style, except for the fact that she will accompany them with a lyre:

> Je veux bien toutefois t'en raconter l'histoire,
> Puisque nous voilà seuls, assis près du foyer.
> Prends cette lyre, approche . . .
>
> ("La Nuit d'octobre")

The feeling of unevenness which so much of Musset's verse generates derives, I think, from a casual mingling of neoclassical conventions like personification with words associated with trivial circumstances. Musset does not exploit the contrast or disparity between the two kinds of style, as Baudelaire was later to do; he seems unaware of the curious effect produced by the mixture. The charges of carelessness that Baudelaire, Flaubert, Leconte de Lisle, Rimbaud, and other writers of the latter part of the century were to bring against Musset apparently stem, in part, from his disparateness of style within single poems. Musset, however, was actually a far more accomplished poet—within a small range of wit or elegiac emotion—than their criticisms would lead one to believe. At times

---

[28]La Fontaine and the eighteenth century's *vers libres* and *rimes mêlées* were rejected by romantic poets, Musset being the principal exception (see, for example, "Silvia"). Ténint finds *vers libres* chilling.

his nonchalant combinations of style create splendid effects of casualness and intimacy. His last great poem "Souvenir" is perhaps the best illustration of Musset's poetic capacities. It is a meandering, allusive poem full of startling shifts in style and topic. The first stanza is filled with conventional solemnity:

> J'espérais bien pleurer, mais je croyais souffrir,
> En osant te revoir, place à jamais sacrée,
> O la plus chère tombe et la plus ignorée
> Où dorme un souvenir!

The tone and the conception of a personally "sacred" spot, as well as the image of the tomb and sleeping memory, are clearly an imitation of Hugo's "Tristesse d'Olympio," which will be obliquely referred to elsewhere in "Souvenir." Having once established Hugo's somewhat monotonously monumental note, Musset breaks it; the apostrophe gives way to a real, not a rhetorical, second-person address:

> Que redoutiez-vous donc de cette solitude,
> Et pourquoi, mes amis, me preniez-vous la main?
> Alors qu'une si douce et si vieille habitude
> Me montrait ce chemin?

"Souvenir" is constructed as a fragmentary dialogue; the poet addresses as many as nine persons or things in the course of it. The result is a kind of dramatic density, a feeling of situation, which, incidentally, is quite lacking in Hugo's poem. The *oui*'s, *non*'s, questions, and exclamations which Musset uses are not simply flat rhetorical devices, but provide the dialectic articulation of the poem.

The description of the Forêt de Fontainebleau is blandly neoclassical in its use of conventional epithets:

> Les violà, ces sapins à la sombre verdure,
> Cette gorge profonde aux nonchalants détours,
> Ces sauvages amis, dont l'antique murmure
> A bercé mes beaux jours.

(11. 13–16)

And when the poet, in a combination of real address and apostrophe, draws attention to the moon, the latter brings in her train a familiar epithet:

> Voyez! la lune monte à travers ces ombrages.
> Ton regard tremble encor, belle reine des nuits;
> Mais du sombre horizon déjà tu te dégages,
>   Et tu t'épanouis.
>
> (11. 33–36)

But the stanza on the moon is followed immediately by lines of considerable novelty; odor and involuntary memory are compared in a way
which we associate normally with *Les Fleurs du mal:*

> Ainsi de cette terre, humide encor de pluie,
> Sortent, sous tes rayons, tous les parfums du jour;
> Aussi calme, aussi pur, de mon âme attendrie
>   Sort mon ancien amour.
>
> (11. 37–40)

Stylistic inventiveness was, however, for Musset, a corollary to indifference toward certain niceties of diction. He did not object to only half-
realized personifications, and a few lines later we find an odd clash of
metaphor:

> O puissance du temps! ô légères années!
> Vous emportez nos pleurs, nos cris et nos regrets;
> Mais la pitié vous prend, et sur nos fleurs fanées
>   Vous ne marchez jamais.
>
> (11. 45–48)

The images of *marcher* and *emporter* are neither parallel nor contrastive;
their juxtaposition is bold, curious, and uneasy.

The effect of slightly strained or mixed metaphors contributes to
Musset's irony, as here where he alludes to "La Tristesse d'Olympio":

> Loin de moi les vains mots, les frivoles pensées,
> Des vulgaires douleurs linceul accoutumé,
> Que viennent étaler sur leurs amours passées
>   Ceux qui n'ont point aimé!
>
> (11. 23–26)

There is something at once serious and comical about real people cover-
ing personified sorrows with winding sheets. As it sometimes happens in
Musset, he achieves the crabbed but witty tone of the metaphysicals. The
swollen, grandiose kind of writing he refers to is exemplified by these
two stanzas of Hugo's:

"O douleur! j'ai voulu, moi dont l'âme est troublée,
Savoir si l'urne encor conservait sa liqueur,
Et voir ce qu'avait fait cette heureuse vallée
De tout ce que j'avais laissé là de mon coeur!

"Que peu de temps suffit pour changer toutes choses!
Nature au front serein, comme vous oubliez!
Et comme vous brisez dans vos métamorphoses
Les fils mystérieux où nos coeurs sont liés!
                                ("La Tristesse d'Olympio," 11. 49–56)

The difference we immediately note between "La Tristesse d'Olympio"
and "Souvenir" is that Hugo's poem is smooth and elegant in its imagery,
orotund in tone, and based on impersonal commonplaces, whereas Musset
likes colloquialness, ironic allusion, brusque changes of mood, and rhetorical figures which range from the banal to the freakish.

A long apostrophe to Dante—one of the many second persons present
in the poem—leads Musset to the central theme of happy memories and
the briefness of pleasure. Musset's capacities for shifting tone are splen-
didly demonstrated in a passage where he addresses mankind (and Victor Hugo in particular): an ancient lyric commonplace, *la vida es sueño*,
is presented as a cliché; then comes the original and bizarrely relevant
image of a man stretching in bed on awakening, which is immediately
followed by intense lyric declarations:

Et vous criez alors que la vie est un songe,
Vous vous tordez les bras comme en vous réveillant,
Et vous trouvez fâcheux qu'un si joyeux mensonge
        Ne dure qu'un instant.

Malheureux! cet instant où votre âme engourdie
A secoué les fers qu'elle traîne ici-bas,
Ce fugitif instant fut toute votre vie;
        Ne le regrettez pas!

Regrettez la torpeur qui vous cloue à la terre,
Vos agitations dans la fange et le sang,
Vos nuits sans espérance et vos jours sans lumière:
        C'est là qu'est le néant!
                                            (11. 93–104)

The passionate tone of the last two stanzas is far more effective for having
been arrived at through a long series of insipidly conventional or fanci-

fully metaphoric lines; "La Tristesse d'Olympio," in comparison, merely proclaims, in an unending monotone, the clichés which "Souvenir" rejects, affirms, or parodies in turn.

The high elegiac mood of the last quotation introduces one of the most interesting moments of the poem: Adam and Eve are represented not in the customary Edenic setting but in one clearly suggested by nineteenth-century science:

> Oui, les premiers baisers, oui, les premiers serments
> Que deux êtres mortels échangèrent sur terre,
> Ce fut au pied d'un arbre effeuillé par les vents
>   Sur un roc en poussière.
>
> Ils prirent à témoin de leur joie éphémère
> Un ciel toujours voilé qui change à tout moment,
> Et des astres sans nom que leur propre lumière
>   Dévore incessamment.
>
> (11. 113–20)

The conception of the earth as a dead rock in the midst of waning stars is one of those numerous scientific notions which are more recent than Western poetic conventions and which entered literature only very slowly. In French poetry we do not expect to find any sort of contemporary scientific assumptions before Leconte de Lisle, Louis Bouilhet, or Laforgue, and Musset's image of the cosmos is therefore all the more surprising.

The grave imagery grows more persistent toward the end of "Souvenir" and undergoes curious elaborations:

> Mes yeux ont contemplé des objets plus funèbres
> Que Juliette morte au fond de son tombeau,
> Plus affreux que le toast à l'ange des ténèbres
>   Porté par Roméo.
>
> J'ai vu ma seule amie, à jamais la plus chère,
> Devenue elle-même un sépulcre blanchi,
> Une tombe vivante où flottait la poussière
>   De notre mort chéri,
>
> De notre pauvre amour, que, dans la nuit profonde,
> Nous avions sur nos coeurs si doucement bercé!
> C'etait plus qu'une vie, hélas! c'était un monde
>   Que s'était effacé!
>
> (11. 137–48)

The transition from the highly romantic Romeo and the Angel of Darkness (the latter an improvement, supposedly, on Shakespeare's text) to the image of the dead child is a fine example of Musset's inventiveness: a comparison taken from bourgeois domestic life creates an unexpected feeling of intimacy in sorrow. The tone is lowered by neoclassical standards, and herein lies a great discovery which was to transform French literature: "low" words, thoughts, and situations can have a serious immediacy lacking in the sublime style.

The key, perhaps, to Musset's style, his tone, and his attitude toward his contemporaries is that he was the principal romantic ironist in France, playing the role that Heine did in Germany, and Byron in England. It is in the nature of the romantic ironist to look with suspicion on new ideals of high style and to preserve traditional elements of technique in the face of his contemporaries' innovations. In respect to skills cultivated by fellow poets, such as descriptions of nature in the romantic period, we expect the ironist to show indifference and condescension. Byron's admiration for Pope is the equivalent of Musset's *classicisme*. At the same time the ironist will show considerable daring in his invention but avoid drawing attention to it. Thus some of the metaphors in "Souvenir" are bolder than almost anything attempted in French before Baudelaire and the symbolists; yet Musset has no general reputation for stylistic audacity. The ironist doesn't pretend to invent; his conservatism has as its ideal the dandy, not the prophet. The image of himself which Musset created ran counter to that of most of his contemporaries, and especially to that of Hugo, who was to be ever more idealogical, revolutionary, and given to high seriousness. Yet when we compare "Souvenir" with "La Tristesse d'Olympio," I am not sure that the latter is a better or more stylistically inventive poem than Musset's.

Musset and Hugo are not the only poets of the 1830's whose works require some discussion of neoclassical diction. Vigny, for example, never broke completely with the stylistic tradition of Chénier and Delille. But Hugo and Musset were more adventurous writers, and therefore their conservation of certain aspects of neoclassicism alongside experimentation is particularly worth examining. The conclusions which impose themselves after such an examination are several. Hugo and his public had by no means lost the sense of genres and levels of style inherited from the seventeenth and eighteenth centuries; Musset, for his part, shows a persistent, if fitful, taste for what we might think to have been worn-out modes of expression. Thus we cannot make a simple classification of the poetic styles of the 1830's into "neoclassical" and "romantic"; these old categories are simply not adequate. The customary notions about French romantic poets and their "revolution" seem therefore somewhat hazy and ungrounded in stylistic facts. There was, of course, no revolution; the essential patterns of neoclassical thought about art remained even though they were modified by the idea of a new genre: the romantic one. In his preface to *Cromwell*, for example, Hugo argues, like a seventeenth-century preface-writer, that the *drame* is valid because it imitates nature. What more neoclassical contention could there be? The whole notion of the *genre romantique* is as neo-Aristotelian as the seventeenth-century debates over *tragicomédie*. It is not surprising therefore that aspects of neoclassical poetic practice survived.

Obviously certain traditional patterns of rhetoric and structure never disappeared from verse, but by the middle decades of the nineteenth century, the high point of French romantic poetry, Hugo, Baudelaire, Nerval, and others had begun to evolve modes of poetic discourse which owed virtually nothing to neoclassical tradition. But before examining these major figures in detail, we must first study the *genre romantique* of the period 1825–45, its peculiar nature, and the lesser poets who helped elaborate it.

III

TOWARD A ROMANTIC ICONOLOGY

The first definition made in France of the adjective *romantique* was an iconological one. Letourneur, the translator of Shakespeare, tried to explain it by evoking English gardens, the Alps, and the paintings of Salvator Rosa, the latter being a curious sort of link between baroque and early romantic taste. The relatively new adjective *pittoresque* was associated with the *romantique* from the very beginning,[1] and it will be useful to recall some of the late eighteenth century's favorite poetical images. Autumnal landscapes, such as we have seen in the verse of De- lille, were popular, as well as suggestions of sunset and night. More in- teresting perhaps, for our purposes, is the fondness for funereal objects: tombs, cenotaphs, mausoleums, urns, and weeping willows. Monasteries, hermitages and their inhabitants belong also to this strain of taste, for monks and nuns were coming, even in Catholic France, to be conceived of as being totally absorbed in thoughts of death—if not of something worse. Ruins, obvious symbols of death and decay, complete the picture, and melancholy is the dominant mood. The sources for these scenes would seem evidently to be English literature—Young's *Night Thoughts* come to mind—but it is easier to observe this phenomenon than to assign precise origins to it.[2]

Well before Hugo and Sainte-Beuve made their first declarations about poetic style in the late 1820's, the French were already beginning to speak of a *genre romantique* which they identified by certain kinds of subject matter, that, while not necessarily new, were not found in the pure

[1]See Charles Bruneau, *Histoire de la langue française* (Paris, 1948), XII, Pt. 1, pp. 117–18.
[2]See Daniel Mornet, *Le Romantisme en France au XVIIIe siècle* (Paris, 1912), 97, and Henri Potez, *L'Elégie en France avant le romantisme* (Paris, 1897), 43–46, 299, 301, 303, 307–10.

stream of neoclassicism. Hugo's first poems in the *genre romantique* will provide a good example. They were published in the fourth and fifth books of *Odes* and retain some of the manner of the more conventional odes while being quite distinct:

> Soeur du hibou funèbre et de l'orfraie avide,
> Mêlant le houx lugubre au nénuphar livide,
> Les filles de Satan t'invoquent sans remords;
> Fuis l'abri qui me cache et l'air que je respire;
> De ton ongle hideux ne touche pas ma lyre,
> De peur de réveiller des morts!
>
> ("La Chauve-souris")

The poet is addressing a bat. He does not appear really to have much to say to the creature, but obviously takes some pleasure in imagining its sinister habits and attributes:

> Sors-tu de quelque tour qu'habite le vertige,
> Nain bizarre et cruel, qui sur les monts voltige,
> Prête aux feux du marais leur errante rougeur,
> Rit dans l'air, des grands pins courbe en criant les cimes,
> Et chaque soir, rôdant sur le bord des abîmes,
> Jette aux vautours du gouffre un pâle voyageur?

It becomes clear that these descriptive details do not support a theme, nor do they have any pattern of development or contrast among themselves. They are there, each for its own sake, to create a certain mood just like the subject matter of a painting. The bat, the owl, the tower, the dwarf, the vultures, the abyss, and the pale face will recur in the work of Hugo and other poets, creating a tone of malaise and fear for which no explanation is given. They are part of the iconography of French romanticism whose function and character can bear some comparison with that of the contemporary plastic arts.

Until recently, romantic painting as a whole has not received the critical attention and public interest accorded to other periods in the history of art. European painting on the eve of modernism has certain characteristics which have made it uncongenial to eyes disciplined by Cézanne, cubism, and the other forms of abstraction current in our century. To begin with, its subject matter seems far more obtrusive than that of earlier periods of art; in romantic painting the subject is determined through its strangeness to draw attention to itself to a degree we do not feel in the more conventionalized work of the renaissance and baroque. The most obvious example that comes to mind is Delacroix, whose subjects seem to vie for our attention with his technical brilliance. In the "Exposition universelle de 1855," Baudelaire even went so far as to say of him, "Another very great, very profound quality of M. Delacroix's talent, one which makes him the favorite painter of poets, is the fact that he is essentially literary." [3] Other romantic artists remain peculiarly associated in our minds with the novelty of their subjects: Goya and his grotesque or sinister figures, Géricault and his madmen, Caspar David Friedrich and his disturbing landscapes, Fuseli and his nightmares. The scornful critic will claim that romantic painting is literary, unpainterly. And conversely much of French romantic poetry can be called pictorial. Like Hugo's "Chauve-souris" it tends to evoke objects for their own sake; it indulges in complacent descriptiveness.

The curious fact is that perhaps at no other period or place have painters and poets shared so similar an iconology as in romantic France. The high periods of painting have often occurred in times and places whose literary activity was mediocre. In the nineteenth century, however, Parisian poets and artists frequented one another, exchanged ideas, and on occasion tried their hand at another art form. Hugo's drawings are well known. The supreme example, of course, of the double artist is to be found in contemporary England: William Blake attempted a union of the arts which others were incapable of. Book illustration, whether practiced with Blake's imagination or more pedestrianly, is a typical nineteenth-century art form, showing the seriousness with which artists treated the verbal image.

The iconography which dominates French romantic verse and European romantic painting is characterized by violence, exoticism, and the sinister. Nightmares, wild animals, ominous birds, threatening landscapes, executions, sensual scenes in Mediterranean lands, and presages of death are favorite motifs. It would be an idle quibble to ascribe the frequency of such images to the *Geist*, dear to Germanic thought, or to an elaborate concatenation of influences. To explain the presence of such material in French verse, however, we should recall two minor literary genres of the early nineteenth century which, because of their popular,

[3]*Oeuvres complètes,* Pléiade edition (Paris, 1951), 700.

even vulgar character, have not perhaps received due recognition for their impact on romantic sensibility. These are the Gothic novel and the commercial theater.

The Gothic novel must have been one of the wonders of the age when the first translations of Anne Radcliffe and Monk Lewis appeared in France. The tradition of literary decorum and urbanity had already been nicked and chipped by certain writers of the revolutionary period,[4] but the wild imagination of the English Gothic novelists is completely irreconcilable with the whole French neoclassical concept of letters. Nor does the palpable sensationalism of the *roman noir* seem to have disgusted serious, elevated writers: Hugo's "Chauve-souris" quoted earlier has an epigraph taken from Mathurin's *Bertram*. To evaluate the novelty and surprise of the Gothic novel, let us summarize certain lurid aspects of *The Monk*, which is perhaps the most utterly Gothic of its genre: the action takes place in a strange country (Spain) where lust and superstition seem to motivate everything; among the characters are monks and nuns torn between God and Satan; the solution to most problems in the novel is violent death, and, finally, the setting is a dangerous labyrinth of chambers, staircases, hidden courtyards, and subterranean vaults. Monk Lewis had created what amounted to a new vision of evil.[5]

The other minor genres which had a surprisingly large influence on French literary sensibility were theatrical ones: the *mélodrame*, the *féerie*, and similar forms of what has been called the *théâtre du merveilleux*.[6] The role of these sub-literary plays in forming taste often tends to be obscured; literary historians like to make far too much of the originality of Hugo's *drame romantique* in order to establish facile antitheses between it and "classical" plays. The truth is less clear cut. In the early nineteenth century, Parisian theater life was divided between the Comédie française, which specialized in verse plays along traditional lines, and the great theaters on the boulevard du Temple, the Gaîté, the Ambigu, and the Porte-Saint-Martin, which welcomed "irregular" plays and novelties of any sort. Guilbert de Pixerécourt was their greatest au-

[4]After Diderot, the most conspicuous independent of the eighteenth century, one might mention Restif de la Bretonne ("le Rousseau du ruisseau") and Sébastien Mercier ("le singe de Diderot"), whose influence on Hugo seems to have been great. See H. Temple Patterson, *Poetic Genesis: Sébastien Mercier into Victor Hugo*, Studies on Voltaire and the Eighteenth Century (Geneva, 1960).

[5]See Lowry Nelson, Jr., "Night Thoughts on the Gothic Novel," *Yale Review*, LII (Winter, 1963), 236–57.

[6]See Marian Hannah Winter, *Le Théâtre du merveilleux* (Paris, 1962).

thor, and his success was international.[7] The dominant genre was the *mélodrame,* a sensational play with incidental music. The source of the plot was sometimes a *roman noir,* and, in any case, the two genres are intimately related by their subject matter. The titles of a few of Pixeré-court's plays will adequately suggest their similarity to Gothic fiction: *Les Maures d'Espagne, Coelina ou l'enfant de mystère, L'Ange tutélaire ou le démon femelle, La Tête de Mort.* We might add *Marguerite d'Anjou* to show how Hugo had been anticipated in historical subjects. The melodrama, like the Gothic novel, represents an important de-velopment in sensibility: both are concerned with evil but see it, not in the traditional theological context, but in a purely secular fashion. The consequences are far-reaching. Violence and bloodshed no longer be-long to a larger scheme of things; they are sensational in the most li-teral meaning of the adjective: sheer unreasoned emotion is their prod-uct. Satan, too, is secularized: the villain emerges as the active agent in these dark matters. The villain is the incarnation of absolute evil, like the devil in Christian thought, but he is all the more sinister for acting gratuitously. The melodrama ceased to believe in the old Christian view of the world and did not yet have any psychological theories to account for evil.

The French romantics' conception of life is often melodramatic in just the way we have been describing. Sinister images like Hugo's arsenal of bats, owls, and demons obtrude for no evident reason. Teratology, the study of monstrosities and abnormalities, is essential. Certain words be-gin to occur incessantly in French verse and critical writings after 1820: *frénétique,*[8] *fantastique, grotesque, macabre. Ange* and *démon* lose their traditional meanings and become terms which the characters in Hugo's plays constantly apply to one another. The old paradox about the "real-ism" of French romanticism can be readily explained by the tremen-dously varied ways which Hugo and his contemporaries found to express unpleasant feelings. We must have recourse to the idea of an iconology, an iconology of evil, in order to account for the shape and detail of much of the poetry of the 1820's and 1830's.

We have seen Hugo, in "La Chauve-souris," handling a quite unex-pected subject in a somewhat overripe neoclassical style. The subject is unexpected because of the traditional character of most of his odes, but

[7]*Ibid.,* 50–51.
[8]Nodier popularized this word after 1814, and applied it to the Gothic novel. See Henri-François Bauer, *Les Ballades de Victor Hugo* (Paris, 1935), 36*n.*

it should not surprise us if we recall that his first prose works, *Han d'Islande* and *Bug-Jargal*, are examples of the *frénétique* manner. From Lamartine's pastiches of Chateaubriand to the reading of *Salammbô* which resulted in Mallarmé's "Hérodiade," nineteenth-century French literary history is filled with examples of prose, always freer, anticipating and nourishing verse. Hugo never had a neoclassical prose style parallel to the manner of his odes; from the start he was committed to the fantastic-realist genre. In verse, however, the *Ballades* and *Orientales* constitute his first lengthy use of the *genre romantique*, and their subject matter will help us elucidate the character of much romantic writing.

The title *Orientales* does not seem really to fit the collection, at least if we take the term—a neologism—to mean poems treating the Near East. At the same time, however, the mood of the book is sustained; we do not feel any discrepancy between the poems about the Greeks and Turks and those about Napoleon or Spain. The reasons for this are complex and involve the whole function of exoticism for the French romantics as well as Hugo's conception of Napoleon. To begin with, the Ottoman Empire is, for Hugo, like Spain, like the Rhineland later, like Italy for some other poets, not a concrete place in historical reality but a fantasy world where actions of a lurid nature can take place. And what are these actions? They are violent or erotic outbursts; they are selfish and libidinous; in short, they are the actions appropriate to a demonic world. Hugo's Turks are not only non-Christian; their love of destruction identifies them as villains or secularized demons. Their harems are a dark paradise.

Spain, though clearly less sinister, has something of the same meaning in Hugo's symbolism. In poems like "La Légende de la nonne," in the *Ballades*, or in the plays *Hernani* and *Ruy Blas*, Spain is a country where lives are under the sway of a somber destiny. For fate is the term Hugo found to summarize his visions of the demonic. It is the key notion of his plays as well as of *Notre-Dame de Paris*, where *ananké* is inscribed on the cathedral. The Middle Ages belong also to the dark realms: the picturesque medieval vignettes of earlier writers undergo a change in high French romanticism. Finally, the figure of Napoleon remained for Hugo, throughout his career, charged with ambivalent grandeur. "Tu domines notre âge; ange ou démon, qu'importe?" he says in the fortieth *Orientale*, and this ambiguous attitude persists in "L'Expiation" and *Les Misérables*.

The unity of *Les Orientales*, and, I suggest, the unity of French romantic poetry lie in the pervasiveness of demonic symbols and themes. These can have varying degrees of intensity. In the *Ballades*, Hugo's first collection marked by a sinister strain, the devils and hobgoblins are presented as quaint, picturesque folklore. The closing of "Les Deux Archers" is characteristic; the poem has told of two archers who have desecrated a sanctuary and have been destroyed by Satan:

> Si quelque enseignement se cache en cette histoire,
> Qu'importe! il ne faut pas la juger, mais la croire.
> La croire! Qu'ai-je dit? ces temps sont loin de nous!
> Ce n'est plus qu'à demi qu'on se livre aux croyances.
> Nul, dans notre âge aveugle et vain de ses sciences,
> Ne sait plier les deux genoux!

The ambivalence and uneasiness of the conclusion are quite typical of Hugo's work before the exile: he was fascinated by the demonic and could not justify this obsession to himself. Other romantic writers tried ironic approaches to the demonic. The Byronic verse tale, which Musset put into fashion with his *Contes d'Espagne et d'Italie*, is an attempt to handle lurid material—any romantic tale taking place in Spain or Italy is bound to have eroticism and violent death in it—with a superficial glaze of sophistication. Other treatments too are possible, and we shall now consider the contributions made to the demonic iconology by Sainte-Beuve, Gautier, Petrus Borel, and Philothée O'Neddy.

The importance of Sainte-Beuve's poetry has often been mentioned but seldom with much explanation. His influence on Gautier,[9] on Baudelaire,[10] and perhaps even on Verlaine is certain, but this influence was of a very special sort. Much of Sainte-Beuve's verse, especially in his first and most famous collection, *La Vie, Poésies et Pensées de Joseph Delorme*, is conventional elegy, whose neoclassical style is only occasionally relieved by oddities of syntax and vocabulary. A contemporary cartoonist had great fun with the following lines, although the curious image is nothing but Racinian metonymy:

---

[9]See Charles-Augustin Sainte-Beuve, *Vie, Poésies et Pensées de Joseph Delorme*, ed. Gérald Antoine (Paris, 1956), cvi-cviii.

[10]See Norman H. Barlow, *Sainte-Beuve to Baudelaire: A Poetic Legacy* (Durham, N.C., 1964).

Pour trois ans seulement, oh! que je puisse avoir
Sur ma table un lait pur, dans mon lit un oeil noir . . .

("Voeu")

In a few poems, however, Sainte-Beuve, spurred perhaps by a sense of
rivalry with Hugo, succeeded in creating a very distinctive tone of his
own, which, while he never exploited it fully, was to suggest further
possibilities to Gautier and Baudelaire. The feeling which Sainte-Beuve
was trying to express is somewhat different from traditional elegiac
sentiment: it is not so much a sense of loss as one of spleen and emptiness,
and in certain poems Sainte-Beuve worked out a quite new and personal
set of "objective correlatives" to render it. Images of city life, of the
dingy, sordid quarters on the fringes of Paris translate his feeling of
universal disgust. Here, for example, is the conclusion of "Les Rayons
jaunes," a poem in which the speaker has thought of various deaths:

— Ainsi va ma pensée, et la nuit est venue;
Je descends, et bientôt dans la foule inconnue
        J'ai noyé mon chagrin :
Plus d'un bras me coudoie; on entre à la guinguette,
On sort du cabaret; l'invalide en goguette
        Chevrote un gai refrain.

Ce ne sont que chansons, clameurs, rixes d'ivrogne,
Ou qu'amours en plein air, et baisers sans vergogne,
        Et publiques faveurs;
Je rentre: sur ma route on se presse, on se rue;
Toute la nuit j'entends se traîner dans ma rue
        Et hurler les buveurs.

After an unctuous poetic meditation on tapers burning yellow in church
and yellow winding sheets, these images of proletarian conviviality (expressed in harsh rhythms and cacophonic juxtapositions of sounds) add
a grotesque complement to the speaker's melancholy: his sorrow is complacent, solitary, and spiritual, while the popular crowd is bestially good
humored. Each reflects unpleasantly on the other, and the city which
brings them together seems to soil both.

A poem of Sainte-Beuve's which Baudelaire particularly admired[11]
was "La Veillée" written for the birth of Hugo's son François-Victor.

[11]See the letter to Sainte-Beuve in Charles Baudelaire, *Correspondance générale*,
ed. Jacques Crépet (Paris, 1949), V, 214–18.

After a conventional description of the parents' watching over the new-born child, he continues:

> — Moi, pendant ce temps-là, je veille aussi, je veille,
> Non près des rideaux bleus de l'enfance vermeille,
> Prés du lit nuptial arrosé de parfum,
> Mais près d'un froid grabat, sur le corps d'un défunt.
> C'est un voisin, vieillard goutteux, mort de la pierre . . .

The Hugolian diction of the first lines yields quite abruptly to a very low level of style exemplified by the mention of kidney stones. This fondness for ugly commonplace material has often been ascribed to Sainte-Beuve's acquaintance with the English lake poets, but no one familiar with Wordsworth is likely to take this hypothesis too seriously. The seventeenth-century satirist Régnier, whose influence in the romantic period we shall come back to, has been proposed as a more likely model.[12] In any case, Sainte-Beuve was clearly determined to exploit subjects which were not only low but also somewhat repulsive in their realistic immediacy. "Moi, j'aime entre deux beaux yeux un sourire un peu louche . . . ," he exclaims in what is also probably an imitation of a baroque model.[13]

As a final example of Sainte-Beuve's imagination, we can isolate in the following "sonnet imitated from Wordsworth" the distinctive note which is his own:

> Je ne suis pas de ceux pour qui les causeries,
> Au coin du feu, l'hiver, ont de grandes douceurs;
> Car j'ai pour tous voisins d'intrépides chasseurs,
> Rêvant de chiens dressés, de meutes aguerries,
>
> Et des fermiers causant jachères et prairies,
> Et le juge de paix avec ses vieilles soeurs,
> Deux revêches beautés parlant de ravisseurs,
> Portraits comme on en voit sur les tapisseries.
>
> Oh! combien je préfère à ce caquet si vain,
> Tout le soir, du silence, — un silence sans fin;
> Etre assis sans penser, sans désir, sans mémoire;

---

[12]See Thomas G. S. Combe, *Sainte-Beuve poète et les poètes anglais* (Bordeaux, 1937), 66.

[13]"Chacun en sa beauté"; Sigogne is the seventeenth-century poet of deformities.

> Et, seul, sur mes chenets, m'éclairant aux tisons,
> Ecouter le vent battre, et gémir les cloisons,
> Et le fagot flamber, et chanter ma bouilloire!

The sonnet of Wordsworth's in question is the first of the series "Personal Talk," which is by no means an encomium of utter silence; a conversation with the poet's sister takes place, in which he compares the delights of reading to the monotony of gossip. As for the details of idle chatter:

> These all wear out of me, like Forms, with chalk
> Painted on rich men's floors, for one feast-night.

We can see how little Sainte-Beuve's imitation really has to do with Wordsworth's sonnet. In the latter the poet's solitude is rich and productive; the scene is intimate rather than bleak. The winter night and pounding wind are Sainte-Beuve's inventions. In his poem the speaker lives in the midst of a distasteful society of brutes and sex-crazed old maids; he longs for insentience—for one infers that memory and desire are his greatest torments. Monotonous, lulling sensation provides an escape from himself, an hypnotic release from inner and outer realities. Though the conclusion of Wordsworth's poem also evokes the sensations of the hearth, Sainte-Beuve makes the final images far more intense by their contrast with the quatrains.

If, through Sainte-Beuve, Wordsworth had any influence on French verse, I think we must conclude that it was in the revival of the sonnet. Sainte-Beuve knew Ronsard's work, but the example of a contemporary English poet exploiting this form may have been decisive. The abundance of sonnets in *Joseph Delorme* inspired three younger poets, Gautier, Nerval, and Musset, but the suitability of the sonnet for intimate reflective poetry was not generally realized until later in the century. Baudelaire points the way, and many of the next generation of poets—Verlaine, Mallarmé, Rimbaud, Corbière, Hérédia—worked with variations on the traditional sonnet forms.

Although the poems of *Joseph Delorme* cannot, in any strict sense, be called demonic or even sinister, they did contribute to French verse a new mood and iconology, which were to merge with darker themes. The feeling of ennui, weariness with the self, and moral indifference, was to obtrude more and more in younger poets, while the imagery of ugly, commonplace urban objects and scenes became an invaluable means of conveying alienation and malaise. There is also in Sainte-Beuve an important strain of decadent religiosity, concerned more with incense and guilt than with redemption or good works. If Sainte-Beuve is only a quite minor poet, still in those few pieces in which he strove after a new manner of verse there occur passages that anticipate French poetry for many decades.

Théophile Gautier's poetry has had, in our century, the curious fate of being seriously mentioned more often in English-speaking countries than in France: the imitations of *Emaux et Camées* that Pound and Eliot made around 1920 have assured him of that even slight renown which he does not enjoy in his own country. And yet his greater contemporaries considered him a poet of some importance. *Les Fleurs du mal* are dedicated to Gautier, and his death elicited superb poems by both Hugo and Mallarmé. As a prose writer, he was one of the most brilliant stylists of his day and greatly expanded the literary vocabulary.[14] His novel *Mademoiselle de Maupin,* a mock confession-novel, is the most elegant blend of parody and seriousness in French romantic prose. In short, the neglect into which Gautier has fallen seems to me more the result of academic obtuseness than of any failing of his splendid if minor gifts. Gautier's poetic production was not immense, yet still, as in the case of many lesser writers, we must discount much of it if we are to get to the truly seminal part of his work. Our concern here is with Gautier's poems of the 1830's. The better known *Emaux et Camées* (1852)—which Baudelaire evidently cared less for[15]—belong to another area of verbal experiment than the high romantic.

Gautier was part of the second generation of romantic poets, along with Musset and Nerval, men of the 1830's rather than of the Restoration. Their careers followed a somewhat different pattern from those of Lamartine, Sainte-Beuve, Hugo, and Vigny: from the very beginning the *genre romantique* constituted the whole scope of contemporary poetry for them. No hesitation between a traditional, neoclassical style and a modernist one occurred in their first published works; Hugo, Sainte-Beuve, and Byron had, in certain poems, set a definitive example to follow. However, the younger poets were not mere imitators. A num-

[14]See Georges Matoré, *Le Vocabulaire et la société sous Louis-Philippe* (Geneva, 1951).

[15]In an *ébauche* of the preface to *Les Fleurs du mal,* Baudelaire significantly praises Gautier's earlier volumes but not *Emaux et camées.* See *Les Fleurs du mal,* ed. Antoine Adam (Paris, 1959), 4*n.*

ber of circumstances imposed on them a rather new conception of the role of poetry and of the poet in society, which is not without some relation to their style and subject matter. To begin with, official honors played little part in their careers: the contemporary public tended to ignore them, at least as poets, and they were among the first writers to evolve that ironic attitude toward society which characterizes much of nineteenth-century French literature. Skepticism seemed the only possible way for them to look at politics, democracy, and nationalism. Gautier and Nerval belonged, furthermore, to the original Bohemia, an independent colony of artists, poets, actors, journalists, and others whose callings were repugnant to bourgeois values.[16] The character of the French public was such as to inspire in these poets a radically modernist attitude toward literature, and this is what Gautier elaborated in his writings on *l'art pour l'art*.

Art for art's sake is a commonly misinterpreted slogan. Even people associated with it, such as Baudelaire, loathed the expression. To try to determine what complex of ideas it represented for Gautier, we must reflect somewhat on polemics over poetry at the time when Gautier began to write. The major young poet of the day was Victor Hugo, and in the prefaces to *Les Orientales* and *Les Feuilles d'automne* he had spoken of "pure poetry" and "a pure work of art." These expressions seem to indicate both exotic subjects and poems which have no reference to public events, for Hugo makes some matter over the propriety of publishing non-political verse in the wake of a revolution. The whole discussion over *l'art pour l'art*, which Gautier fed with his prefaces to *Albertus* and *Mademoiselle de Maupin*, seems to center around Hugo, local color, and the freedom of the imagination.[17] It is directed against the neoclassical conception of the poet as a composer of odes on public questions. As an affirmation of the autonomy of art, the theory of *l'art pour l'art* is an essential hypothesis of modern esthetics, but it acquired several corollaries in the course of the nineteenth century which are of less value. Opposition to both industrialism and movements of social reform came to color what at first had been merely a reaction to neoclassicism. Finally, immoralism was associated with *l'art pour l'art*. What the phrase most generally and essentially meant, however, can be summed

[16]The romantic *cénacles* had not been Bohemian. For the growth of Bohemia, see Enid Starkie, *Petrus Borel: The Lycanthrope* (New York, 1954), 19–85.

[17]See Marcel A. Ruff, *L'Esprit du mal et l'esthétique baudelairienne* (Paris, 1955), 432. Hugo always claimed to have invented the phrase *l'art pour l'art*.

up as follows: the artist and public have no mutual obligations. In theory at least, the way was prepared for the unprecedented and interlocking series of poetic experiments which form the history of French verse from the 1830's to the end of the century.

In accordance with the theory of *l'art pour l'art*, Gautier's poems display right from the beginning a descriptive richness and intimacy of tone judiciously derived from Hugo and Sainte-Beuve. Symbols of death and urban imagery abound:

> ... la ville aux cent bruits
> Où de brouillards noyés les jours semblent des nuits,
> Où parmi les toits bleus s'enchevêtre et se cogne
> Un soleil terne et mort comme l'oeil d'un ivrogne ...
> ("Paris")

Something of Gautier's originality can be felt in these lines: despite the inversion of *de brouillards,* a device which Gautier normally avoids, the language is free of self-consciously poetic usage.[18] The bleakness of the city, which Sainte-Beuve had less concretely depicted, is reinforced by the imagery of an infernal sky, heavy and dark. The avoidance of banality and the pursuit of the pictorial were Gautier's guiding principles in style.

Although many fine passages occur in all of Gautier's verse, we need not dwell on his second volume, *Albertus:* this is a Byronic verse tale about witches and *sabbats,* which must be seen as a parody, for as seriously and complacently as the French romantics took demonology, their self-irony could also be immense. Demonic imagery is handled quite gravely, however, in *La Comédie de la mort* (1837), in many ways Gautier's most interesting collection and certainly the one which most profoundly influenced Baudelaire. The title poem is intentionally Dantesque: a romantic visit to the underworld forms its subject and "La Comédie de la mort" is almost a summa of the imagery of spleen and death which the 1830's cultivated. The poem begins at the end of autumn; the sky is prison-like:

> C'était le jour des Morts : une froide bruine
> Au bord du ciel rayé, comme une trame fine,
>   Tendait ses filets gris;

[18]Bruneau, *Histoire de la langue française,* XII, Pt. 1, p. 264, suggests that Gautier avoided, except for special effects, anything suggestive of *mots nobles.*

> Un vent de nord sifflait; quelques feuilles rouillées
> Quittaient en frissonnant les cimes dépouillées
>   Des ormes rabougris . . .

There follows a long meditation on the dead in their coffins, which
Baudelaire was to make use of in "La Servante au grand coeur . . . ."
Night falls and the crows, owls, vampires, and other creatures of the
sinister, romantic bestiary emerge. The poet hears a dialogue between
a dead girl and the worm whose "marriage" to her is about to be con-
summated: necrophilia is a favorite demonic mode of sexuality. The
speaker then returns home to a room furnished with a coffin-like bed,
a picture of the dying Christ, and a skull. Raphael appears in order to
announce the end of the human race. "Death in life" is the subject of the
following section and a guide presents herself to lead the poet down the
funèbre spirale:

> Pour guide nous avons une vierge au teint pâle
> Qui jamais ne reçut le baiser d'or du hâle
>   Des lèvres du soleil.
> Sa joue est sans couleur et sa bouche bleuâtre,
> Le bouton de sa gorge est blanc comme l'albâtre
>   Au lieu d'être vermeil.

The figure of the pale woman with black hair occurs regularly in romantic literature and painting. Virginity, frigidity, or sterility are among
her attributes, and sexual barrenness can carry numerous symbolic
meanings as it later does in Mallarmé's "Hérodiade." Here the guide
represents not simply death but the poet's muse, statue-like, *sinistre et
charmante.* The Dantesque pattern of the journey is continued, and the
poet meets successively Faust, Don Juan, and Napoleon, three personages who fired the romantic imagination through their defiance of deity
and mortal bounds. The description of Don Juan is a fine example of the
grotesque:

> Tout ce luxe, ce fard sur cette face creuse,
> Formaient une alliance étrange et monstrueuse.
>   C'étaient plus triste à voir
> Et plus laid qu'un cercueil chez des filles de joie,
> Qu'un squelette paré d'une robe de soie,
>   Qu'une vieille au miroir.
>   . . . .
> Dis, que fais-tu donc là, vieillard, dans les ténèbres,

> Par une de ces nuits où les essaims funèbres
> S'envolent des tombeaux?
> Que vas-tu donc chercher si loin, si tard, à l'heure
> Où l'Ange de minuit au beffroi chante et pleure,
> Sans page et sans flambeaux?

Don Juan, Faust, and Napoleon admit defeat in their search for love, knowledge, and power, and the poet returns from the underworld overwhelmed by the idea of death. He makes a last attempt to throw off this obsession, but in place of the healthy Hellenic muse he has invoked there appears, in a new guise, the infernal guide:

> Chantons Io, Péan!... Mais quelle est cette femme
> Si pâle sous son voile? Ah! c'est toi, vieille infâme!
> Je vois ton crâne ras;
> Je vois tes grands yeux creux, prostituée immonde,
> Courtisane éternelle environnant le monde
> Avec tes maigres bras!

The association of death and eroticism is reaffirmed, and the poem closes on a note of inexorability.

Most of Gautier's poems are more interesting for their details than for their overall structure. "La Comédie de la mort" is characteristic in this respect: a certain colloquial note—evident in our citations—lends itself to discursiveness and rambling. Indeed, the relation between Gautier and Baudelaire becomes clearer when we compare the concision of the younger poet to Gautier's wordiness: often, as in the opening of "La Comédie de la mort," many scattered phrases in Gautier will be drawn together by Baudelaire and forced into a tighter, more dramatic form. But in mood and phrasing Gautier frequently anticipated effects which we commonly ascribe to Baudelaire. The complex of feelings connected with spleen, horror of movement, ebbing life, and nostalgia for the cloister is eloquently expressed in such a poem as "Thébaïde":

> Donc, reçois dans tes bras, ô douce Somnolence,
> Vierge aux pâles couleurs, blanche soeur de la Mort,
> Un pauvre naufragé des tempêtes du sort!
> Exauce un malheureux qui te prie et t'implore,
> Egrène sur son front le pavot inodore,
> Abrite-le d'un pan de ton grand manteau noir,
> Et du doigt clos ses yeux qui ne veulent plus voir.
> Vous, esprits du désert, cependant qu'il sommeille,

> Faites taire les vents et bouchez son oreille,
> Pour qu'il n'entende pas le retentissement
> Du siècle qui s'écroule, et ce bourdonnement
> Qu'en s'en allant au but où son destin la mène
> Sur le chemin du temps fait la famille humaine!

The ancient Christian adoration of immobility as the perfect state, which Pascal so movingly represents, is summed up in lines which convey a dread of historical process, seen not as progress but as decay.

Gautier is so seldom credited with having any thoughts or deep feelings that it may come as a surprise to realize that, in a completely secularized and rather esthetic way, he saw his own age as the end of a great classical-Christian historic cycle, in which a spiritual night was drawing over the West. Predictably, he conceived of human history only as the history of the *beaux arts*, but he had sufficient taste to recognize the relatively impoverished and derivative character of painting, sculpture, and architecture in his day. "Melancholia," suggested by the Dürer engraving, is a meditation on Northern Renaissance painting and Trecento frescoes: it attempts to order the stages of our civilization's decay and concludes that the nineteenth century will remain unredeemed by its art. (Perhaps for the first time in French poetry, a religious vocabulary is here transferred to esthetic matters.) The most thorough statement of Gautier's feelings about history, however, is "Ténèbres," a poem in which thoughts on individual spleen and contemporary decay are cast in terza rima, a form particularly associated with Gautier:

> Taisez-vous, ô mon coeur! taisez-vous, ô mon âme!
> Et n'allez plus chercher de querelles au sort;
> Le néant vous appelle et l'oubli vous réclame.
>
> Mon coeur, ne battez plus, puisque vous êtes mort;
> Mon âme, repliez le reste de vos ailes,
> Car vous avez tenté votre suprême effort.

A theme which Baudelaire and Gautier share, and which is connected with the mood called spleen, is the voluntary imitation of death: through spite at life and apprehension of the future, the soul tries to anticipate its inevitable destruction, the thought of which is tinged with overtones of consolation.

The same imagery of futile movement which Baudelaire was to em-

ploy in "Le Voyage" occurs as the poet begins to résumé his experience
of life:

> Hélas! le poète est pareil à l'amant,
> Car ils ont tous les deux leur maîtresse idéale,
> Quelque rêve chéri caressé chastement:
>
> Eldorado lointain, pierre philosophale
> Qu'ils poursuivent toujours sans l'atteindre jamais;
> Un astre impérieux, une étoile fatale.
>
> L'étoile fuit toujours, ils lui courent après;
> Et le matin venu, la lueur poursuivie,
> Quand ils la vont saisir, s'éteint dans un marais.

The plaint of the despairing artist, so frequently echoed by later poets,
seems to have been an invention of Gautier's. The antinomy of aspiration
and achievement is expanded on:

> Il est beau qu'un plongeur, comme dans les ballades,
> Descende au gouffre amer chercher la coupe d'or,
> Et perce triomphant les vitreuses arcades.
>
> Il est beau d'arriver où tendait son essor,
> De trouver sa beauté, d'aborder à son monde,
> Et, quand on a fouillé, d'exhumer un trésor;
>
> De faire, du plus creux de son âme profonde,
> Rayonner son idée ou bien sa passion,
> D'être l'oiseau qui chante et la foudre qui gronde;
>
> D'unir heureusement le rêve à l'action ...

"Certes, je sortirai, quant à moi, satisfait / D'un monde où l'action n'est
pas la soeur du rêve ..." wrote Baudelaire, taking up Gautier's antithesis, which is another variation on the opposing realms characteristic
of nineteenth-century thought: being and becoming, the ideal and the
real, appearance and reality, and so forth. The feeling of disparity
or *décalage* is typical of the romantics, and Gautier attributes it to the
late and fallen character of his epoch; "Ténèbres" concludes with the
world waiting for a redemption that will never come:

Le Christ, d'un ton railleur, tord l'éponge de fiel
Sur les lèvres en feu du monde à l'agonie,
Et Dieu, dans son Delta, rit d'un rire cruel.

Quand notre passion sera-t-elle finie?
Le sang coule avec l'eau de notre flanc ouvert;
La sueur rouge teint notre face jaunie.

Assez comme cela! nous avons trop souffert;
De nos lèvres, Seigneur, détournez ce calice,
Car pour nous racheter votre Fils s'est offert.

Christ n'y peut rien : il faut que le sort s'accomplisse;
Pour sauver ce vieux monde il faut un Dieu nouveau,
Et le prêtre demande un autre sacrifice.

Voici bien mille ans que l'on saigne l'Agneau;
Il est mort à la fin, et sa gorge épuisée
N'a plus assez de sang pour teindre le couteau.

Le Dieu ne viendra pas. L'Eglise est renversée.

This vision of the cycle of Christian history drawing to its sinister close is an important aspect of romantic historical theory with its Hegelian penchant for sharply defined ages. But Gautier does not place it in the context of prophetic poetry as Nerval, Hugo, and Yeats were to do; for him the imminence of a new cycle is unthinkable. Gautier had not evolved a framework of poetic thought in which he could thoroughly exploit his feeling about history, for his intellect was perhaps too timid to lead him into the abstruse metaphysical concepts cherished by his friend Nerval. But the intuition of a demonic God—a central theme in French romanticism as we shall see—was perfectly consonant with his temperament. His mocking Christ and sardonic God anticipate many later and greater visions of an evil deity.

Before we leave the subject of Gautier, there is one other question which can most pertinently be brought up. Although it is subordinate to the principal themes of this book, something must be said about Gautier's and the other romantics' relation to baroque poetry—just as with Sainte-Beuve it was necessary, in conclusion, to sketch out his importance in reviving the sonnet and the sonnet's subsequent fortune in French poetry, despite the fact that other aspects of Sainte-Beuve's verse concern us more. We shall now briefly have to take account of the romantics' interest in the early seventeenth century and their use of baroque themes and vocabulary.

The romantics' attraction to the baroque—which they called "style Louis XIII"—was so immense that one can only explain critical neglect of this fact by the general modern ignorance of French baroque literature, an ignorance which is only now being dissipated. Through weariness at the late seventeenth-century writers, whom eighteenth-century critics had so fatiguingly extolled as the exemplars of literature, the romantics turned, with excitement, to the somewhat forgotten poets and playwrights who flourished before the courtly age of Louis XIV. Hugo, for example, declared the French language of the baroque period to be superior to that of any other time.[19] The resemblance of his eerie landscapes in the *Ballades* and elsewhere to those of Saint-Amant was generally recognized,[20] for certain baroque poets had a taste for the macabre and ghoulish that clearly anticipates the romantics.[21] In his plays Hugo was also, in certain respects, the disciple of Corneille, Scudéry, and the seventeenth-century Spaniards: the figure of Don César in *Ruy Blas*, with his comic exuberance of metaphor, is definitely reminiscent of both *précieux* styles and *graciosos*. Hugo was not, of course, alone in his fondness for the unexpected, bizarre side of seventeenth-century literature. At least one of Sainte-Beuve's poems is a eulogy of ugliness in the tradition of Sigogne, and Baudelaire's knowledge of baroque poets was remarked on during his lifetime.[22]

The impact of certain rather baroque facets of Shakespeare's plays should not be forgotten either. Musset made considerable use of *Twelfth Night* and *Measure for Measure* in *Les Caprices de Marianne:* the clowns, the elaborate plays on words and spun-out metaphors, and most of all the somber turns of plot in the Dark Comedies give a strange and original coloring to the play. Gautier's tribute to Shakespeare is *Mademoiselle de Maupin*, where a performance of *As You Like It* mirrors the whole novel: transvestite disguise and pastoral create a late-renaissance ambiance. And, finally, the skulls ever-present in French romantic literature are, to some extent, reminiscences of Yorick's, for the gravedigger's

---

[19]*Ibid.*, 232.

[20]See René Jasinski, *Les Années romantiques de Théophile Gautier* (Paris, 1929), 220–22.

[21]See Mario Praz, *The Romantic Agony* (London, 1933), 32–41.

[22]See *Les Fleurs du mal*, ed. Antoine Adam, xii–xiii.

scene in *Hamlet* enchanted partisans of the new literature by its dramatic audacity and philosophic depth.

Gautier's acquaintance with baroque poetry is even more fully attested than that of the other romantics, for he wrote the first study of "Louis XIII" verse, *Les Grotesques* (1835). Although the work is by no means scholarly or complete, it bears witness to the romantics' bemused delight at discovering to what outlandish lengths certain baroque poets went in their search for novelty and surprise. It is probably not very fruitful or even interesting to ascribe the genesis of this or that romantic poem to this or that baroque one, but many striking parallels in subject and style are worth observing in order to clarify the history of French poetry. Skulls, for example, were not exclusively the province of Shakespeare: we can find a death's-head meditation in Pierre de Saint-Louis, one of the poets treated in *Les Grotesques:*

> Au pied d'un crucifix, une teste de mort,
> Ou de morte plutôt, lui déclare son sort,
> Y voyant, sur son front, ces paroles écrites,
> Qu'avec elle, lecteur, il faut que tu médites :
> "Dans les trous de mes yeux, et sur ce crâne ras,
> Vois comme je suis morte, et comme tu mourras,
> J'avois eu, comme toi, la chevelure blonde,
> Les brillans de mes yeux ravissoient tout le monde,
> Maintenant je ne suis que ce que tu peux voir,
> Sers-toi doncques de moi, comme de ton miroir."
>
> ("Une Teste de mort" [23])

Skeletal women are another recurring theme. Under the influence perhaps of the *marinisti*, certain seventeenth-century French poets explored the idea of gruesome ugliness and painful, death-like copulation:

> Non, je ne l'ayme point ceste carcasse d'os,
> Qu'on ne m'en parle plus, quoy qu'il y ait du lucre,
> J'ayme autant embrasser l'image d'Atropos
> Ou me laisser tomber tout nud dans un sepulcre.
> Dés la premiere nuict de nos embrassemens,
> J'imaginay sa chambre estre un grand cimetiere,
> Son corps maigre sembloit un monceau d'ossemens,
> Son linceul un suaire et sa couche une biere.
>
> (Auvray, "Contre Une Dame trop maigre" [24])

[23]Quoted in Jean Rousset, *Anthologie de la poésie baroque française* (Paris, 1961), II, 144.
[24]Quoted in Rousset, *ibid.*, II, 147.

In the hands of the romantics this theme becomes more diabolical. Interest in succubae and the importation of vampire myths from eastern Europe enriched its detail, and Gautier, Philothée O'Neddy, and Baudelaire all wrote variations on it. Gautier's description of Albertus in the arms of his witch introduces the element of metamorphosis, itself a rather baroque motif:

> Tout à coup, sous ses doigts, ô prodige à confondre
> La plus haute raison! Albertus sentit fondre
> Les appas de sa belle, et s'en aller les chairs.
> — Le prisme était brisé. — Ce n'était plus la femme
> Que tout Leyde adorait, mais une vieille infâme
> Sous d'épais sourcils gris roulant de gros yeux verts,
> Et pour saisir sa proie, en manière de pinces,
> De toute leur longueur ouvrant deux grands bras minces.
> (*Albertus*, CV)

Baudelaire's "Métamorphoses du vampire" was to be, like a number of his poems, a reworking of Gautier.

Thematic relations between baroque poetry and romantic literature are too numerous and evident for one to attempt a complete catalogue of them. However, something must be said about certain stylistic similarities, which are perhaps harder to uncover. The abundance of satire, in the early seventeenth century, with its attendant freedom of style, is obviously related to the romantic *grotesque*, but we might also recall the rich descriptive detail of certain seventeenth-century authors, which made them unique in French before the romantic movement. To confine ourselves to merely one facet of style, the use of color adjectives is astonishingly similar at times in certain baroque poets and in Gautier, who, following Hugo and Sainte-Beuve, made color notation the object of a virtual cult. Here is a seventeenth-century description of a butterfly:

> As-tu jamais veu de l'Albastre
> Plus net et plus pur que ce blanc?
> Vois-tu cette couleur de sang?
> Ce noir, ce tané, ce jaunastre?
>
> Remarque icy le sombre éclat
> De la pourpre et de l'amarante,
> Voy comme elle devient mourante,
> Auprès de ce vif incarnat.

> Observe une belle nuance
> Dans ce petit cerne azuré,
> Et que ce verd et ce doré
> Font une discrette nuance.
>
> (Perrin, "Le Papillon" [25])

The very verse form anticipates the "Symphonie en blanc majeur" (in *Emaux et camées*), while the richness and precision of the color terminology is such as one would have hardly thought possible in French before the nineteenth century. We should not however be astonished: the late sixteenth and early seventeenth centuries were marked by a great wave of descriptive verse in the romance literatures. This pictorial poetry has some analogies with French romantic styles, but I think we can discern patterns in the latter that are particularly characteristic of the nineteenth century.

Descriptions of scenes and actions need not be offered as having any ulterior motive, but in poetry of any great weight we expect to infer, by symbolism or analogy, more than one plane or level of sense. The most obvious kind of extended meaning which we find in the earlier centuries of European literature is, of course, the allegorical and typological. In the nineteenth century there was no lack of theoretical statements on symbolism: Hugo's "book of nature" and Baudelaire's "universal analogy," whatever we may think of them as philosophy, are only two of the best-known phrases about the matter. In practice, however, the French romantics liked a particular kind of analogical poem which first seems to become dominant in Gautier.

Although the use of analogy is, of course, too general a characteristic of poetry to dispose of in a few words, certain useful distinctions can be readily made. When Ronsard invites Mignonne to go observe the fate of a rose, an ancient body of poetic commonplaces prepares us for the conclusions he will draw: the analogy is more authoritative than surprising, for we are reading in terms of a familiar convention. But when we begin a poem like Gautier's "Terza Rima," we cannot be sure it is anything but anecdote:

> Quand Michel-Ange eut peint la chapelle Sixtine,
> Et que de l'échafaud, sublime et radieux,
> Il fut redescendu dans la cité latine,

[25]Quoted in Rousset, *ibid.*, I, 153.

Il ne pouvait baisser ni les bras ni les yeux;
Ses pieds ne savaient pas comment marcher sur terre;
Il avait oublié le monde dans les cieux.

Trois grands mois il garda cette attitude austère;
On l'eût pris pour un ange en extase devant
Le saint triangle d'or, au moment du mystère.

The following tercet begins, however, "Frère, voilà pourquoi les poètes . . . ." With this apostrophe, the poem seems to break into two parts, the first and second terms of the analogy; the movement is particularly brusque because of the absence of *ainsi, comme,* or *tel,* which are the usual words bridging the two sections of this kind of analogical poem. Although the shift of subject is abrupt, the Michelangelo anecdote is not extrinsic and gratuitous: Michelangelesque references—a return to the first term of the analogy—come back in the description of poets' state of mind which closes the poem:

Notre jour leur paraît plus sombre que la nuit;
Leur oeil cherche toujours le ciel bleu de la fresque,
Et le tableau quitté les tourmente et les suit.

Comme Buonarotti, le peintre gigantesque,
Ils ne peuvent plus voir que les choses d'en haut,
Et que le ciel de marbre où leur front touche presque.

Sublime aveuglement! magnifique défaut!

What we should note in the structure of "Terza Rima" is the absence, in the beginning, of any indication of theme or direction: while the comparison between Michelangelo's infirmity and the poets' ecstasy is not really odd, it is not in any way foreseeable.

Many of Gautier's poems are built up in the same fashion as "Terza Rima," but the one we shall turn to now seems to me particularly important for its anticipation of Baudelaire's poetic practice. "Niobé" first describes a statue:

Sur un quartier de roche, un fantôme de marbre,
Le menton dans la main et le coude au genou,
Les pieds pris dans le sol, ainsi que des pieds d'arbre,
Pleure éternellement sans relever le cou.

This is one of those *transpositions d'art* which Gautier thought so highly of and which tend to remind us of Pater's unfortunate dictum that art can only be talked about artistically. One of the salient characteristics of this kind of analogical poem in French is the use of specific objects, especially artifacts, as the initial term of comparison. In the conclusion, where the second term of comparison is introduced, Gautier frankly uses the term "symbol":

> O symbole muet de l'humaine misère,
> Niobé sans enfants, mère des sept douleurs,
> Assise sur l'Athos ou bien sur le Calvaire,
> Quel fleuve d'Amérique est plus grand que tes pleurs?

Because we associate the word "symbol" with the poetic practice of Mallarmé and Rimbaud, I should like to call a poem like "Niobé" emblematic: an action, object, or figure is presented and its meaning subsequently glossed. From a formal standpoint the structure seems rather simple: we are reminded somewhat of fables. The closest analogy these emblematic poems have in earlier literature is perhaps the allegory, and it is not surprising that Baudelaire praised allegory or that Gautier wrote an imitation of Petrarch's *Trionfi*.[26] Allegory seemed to have for them the charm of a *pre-classical* mode of poetry. The bipartite emblematic poem was to be more richly exploited by Vigny, Hugo, and Baudelaire but, as in so many matters, Gautier's role as predecessor and innovator is capital.

Gautier's verse is many-faceted, if minor, and has led us away from the imagery of the sinister into other technical considerations. To conclude our examination of demonic iconology, however, we shall consider the verse of two of Gautier's friends of the 1830's. Both are lesser poets and were probably not influential, but their work represents the extremes of early romantic sombreness and linguistic perversity. Philothée O'Neddy and Petrus Borel—to use their chosen names—were among the great literary eccentrics of their day. Often their verse is conventional, but occasionally their reputation for bizarreness is fully justified. O'Neddy was the less peculiar of the two; here is his version of the metamorphosis of woman into skeleton:

> Je rêvais, l'autre nuit, qu'aux splendeurs des orages,
> Sur le parquet mouvant d'un salon de nuages,
> De terreur et d'amour puissamment tourmenté,

[26]"Le Triomphe de Pétrarque."

Avec une lascive et svelte Bohémienne,
 Dans une valse aérienne,
 Ivre et fou j'étais emporté.
. . . .
Oh! pitié! — je me meurs. — Pitié! ma blanche fée!
Disais-je d'une voix électrique, étouffée.
Regarde. — Tout mon corps palpite incandescent. —
Viens, viens, montons plus haut, montons dans une étoile.
— Et là, que ta beauté s'abandonne sans voile
 A ma fougue d'adolescent!

Un fou rire la prit... rire désharmonique,
Digne de s'éployer au banquet satanique.
J'eus le frisson, mes dents jetèrent des strideurs.
Puis, soudain, plus de fée à lubrique toilette!
 Plus rien dans mes bras qu'un squelette
 M'étalant toutes ses hideurs!

         ("Succube")

The living room of clouds with its shifting floor is a striking way of rendering acrophobic dreams, and the luminous storm (*splendeurs* suggests brightness) anticipates the odd and novel adjective "electric," as well as "incandescent," freakily placed in an adverbial position. Linguistic oddity at any cost was O'Neddy's great concern: the colloquial *fou rire* mingles with neologisms like *strideurs* and *désharmonique*, while the expression *sans voile* is pure neoclassicism. The abundance of k-sounds in the last stanza quoted violates the traditional canons of euphony, in order apparently to suggest the clatter of bones. What we have in "Succube" is a good example of Bohemian taste, which values insubordination above all. To some degree, the *espirit de bohème* penetrated nearly all of French romanticism, but it is more covert in major figures. O'Neddy's poem can be taken as a common denominator of the romantic impetus to find the *new* at any cost.

 Petrus Borel was a stranger figure than O'Neddy: "one of the stars in the somber romantic sky," to quote Baudelaire's words. In the preface to his *Rapsodies* Borel wrote, "Je suis républicain comme l'entendrait un loup-cervier; mon républicanisme, c'est de la lycanthropie." The Werewolf, as Borel called himself, seems to have been a deeply disturbed person, incapable of subsisting even in the *bohème* of journalists and lesser poets. Baudelaire regretted the incompleteness and botched character of his talent while maintaining that Borel was essential to romanticism. His linguistic imagination was certainly at times impressive:

Autour de moi voyez la foule sourcilleuse
S'ameuter, du néant son haut coeur est marri. —
Dites de ce vieux chêne où va le tronc pourri? —
Poudre grossir la glèbe. — Et vous, souche orgueilleuse!
Un ogre appelé Dieu vous garde un autre sort!
Moins de prétentions, allons, race servile,
Peut-être avant longtemps, votre tête de mort
Servira de jouet aux enfants par la ville !...
Peu vous importe, au fait, votre vil ossement;
Qu'on le traîne au bourbier, qu'on le frappe et l'écorne...
Il renaîtra tout neuf, quand sonnera la corne
    Du jugement!

                             ("Rêveries")

The archaisms of the first lines are not gratuitous but ironically characterize the crowd as high minded. The blunt dialogue heightens the angry undertone, as does the strange use of *poudre*. Borel is either omitting subject and verb (*il va, poudre . . .*) or else construes it as an infinitive ("to crumble or rot") by analogy with a series of unusual and defective verbs,[27] and treats it as a verb of motion like *aller grossir la terre*. *Glèbe*, a poetic term suggesting fertility, is again ironic: death is meaningless, and proof of God's malevolence. And, finally, the advent of the Last Judgment demonstrates the senseless incoherence of God and His scheme of things: sloughing off one's body only to get it back again is offered as a sardonic consolation.

    Borel did not write much verse; after the volume of *Rapsodies* there remains only the Prologue to the novel *Madame Putiphar*. This piece is an allegory about three apocalyptic horsemen who war in the poet's heart. The world and the cloister are the first two, but his favorite is death:

Le dernier combattant, le cavalier sonore,
Le spectre froid, le gnôme aux filets de pêcheur,
C'est lui que je caresse et qu'en secret j'honore,
Niveleur éternel, implacable faucheur,
C'est la mort, le néant !... D'une voix souterraine
Il m'appelle sans cesse : — Enfant, descends chez moi,
Enfant, plonge en mon sein, car la douleur est reine
De la terre maudite, et l'opprobre en est roi!
Viens, redescends chez moi, viens, replonge en la fange,
Chrysalide, éphémère, ombre, velléité!

[27]Cf. *ardre, sourdre, tistre, poindre, moudre*.

Viens plus tôt que plus tard, sans oubli je vendange
Un par un les raisins du cep Humanité.
Avant que le pilon pesant de la souffrance
T'ait trituré le coeur, souffle sur ton flambeau;
Notre-Dame de Liesse et de la Délivrance,
C'est la mort! Chanaan promis, c'est le tombeau!

These lines are cast in an odd verse form: they are arranged as if in verse-paragraphs, but the rime pattern is stanzaic. The poet seems to be striving for a combination of sustained discourse and lyrical effect. The especially interesting thing about this passage is its cosmology: the underground is seen both as man's origin and end. "*Re*descends," "*re*plonge," cries the horseman, who offers the liberation of original insentience—a theme we have already encountered in Gautier. The colorfulness of the language is also worth noting: "Notre-Dame de Liesse et de la Délivrance" introduces an unctuous note of religiosity, while "cep Humanité" is a super-concise construction usually associated with the late work of Hugo.

In the Prologue to *Madame Putiphar*, as elsewhere in Borel, as in the work of Gautier, or in Hugo's volumes before the exile, the abundance of imagery connected with death, the demonic supernatural, or the absence of God cannot be said to correspond to a stable, coherent pattern of thought. It would be vain to construct a "philosophy" from this verse. As yet, death and the devil are merely obsessive preoccupations. In this sense, we may speak of them as belonging to a French romantic iconology: they create favorite moods rather than symbolize ways of thinking. In the course of the nineteenth century, however, as the strain of poetry darkens and diversifies, several figures stand out for the breadth of their poetic vision and its coherence. After 1840, the poetry of Vigny, Baudelaire, Nerval, and Hugo absorbs and orders the fragments of romantic thought and sensibility.

IV

VIGNY'S DEMONIC WORLD

We have seen that the imagery of the sinister recurs ever more frequently in poetry from 1825 to 1845. For convenience we can distinguish several modes of it. Victor Hugo's *Ballades* illustrate the folkloric and medieval mode of demonic imagery. This is allied more with superstition than with religious feeling and is usually treated in a mock-serious fashion. We can associate it with the term "grotesque" which Hugo liked and which has been defined as "an attempt to invoke and subdue the demonic aspects of the world." [1] Closely related is the Oriental-Spanish strain of local color: from Musset's Byronic verse tales to Hugo's *Hernani* and *Ruy Blas*, the southern and eastern countries represent the realm of fatal *volupté*. The melodrama is another demonic mode and can best be defined as a world where evil is secularized and violent, the villain substituting for the more traditional Christian devil. Sometimes in French romantic literature, we even encounter the Byronic inversion of values by which Cain becomes a hero: Balzac's Vautrin and his criminal antisociety are opposed to the rotten world of conventional goodness. In the case of Balzac, however, a distinction is to be made: his depiction of Vautrin is not merely designed to shock but is supported by a coherent sociological theory. Most of the early romantic forms of demonology are, on the other hand, purely gratuitous: they do not seem to embody a view of the world so much as an idle taste for the disagreeable. A somewhat more serious handling of the demonic occurs, as we have seen, in Gautier's *Comédie de la mort*, where the emphasis is less on objects of superstition than on a view of history as the decay of art and the drying up of religious feeling. Yet admirable as certain fragments

[1] Wolfgang Kayser, *The Grotesque in Art and Literature*, trans. Ulrich Weisstein (Bloomington, 1963), 188.

70

of Gautier are, it is not until we come to Vigny's later poetry that we find a coherent vision of mankind under the sway of the inhuman.

Vigny's imagination seems to have been early and strongly influenced by Milton,[2] who, as the last great mythic poet before the nineteenth century, forms a kind of link between the orthodox Christian imagination and the various changes wrought in the Christian world view by the romantics. "Eloa ou la soeur des anges," Vigny's earliest attempt at mythopoeia, derives obviously (in its embellished style as well as in its subject) from Milton's elevation of biblical and para-biblical matter to the sublime style, as well as from the romantic fascination and dissatisfaction with the old Christian dogma. However, "Eloa" is not as clear in its theological implications as Blake's criticisms of Milton or even Vigny's later notions of good and evil. It is obviously a youthful work, somewhat spoiled by a Byronic urge to shock, while remaining ambiguous in intention. An angel, Eloa, has been born from a tear shed by Jesus over Lazarus' death. The point seems to be that friendship and pity have begotten the first earth-born angel, who eventually will succumb to Satan through her desire to console him. Compassion is a virtue belonging to the devil's party in Vigny's thought. And Satan, when he appears, eagerly assures Eloa of his solicitude for mankind:

> "J'ai pris au Créateur sa faible créature;
> "Nous avons, malgré lui, partagé la Nature :
> "Je le laisse, orgueilleux des bruits du jour vermeil,
> "Cacher des astres d'or sous l'éclat d'un Soleil;
> "Moi, j'ai l'ombre muette, et je donne à la terre
> "La volupté des soirs et les biens du mystère.
> . . . .
> "La voilà sous tes yeux l'oeuvre du Malfaiteur;
> "Ce méchant qu'on accuse est un Consolateur
> "Qui pleure sur l'esclave et le dérobe au maître,
> "Le sauve par l'amour des chagrins de son être,
> "Et, dans le mal commun lui-même enseveli,
> "Lui donne un peu de charme et quelquefois l'oubli."

These direct declarations anticipate the best in Vigny's later work: given the poverty-stricken character of early nineteenth-century French, they constitute a very admirable example of "sublime" style. Above all, their thought is incisive and gnomically expressed. Our reading of "Eloa" as

[2]See Charles Bruneau, *Histoire de la langue française* (Paris, 1948), XII, Pt. 1, p. 112.

a myth about the secret bonds between man's lot and Satan's is, however, somewhat thrown out of line by a coda tacked on to the poem, a passage rather difficult to interpret, in which Eloa and Satan fall through eternity endlessly reproaching one another. This conclusion is clever as a shift in tone (it was perhaps meant to be a criticism of marriage), but it confuses the theological notions which had previously been quite sharp. Perhaps Vigny meant one to conclude that, regardless of God or Satan, all personal relationships are hellish, which, given his personality, might not be too improbable.

Vigny's later and more important work also offers enigmas in interpretation. We know that Vigny, like Hugo and Lamartine, was always tempted by the urge to write one of those great metaphysical poems of the sort that Blake, Goethe, Shelley, and (later) Rimbaud managed to produce. The idea of a *Fin de Satan*—a kind of *suite* to "Eloa" in which the eternal dualism of God and Satan would be transcended—apparently occurred to Vigny long before it did to Hugo,[3] but we have no samples of this project. On the other hand, the posthumous collection that we know as *Les Destinées* (1864) was planned and replanned by Vigny for the last twenty years of his life. Its publication was attended to by a friend of the poet's, and all evidence points to the fact that *Les Destinées* remains a compromise between what Vigny really wanted to say and what he succeeded in expressing. Up to within a year of his death Vigny was still trying to work his last volume into a coherent whole and still foreseeing parts of it that he was never to write.[4]

The critical reaction to *Les Destinées* has a curious history. The work did not cause much stir upon publication: Vigny had long ceased to be prominent in literary circles, and he had published so little since the 1830's that the book must have seemed really to come from beyond the tomb. Furthermore, Vigny's style, with its roots in late eighteenth-century and Empire poetry could hardly have been revelatory to readers of the future Parnassians—much less to Leconte de Lisle (who found this late volume a decline), or to Verlaine and Mallarmé, who were beginning their careers under the aegis of Baudelaire. In 1871, when Rimbaud drew up a sketch of the history of nineteenth-century French poetry, he did not, in his endless lists of famous and forgotten poets, mention

[3]See H. J. Hunt, *The Epic in Nineteenth-Century France* (Oxford, 1941), 145–49.

[4]See Alfred de Vigny, *Les Destinées*, ed. Verdun L. Saulnier (Paris, 1947), xv–xix.

Vigny. The latter's true fame seems only to have begun somewhat later, at a time when pedagogues were defining what was to be considered important in French literature: a spurt of attention in the late 1880's and 1890's suddenly made Vigny into a schoolroom classic. (Marcel Proust, that best of students, found Vigny second only to Baudelaire among French lyric poets.) Since that time, academic research has gradually illuminated Vigny's life, sources, and private musings. Yet one feels that in some ways the real interest of Vigny's work has been neglected in the desire to make of him some necessary complement to the *pléiade* of French romantic poets.

"Optimist" and "pessimist," "symbolist" and "philosopher," the tags attached to Vigny recur with the tiresome finality of terms that never settle anything. Elaborate schemes have been drawn up to resolve any antithetical patterns among them.[5] Provisionally we might best simply refute these labels in a categoric fashion: Vigny can hardly be charged with having a philosophy in the modern sense of the term; his acquaintance with technical philosophy was so slight that he could not make out what Kant had been up to.[6] Vigny was no more and no less a metaphysician than Hugo, Nerval, Lamartine, and Baudelaire. Perhaps *moraliste* would be a better word to describe his train of thought. As for his "symbolism," Vigny relished the ancient conventions of allegory, and it is pointless to suggest any bond between him and the *symbolistes*. Finally, one who is both an optimist and a pessimist is really neither; Vigny's cogitations on the question of evil are those of a hesitant dualist: like so many French romantics Vigny was a Manichaean groping, with only partial success, toward some dialectic that might resolve his antithetical feelings.

With as few preconceptions as possible, therefore, we can now approach *Les Destinées* in search of the work's distinctive poetic qualities, postponing, at least initially, any attempt to synthesize the author's view of life. At the same time, we shall limit our discussion to those poems which have some breadth of meaning. For example, we shall leave aside "Les Oracles" (although for the *amateur* of poetic styles, it is a fascinating attempt to discuss the politics of the Second Republic in periphrases) and "Wanda," from which we can learn something about Western European attitudes toward Czarist Russia and its plight. Rather,

---

[5]See, for example, *ibid.*, xix–xlv.
[6]See Alfred de Vigny, *Oeuvres*, ed. F. Baldensperger (Paris, 1960), II, 1251–53.

we shall deal with Vigny as an anti-Christian thinker, eager to subvert, on their own serious grounds, the orthodox conceptions of God and Saviour.

The title-poem of *Les Destinées* was evidently conceived as the first stage in a dialectic to be explored throughout the volume. It is built around one of the dominant symbols of French romanticism: the sinister sky. The sky is, of all objects of contemplation, the one most closely identified with godhead in Western symbolism. The Romance languages confuse it with heaven, while Greek and Latin sometimes call it by the name of the principal ancient divinity (*sub Jove, Zeùs hùei*). The French romantic preoccupation with the Christian God and his tyranny led to a great elaboration of sky imagery in its demonic modality: the atmosphere is represented as not only dark, but also solid and heavy; frequently it is compared to metal, and sometimes even to a prison; the sky is seen as an enclosure rather than as an access to higher regions. Behind this conception lurks, of course, a covert analogy with hell, which has always been thought of as confined, in opposition to the boundlessness of heaven.

One wonders whether Vigny did not choose to put the title-poem "Les Destinées" into terza rima in order to recall Dante and the *Inferno*, since Vigny never used this prosodic form elsewhere and since it is, in any case, uncommon in French. The style, however, is not Dantesque but follows the adjective- and participle-laden sentence patterns of the abbé Delille:

> Depuis le premier jour de la création,
> Les pieds lourds et puissants de chaque Destinée
> Pesaient sur chaque tête et sur toute action.
>
> Chaque front se courbait et traçait sa journée,
> Comme le front d'un boeuf creuse un sillon profond
> Sans dépasser la pierre où sa ligne est bornée.
>
> Ces froides déités liaient le joug de plomb
> Sur le crâne et les yeux des hommes leurs esclaves,
> Tous errants, sans étoile, en un désert sans fond;
>
> Levant avec effort leurs pieds chargés d'entraves,
> Suivant le doigt d'airain dans le cercle fatal,
> Le doigt des Volontés inflexibles et graves.

Tristes divinités du monde oriental,
Femmes au voile blanc, immuables statues,
Elles nous écrasaient de leur poids colossal.

The imagery of the sinister is carefully established: there is pressure on man's head, while his feet are shackled and his actions controlled like those of a domestic animal. In short, he has been reduced to the sub-human. The landscape is a wasteland marked only by a stone; no plant life softens it. The yoke is a pivot image used of both oxen and slaves, and the lead it is made of constitutes the basest element in the hierarchy of metals, the one associated not only with the infernal, but with the ultimate decline from the Golden Age. Vigny has furthermore enriched the symbol of the demonic sky with female deities patterned after the Eumenides. Fate is the metaphysical conception most suited to the image of an infernal universe, for it creates a figurative prison analogous to the material one. Since fate implies a preordained course of events, images of immobility also belong to this complex: the deities are statues and the world consists of a "circle."

The *cercle fatal* recalls another fact about demonic imagery, which is essential to the sense of the poems as a whole. Circles have often been used as symbols of godhead—for example, Dante's *tre giri*—and immobility is an attribute of divine perfection. But certain symbols can be read in both a divine and a demonic sense; here the demonic mode prevails. Likewise, broader conceptions can be susceptible of opposite interpretations: as "Les Destinées" progresses and the ancient idea of fate is equated with the Christian principle of grace, we realize that the poem offers a demonic interpretation of Christian theology.

"Les Destinées" is closely related to another poem, which is a reading of the Bible "in its infernal or diabolical sense," as Blake put it in *The Marriage of Heaven and Hell.* "Le Mont des Oliviers," which Vigny had once decided would set the tone of his whole volume, is a demonic version of the Gospel. Nineteenth-century French writers were much given to reinterpreting Jesus' life, but while some sought above all to find democratic teachings in the Gospel, others saw in it a confirmation of their feeling that the Christian God was essentially sinister. Vigny was of both persuasions: his Christ preaches fraternity and has been abandoned by His evil father. The Crucifixion thus becomes a meaning-less, purely human event—simply another example of God's indifference to mankind, symbolized by the impenetrable black sky stretched over the agony in the garden.

A moral emerges in the famous *septain* which Vigny added to his poem long after its composition. Vigny has earlier been elaborating on Jesus' prayer: "O my father, if this cup may not pass away from me, except I drink it, thy will be done" (Matthew 26:42). Since God does not speak or answer in the Gospel, especially to the crucial question "Eli, Eli, lama sabachtani," Vigny draws the conclusion of his myth by inference from the night in Gethsemane and the Crucifixion:

LE SILENCE
S'il est vrai qu'au Jardin sacré des Ecritures,
Le Fils de l'homme ait dit ce qu'on voit rapporté;
Muet, aveugle et sourd au cri des créatures,
Si le Ciel nous laissa comme un monde avorté,
Le juste opposera le dédain à l'absence,
Et ne répondra plus que par un froid silence
Au silence éternel de la Divinité.

We can clearly perceive here the impetus behind Vigny's creation of demonic myth: the potential of mankind is felt to be circumscribed by the conception of a father-sky-god like the Christian one. None of the French romantics wrote so explicitly about God's hindering effect on man as did Blake, but one senses in many of them the same awe at human powers of revolt and the same disgust at the hoary figure of Nobodaddy sitting in the clouds.

I have spoken of "Le Mont des Oliviers" and "Les Destinées" as myth, but perhaps the term had best be qualified. Vigny's taste, nurtured on the Bible, *Paradise Lost*, *Le Génie du christianisme*, and on Byron, was partial to epic and legendary material, but his handling of it reflects the allegorizing urge of neoclassicism. A didactic, moral-imperative tone distinguishes Vigny's work from pure forms of mythopoeia and symbolism. Sometimes, as in "La Colère de Samson," the ethical, hortatory element is skilfully subordinated to the framework of the myth; elsewhere, however, as in "La Mort du loup," we feel the contrived quality which is the greatest pitfall of allegory and which can only be redeemed by magnificance of detail. Certainly "La Mort du loup" suffers in its initial, descriptive part from just such contrivance. Vigny's art often lies on some ill-defined borderline between versified narration with comments and the indestructible wholeness of mythopoeic poetry. The recent discovery that he often, if not always, wrote out his poems in prose versions which he later versified,[7] suggests the precarious nature of his imagination: probably none of his poems is free of mechanical elaboration, but most of them attain, at some point, a high order of poetry, even if only for a line or two.

To judge the real scope of Vigny's art, we must examine "La Maison du Berger" in some detail. Like "Les Destinées," this poem had a particular importance in Vigny's mind. According to his plan of 1847—the year when he had already made the prose version of "Les Destinées"— "La Maison du Berger" would open his volume, which was to be closed by Eva's never-written reply. Vigny's critics have been especially obtuse in regard to this longest, most complex, if not most perfect of his later poems.[8] It surely contains the greatest number of Vigny's unforgettable lines, and I feel it gives the true measure of his talent. The opening passage, uneven though it be, shows a wonderful command of rhetoric. First:

> Si ton coeur, gémissant du poids de notre vie,
> Se traîne et se débat comme un aigle blessé,
> Portant comme le mien, sur son aile asservie,
> Tout un monde fatal, écrasant et glacé;
> S'il ne bat qu'en saignant par sa plaie immortelle,
> S'il ne voit plus l'amour, son étoile fidèle,
> Eclairer pour lui seul l'horizon effacé . . .

The ample *septain*—already an archaically long stanza when the poem was written—is handled with sophistication: the sentence form is not yet resolved, though the imagery comes to a resting point; the initial, slightly incoherent image of the wounded eagle-heart crushed in the wing by a heavy world (we encounter again the symbolism of "Les Destinées") is followed by the vision of a night sky where no star shines —stars always mean hope. The second stanza borrows its imagery from the prison galleys which subsisted until 1748:

> Si ton âme enchaînée, ainsi que l'est mon âme,
> Lasse de son boulet et de son pain amer,
> Sur sa galère en deuil laisse tomber la rame,
> Penche sa tête pâle et pleure sur la mer,

---

[7]See Henri Guillemin, *M. de Vigny: homme d'ordre et poète* (Paris, 1955), 65–66, 69–70, 73–77.

[8]See, for example, Vigny, *Les Destinées*, 25.

> Et, cherchant dans les flots une route inconnue,
> Y voit, en frissonnant, sur son épaule nue,
> La lettre sociale écrite avec le fer . . .

The sentence pattern is still not resolved. Skipping the third stanza which again consists of a series of if-clauses, we find a tonic shift of verbal mode from the most indirect of tense usages—the hypothesis—into the firm imperative:

> Pars courageusement, laisse toutes les villes;
> Ne ternis plus tes pieds aux poudres du chemin;
> Du haut de nos pensers vois les cités serviles
> Comme les rocs fatals de l'esclavage humain.

The image of the infernal city standing in a wasteland of dust and rock is, as we have seen in regard to Sainte-Beuve and Gautier, the principal way for the French romantics to express the character of modern life.

Now the sentences become declarative, as the refuge of Nature is invoked:

> La Nature t'attend dans un silence austère;
> L'herbe élève à tes pieds son nuage des soirs,
> Et le soupir d'adieu du soleil à la terre
> Balance des beaux lis comme des encensoirs.
> La forêt a voilé ses colonnes profondes,
> La montagne se cache, et sur les pâles ondes
> Le saule a suspendu ses chastes reposoirs.

Something of the heteroclite character of Vigny's style is suggested by this *septain*: the *-oir* rimes are strikingly rare, as is the ecclesiastical imagery (Baudelaire later was to imitate them), but at the same time banal, late neoclassical epithets and images abound. The effect is not unlike that of Chateaubriand's vocabulary, in which genuine invention is mingled with all the poetic insipidities of rococo taste. Exactly the same mixture occurs two stanzas later where, following his rhetorical principle of elegant variety, Vigny avoids the noun-plus-verb declarative sentence pattern hitherto used:

> Il est sur ma montagne une épaisse bruyère
> Où les pas du chasseur ont peine à se plonger,
> Qui plus haut que nos fronts lève sa tête altière,
> Et garde dans la nuit le pâtre et l'étranger.

Viens y cacher l'amour et ta divine faute;
Si l'herbe est agitée ou n'est pas assez haute,
J'y roulerai pour toi la Maison du Berger.

The conventions of pastoral are imaginatively renovated here: keeping
the figure of the shepherd, Vigny places him in the surroundings of
real, contemporary shepherds. The return to the first person singular
creates a sudden note of intimacy, as does the suggestion of secrecy,
beds, and night. In order to bring out Vigny's originality we might recall, by way of contrast, some of the innumerable but not very individ-
ualized love-in-a-landscape poems of Hugo, like "Tristesse d'Olympio."

Having established a version of pastoral, Vigny contrasts traveling in
the shepherd's wagon with the latest mode of transportation, the railroad.
Much fun has been made of Vigny's supposed anger at the locomotive,
but little thought has been given to the appropriateness of this famous
seeming excursus on railway accidents. The metallic, the forged, the
built, in short, anything pertaining to machines or constructions has always been part of demonic symbolism. Vigny has simply taken the latest
embodiment of the Satanic urge to invent (of which the first example,
he knew from *Paradise Lost*, was the cannon) and set it in opposition to
the old, natural way of life.

Stylistically the passage on the railroad is at once magnificent and
vaguely comic:

Que Dieu guide à son but la vapeur foudroyante
Sur le fer des chemins qui traversent les monts,
Qu'un ange soit debout sur sa forge bruyante,
Quand elle va sous terre ou fait trembler les ponts
. . . .
Oui, si l'ange aux yeux bleus ne veille sur sa route,
Et le glaive à la main ne plane et la défend,
S'il n'a compté les coups du levier, s'il n'écoute
Chaque tour de la roue en son cours triomphant,
S'il n'a l'oeil sur les eaux et la main sur la braise,
Pour jeter en éclats la magique fournaise,
Il suffira toujours du caillou d'un enfant.

The stern Miltonic angel is one of Vigny's most successful attempts at
mythmaking, and the suspenseful syntax, building up to a blunt, detached clause with an attendant shift of tone, demonstrates Vigny's
mastery of his beloved *septain*. But the periphrases make one vaguely un-

comfortable: it is not so much that Vigny, like the neoclassicists, abhorred the normal terms for objects; rather, we are disturbed by the way Vigny readily assimilates the locomotive into his poetic world, as if the industrial age did not need a new style. Later he refers to the "bull" and the "dragon": the particularness of the locomotive is passed over. The stylistic problem involved here was a major one for nineteenth-century poets: Could old conventions of poetic diction and meter suffice to express the flavor of contemporary life? Before Rimbaud's time we find, without there being much written about the matter, some curious hestitations in practice, of which Vigny's is perhaps the most memorable.

According to the historical perspective he has been slowly establishing in the first part of "La Maison du Berger," the present and the urban betoken decay of the imagination and imprisonment of the spirit. Pastoral returns in a lament over the passing of travel by stagecoach:

> On n'entendra jamais piaffer sur une route
> Le pied vif du cheval sur les pavés en feu :
> Adieu, voyages lents, bruits lointains qu'on écoute,
> Le rire du passant, les retards de l'essieu,
> Les détours imprévus des pentes variées,
> Un ami rencontré, les heures oubliées,
> L'espoir d'arriver tard dans un sauvage lieu.

The underlying image in this stanza is one of irregular motion toward an unknown end point. It is followed immediately by the introduction of the demonic circular symbolism, and, in a curious passage, people become locomotives:

> La distance et le temps sont vaincus. La science
> Trae autour de la terre un chemin triste et droit.
> Le Monde est rétréci par notre expérience,
> Et l'équateur n'est plus qu'un anneau trop étroit.
> Plus de hasard. Chacun glissera sur sa ligne,
> Immobile au seul rang que le départ assigne,
> Plongé dans un calcul silencieux et froid.

A Satanic world of metal, coal, and regular, geometric motion—which is as deadly as stillness—has banished the plants and animals of nature.

A reflexion on the death of Revery closes Part I of the poem and provides an adequate transition to the next section, which begins as a history of the decline of poetry from its biblical and Homeric estate. There are dark allusions to contemporary poets (Lamartine, evidently) who dabble in politics, and aspersions cast on industrialism and the government. This section can best be described as a rebuttal of *Saint-Simonisme*,[9] the doctrine, widespread in both bourgeois and socialist quarters, that industrialism would lead to universal well-being. A meditation on the "diamond" of human thought (Vigny's principal non-demonic symbol[10]) leads, somewhat unexpectedly, to intuitions of the future, accompanied by imagery of dawn and awakening. Most surprising of all, the section concludes with the occultist jargon common to many romantics, especially Hugo:

> Mais notre esprit rapide en mouvements abonde;
> Ouvrons tout l'arsenal de ses puissants ressorts.
> L'invisible est réel. Les âmes ont leur monde
> Où sont accumulés d'impalpables trésors.
> Le Seigneur contient tout dans ses deux bras immenses,
> Son Verbe est le séjour de nos intelligences,
> Comme ici-bas l'espace est celui de nos corps.

The relation of this passage to Part I of the poem is only superficially obscure: Vigny is exposing a dialectic of history in which the Age of Nature has yielded to that of machinery which, in turn, will be followed by the reign of immaterial *Geist*. The prophetic turning toward the future characteristic of romanticism thus promises, at least momentarily, to lead out of the demonic world.

By a slightly tenuous train of thought, Vigny passes from the question of mankind's potential to Eva's nature at the beginning of Part III. Seven stanzas of the maxim-like declarations which Vigny prized then lead to the final and most curious turning point in the thematics of the poem:

> Eva, j'aimerai tout dans les choses créées,
> Je les contemplerai dans ton regard rêveur
> Qui partout répandra ses flammes colorées,
> Son repos gracieux, sa magique saveur :
> Sur mon coeur déchiré viens poser ta main pure,
> Ne me laisse jamais seul avec la Nature;
> Car je la connais trop pour n'en pas avoir peur.

Nature, which had originally represented the higher, pastoral state of existence, is now dissociated from the human. She speaks, cold and statue-like, reminding one of the goddesses of Destiny:

---

[9] See *Ibid.*, 25–26.
[10] See François Germain, *L'Imagination d'Alfred de Vigny* (Paris, 1962), 528.

> Elle me dit : "Je suis l'impassible théâtre
> "Que ne peut remuer le pied de ses acteurs;
> "Mes marches d'émeraude et mes parvis d'albâtre,
> "Mes colonnes de marbre ont les dieux pour sculpteurs.
> "Je n'entends ni vos cris ni vos soupirs; à peine
> "Je sens passer sur moi la comédie humaine
> "Qui cherche en vain au ciel ses muets spectateurs.

The metaphor of life as a play was much used by nineteenth-century French poets. Its effect is usually one of diminution: the fragility, brevity, and insignificance of human existence are stressed.

It is usually asserted that Vigny disliked nature out of spite because other romantic poets wrote so affectionately of it. However, we have seen that Vigny's concern in "La Maison du Berger" is to represent mankind's spiritual potential, which can only be dwarfed by the immensity of the material world. Nature, therefore, is depressing in her magnificence:

> C'est là ce que me dit sa voix triste et superbe,
> Et dans mon coeur alors je la hais, et je vois
> Notre sang dans son onde et nos morts sous son herbe
> Nourrissant de leurs sucs la racine des bois.
> Et je dis à mes yeux qui lui trouvent des charmes :
> "Ailleurs tous vos regards, ailleurs toutes vos larmes,
> "Aimez ce que jamais on ne verra deux fois."
> . . . .
> Vivez, froide Nature, et revivez sans cesse
> Sous nos pieds, sur nos fronts, puisque c'est votre loi;
> Vivez, et dédaignez, si vous êtes déesse,
> L'homme humble passager, qui dut vous être un roi;
> Plus que tout votre règne et que ses splendeurs vaines,
> J'aime la majesté des souffrances humaines;
> Vous ne recevrez pas un cri d'amour de moi.

Many of the essential tendencies of Vigny's art are evident in this section of "La Maison du Berger." If much of his verse is ornamented in neoclassical fashion, the heightened passages frequently show traits that are Vigny's own. Often it is a sententious speech which constitutes the most eloquent part of the poem, as is the case here. Imperatives and declarative verse-sentences—especially at the end of stanzas—are the syntactic signs of Vigny's most elevated style, and the didactic tone of allegory prevails. Vigny is primarily a gnomic poet: his imagination sought lapidary statements, and the inevitable introductory and circumstantial material suggests all too frequently that Vigny is versifying a prose sketch.

As "La Maison du Berger" draws to a close the time is again evening, as in Part I; this recurrence forces on our attention the dialectic character of the poem and the enrichment of the speaker's point of view which has occurred in the course of its 336 lines. The elegiac mood, created by the contrast between man's cycle of life and that of nature, intensifies in what is perhaps the most lyrical stanza in Vigny's *oeuvre*:

> Nous marcherons ainsi, ne laissant que notre ombre
> Sur cette terre ingrate où les morts ont passé;
> Nous nous parlerons d'eux à l'heure où tout est sombre,
> Où tu te plais à suivre un chemin effacé,
> A rêver, appuyée aux branches incertaines,
> Pleurant, comme Diane au bord de ses fontaines,
> Ton amour taciturne et toujours menacé.

The closing line consists of one of those great quadripartite alexandrines in which four words assume massive proportions. The simile it completes demands some elucidation: most commentators learnedly observe that the source is *As You Like It* and that the reference is not to the goddess but to Montemayor's *Diana enamorada*. But in Vigny the allusion is to the Diana of antiquity, by which name he, like most Frenchmen of his day, designated three Greek deities as well as the Roman one. He actually seems to mean Selene, the moon-goddess enamored of Endymion, who, sunk in eternal sleep, lay exposed on a mountain. The associations of the myth are nice: nighttime and mortal frailty. The imagery of vanishing light which runs through the stanza provides a symbol of mortality, and, after the intermediary vision of a future Golden Age, we are brought back to the confines of our present condition.

What Vigny's definitive view of man in history was cannot be ascertained—it is perhaps significant that he never expressed it. The importance of his verse, though, is clear: Vigny presents us, for the first time in French romantic poetry, with a fully elaborated vision of a demonic universe. Fragments of such a vision occur in Hugo's earlier work and even in certain passages of Lamartine,[11] but in Vigny it is whole: the

---

[11]For Lamartine see "Novissima verba," 11.380 et seq. *La Chute d'un ange*, part of Lamartine's unfinished attempt at a great philosophical epic, contains another theme, which, if not really demonic, displaces man's focus from God to himself: Cédar abandons his fellow angels to live with the mortal Daïdha.

world is a wasteland of rock and metal covered with a black lid; eroticism is perverted, as in "La Colère de Samson," and a general mood of
alienation prevails. Fate, set in motion by a sinister, withdrawn deity,
provides the mechanism underlying the universe. In short, Vigny presents us with the essential categories of demonic symbolism coherently
worked out. Although he evidently did not feel that such a view of the
world was complete, it was congenial to his imagination and he treated
it with the utmost seriousness. Vigny's handling of Satanic imagery
might be called philosophical in order to distinguish it from a theological
conception of an evil world. The difference is one of sensibility: using
similar materials, Baudelaire, as we shall see presently, constructed a more
nearly religious vision of demonic forces.

V

BAUDELAIRE:
INNOVATION AND ARCHAISM

"The day will come, undoubtedly, when . . . the date of *Les Fleurs du mal* will no longer seem like the beginning of modernism in poetry. Baudelaire will then seem much closer to the romantics, from whom he has been excessively separated . . . ." [1] Baudelaire has, by now, ceased to interest us for the reasons which once appeared important: his diabolical Catholicism is a familiar, historical mode of sensibility which neither shocks nor has morbid appeal, particularly in its erotic applications; his estheticism has the outmoded charm of *art nouveau;* finally, as an experimental writer he was timid in comparison with Rimbaud and Mallarmé, whose audacious attempts to isolate the essence of poetry have not been surpassed; in short, Baudelaire is taking his proper place among the French romantics and must be seen in the same perspective as his contemporaries.

Since Baudelaire had an acute, epigrammatic intelligence, reminiscent of the seventeenth-century moralists, critics have largely tended to deal with philosophical themes and statements in his work: they have pursued the dangerous game of inventing for him an immutable system of thought. Recent research, however, has stressed the diversity and changes in Baudelaire's intellectual development. [2] He wavered, for example, between Gautier's conception of *l'art pour l'art*, with its attendant admiration for Greek sculpture, and a para-Christian theory of art as repentance and salvation. [3] Such inconsistencies are somewhat masked by the structure of *Les Fleurs du mal* where Baudelaire evidently tried

---

[1] Henri Peyre, *Connaissance de Baudelaire* (Paris, 1951), 155.

[2] See Charles Baudelaire, *Les Fleurs du mal*, ed. Antoine Adam (Paris, 1959), viii–xvi.

[3] See Marcel Ruff, *L'Esprit du mal et l'esthétique baudelairienne* (Paris, 1955), 233–43.

to arrange his poems in a dialectic pattern which could countenance paradoxes and antithetical themes, but any close chronological study of his work reveals that Baudelaire was more a master of the maxim than a systematic theologian or philosopher.

As a corollary to Baudelaire's fragmented and varied patterns of thought, we find that stylistically his poetry does not seem to show the clear schema of change and evolution that we can trace in the works of Mallarmé, Rimbaud, Hugo, or virtually any other major nineteenth-century French poet. There is, of course, some difficulty in dating much of his verse: poems which Baudelaire's friends claimed to have seen in the 1840's may have been later reworked and no longer represent Baudelaire's early style, whereas among those published as late as the 1860's we cannot always be sure that certain ones were not youthful works finally offered to the public through some caprice of the poet's.[4] Furthermore, in his criticism Baudelaire tended to avoid discussing matters of style and diction: we really have no clues to his theories about rhetoric, levels of style, vocabulary, and imagery. From the evidence of the texts, however, we can say that Baudelaire was more influenced than any of his contemporaries by pre-nineteenth-century poets, and that a taste for idiosyncratic archaisms abided with him to the end.

Using whatever evidence we have for dating Baudelaire's poems, we can tentatively make some distinctions between earlier work and his style around 1860, but great divergencies still subsist in the poems of any one period. "J'aime le souvenir . . . " will serve as a convenient point of departure, since, for excellent reasons, it is ascribed to the very earliest phase of Baudelaire's career:

> J'aime le souvenir de ces époques nues,
> Dont Phoebus se plaisait à dorer les statues.
> Alors l'homme et la femme en leur agilité
> Jouissaient sans mensonge et sans anxiété,
> Et, le ciel amoureux leur caressant l'échine,
> Exerçaient la santé de leur noble machine.

The correspondence of clause and couplet suggests the work of an unpracticed poet for whom Hugo's innovations in prosody do not yet exist; the second rime, furthermore, belongs both to the categories of poor rime and facile rime. "Noble machine" is patterned after neoclassical

---

[4]A case in point is that of "La Lune offensée," which most critics would take to be early Baudelaire although it was not published until 1862.

rhetorical principles: by metonymy "body" becomes "machine," but since the latter is not inherently sublime, it is ennobled by the epithet. Yet we must not assume that Baudelaire was to avoid such old-fashioned devices later on; as a matter of fact, he added the mythological touch for the second edition of *Les Fleurs du mal;* in the first one, the text had read "le soleil se plaît . . . " rather than "Phoebus se plaîsait . . . ." [5] The theme of "J'aime le souvenir . . . " belongs to the minor strain of neo-Hellenism in nineteenth-century French poetry; its style is bland and colorless:

> L'homme, élégant, robuste et fort, avait le droit
> D'être fier des beautés qui le nommaient leur roi . . .

We must remember that, although Baudelaire's work is commonly associated with exoticism, synesthesia, and lurid colors, he has at least one other manner as well.

To turn from "J'aime le souvenir . . . " to "Sed non satiata" is to leave placid neo-Hellenism for the darker levels of *bas-romantisme* and a more intricate kind of poetry. "Sed non satiata" dates, like the previous poem, from the early 1840's:

> Bizarre déité, brune comme les nuits,
> Au parfum mélangé de musc et de havane,
> Oeuvre de quelque obi, le Faust de la savane,
> Sorcière au flanc d'ébène, enfant des noirs minuits,
>
> Je préfère au constance, à l'opium, au nuits,
> L'élixir de ta bouche où l'amour se pavane;
> Quand vers toi mes désirs partent en caravane,
> Tes yeux sont la citerne où boivent mes ennuis.

The rime scheme of the quatrains contains the most extraordinary examples of rich, rare rime in all of Baudelaire's work, and the impression of lexical *recherche* is further increased by the unusual nouns *déité* and *obi*, to say nothing of the wine names *nuits* and *constance*, which are masculine unlike their commonplace homophones. Rhetorically, the lines are a succession of baroque conceits and hyperboles carefully chosen so that most words refer to non-French things: *se pavane* suggests a Spanish dance, ebony comes from the Orient, *constance* was imported from South Africa, obis or obeah-men practiced magic in the West Indies, and

---

[5] Similarly, the "banquier" in the 1857 version of "Les Litanies de Satan" later became "Crésus."

so forth. In the tercets the imagery suddenly reverts to classical sources, thus complementing the title (which is a quote from Juvenal referring to Messalina):

> Par ces deux grands yeux noirs, soupiraux de ton âme,
> O démon sans pitié! verse-moi moins de flamme;
> Je ne suis pas le Styx pour t'embrasser neuf fois,
>
> Hélas! et je ne puis, Mégère libertine,
> Pour briser ton courage et te mettre aux abois,
> Dans l'enfer de ton lit devenir Proserpine!

The poet is saying, through these elegant circumlocutions, that he cannot repeatedly satisfy his mistress' desire as if he were a Lesbian. The initial image is of hell's being located within her, the eyes serving as outlets like the Avernus in antiquity; through a pun on *embrasser*, a modulation occurs, and now hell is her bed, surrounded by the Styx. Other linguistic details are chosen for density of meaning: *mégère* is a common noun designating a shrew as well as the name of one of the Eumenides; *mettre aux abois* recalls Cerberus and the guardian monsters of Hades. The conceits and mythology of "Sed non satiata" bring to mind earlier phases of French poetry, but here it is the contorted and vituperative style of Sigogne and the *satyriques* we think of, rather than the neoclassical mode.

It would be rash to suggest that between "J'aime le souvenir . . ." and "Sed non satiata" one is more characteristic of Baudelaire's earlier verse; our information about the composition and subsequent revision of most of his poems is simply not adequate. But one thing seems certain: Baudelaire continued to study and imitate older traditions of poetry. For example, in the poems addressed to Madame Sabatier (numbers XL to XLVIII of the 1861 edition of *Les Fleurs du mal*, the one usually reprinted) we encounter sometimes an imagery of suns, flames, angels, and ascension, which suggests baroque devotional verse.[6] In his fondness for imitating older styles Baudelaire even wrote one poem in another language than French: "Franciscae meae laudes" is, to my knowledge, the only adult attempt by any important nineteenth-century French poet to work in the conventions of a foreign tongue.

In certain of the poems written after the 1857 edition of *Les Fleurs du mal* we can isolate another aspect of Baudelaire's style and can be fairly sure it is not the result of accretions upon a piece conceived years be-

[6]See Ruff, *L'Esprit du mal*, 175.

fore. A passage from "Les Petites Vieilles" will serve as illustration, although, surprisingly enough, Baudelaire claimed in this poem to have imitated Hugo, to whom it was dedicated:

> — Avez-vous observé que maints cercueils de vieilles
> Sont presque aussi petits que celui d'un enfant?
> La Mort savante met dans ces bières pareilles
> Un symbole d'un goût bizarre et captivant,
>
> Et lorsque j'entrevois un fantôme débile
> Traversant de Paris le fourmillant tableau,
> Il me semble toujours que cet être fragile
> S'en va tout doucement vers un nouveau berceau;
>
> A moins que, méditant sur la géométrie,
> Je ne cherche, à l'aspect de ces membres discords,
> Combien de fois il faut que l'ouvrier varie
> La forme de la boîte où l'on met tous ces corps.

Hugo certainly never wrote anything like this aside, in which the poet assumes a mask of amused detachment and almost maniacal precision in order to cover up his feelings of guilt, identification, distaste, and sympathy at the sight of ancient crones. The covert theme of the poem is a brief against God for permitting decrepitude and death to exist, and its form is that of a one-sided conversation. The passage above exemplifies the delicate and dramatic shifts of tone around which the poem is organized. The language of "Les Petites Vieilles" can immediately be distinguished from that of the poem we considered earlier: it is both colorless and precise, the expression of the analytical intellect. No complexities of metaphor distract us from the exact force of what the speaker has to say. Indeed, it is only on reflection that one realizes that the whole passage develops a daring conceit; the coffins of old people and of children are not really the same: one shrinks slightly with age, but one does not grow in reverse.

Whereas Baudelaire, in "Les Petites Vieilles," has pruned from his language certain of the more obvious poetic devices the nineteenth century loved—adjectives denoting sense impressions, intricate images, and rare words—he keeps two neoclassical conventions which his contemporaries, under the sway of Hugo, tended to avoid: hyperbaton with *de*-phrases and a generous use of predictable epithets. Other mid-century poets disliked lines like "Traversant de Paris le fourmillant tableau" on the grounds that they were stilted and lifeless. It has even been suggested

that Baudelaire's inversions and epithets resulted from ineptitude at versification.[7] On the contrary, I think we must see in these archaisms one of
Baudelaire's finest inspirations: they lend gravity, even solemnity to the
speaker's language and prevent the irony from seeming facile or imperti-
nent. This is an ambivalent poem in which a superficial delight in the grotesque conceals the seriousness of the theme. The language is appropriately a mixture of minute, prosaic observations and the muffled
grandeur of faded rhetoric.

It might seem that the dry but subtly dramatic language of "Les Petites Vieilles" would be suitable for a poet's later work, in contrast with
the gaudy violence of "Sed non satiata." Yet Baudelaire did not lose his
taste for lurid baroque effects, witness "A une madone." This "ex-voto
dans le goût espagnol" was written in 1859, the same year as "Les Petites
Vieilles":

> Je veux bâtir pour toi, Madone, ma maîtresse,
> Un autel souterrain au fond de ma détresse,
> Et creuser dans le coin le plus noir de mon coeur,
> Loin du désir mondain et du regard moqueur,
> Une niche, d'azur et d'or tout émaillée,
> Où tu te dresseras, Statue émerveillée.
> Avec mes Vers polis, treillis d'un pur métal
> Savamment constellé de rimes de cristal,
> Je ferai pour ta tête une énorme Couronne;
> Et dans ma Jalousie, ô mortelle Madone,
> Je saurai te tailler un Manteau, de façon
> Barbare, roide et lourd, et doublé de soupçon,
> Qui, comme une guérite, enfermera tes charmes;
> Non de Perles brodé, mais de toutes mes Larmes!

One of the generally accepted principles about Baudelaire's stylistic development is that he used verse-paragraphs of alexandrines only in his
early work; "A une madone" provides us with another of those exceptions which make it futile to trace neat patterns of change in Baudelaire's
style. In addition, the use of allegory is far more extravagant than that
in his early poems, when he supposedly was most steeped in sixteenth-
and seventeenth-century poetry. Such a sustained, formal use of conceit
—for each real detail of the *ex-voto* a moral quality is substituted—is unlike nineteenth-century poetry in that its rhetoric is too intellectualized,

---

[7]See Albert Cassagne, *Versification et métrique de Charles Baudelaire* (Paris,
1906), 31.

too "witty" in the old sense of the term. It betrays in Baudelaire an almost perverse taste for traditional figures of speech which he shared with none of his contemporaries.

Having observed the stylistic variety of *Les Fleurs du mal*, we must still face the fact that Baudelaire's poetry is nearly always recognizable as his own: there are certain underlying principles beneath the varied surface. The first of these is obviously archaism: Baudelaire is alone among nineteenth-century French poets in his dedication to renaissance and neoclassical rhetoric. Hugo's use of baroque conceits in *Ruy Blas* and Gautier's emulation of medieval Italian in "Le Triomphe de Pétrarque" are merely episodes in their development as poets; even Mallarmé tired of traditional figures of speech after having magnificently revived them. For Baudelaire, epithet, personification, and allegory—to name only a few favorite devices—remained identified with poetry itself. Our first task will therefore be the examination of what the value of rhetoric was for him.

If one closely studies a good many of the *Fleurs du mal*, it becomes apparent that adjectives and participles are more numerous than finite verbs,[8] that the syntax is not characterized by elaborate clauses; in short, that despite all differences in vocabulary and subject, Baudelaire's style, like Vigny's, continues the phrasal, epithetical tendencies of the abbé Delille's manner. But in Baudelaire's case, of course, we have no reason to expect such a filiation: unlike Vigny, who became a poet in an age of neoclassicism and never had sufficient verbal imagination to free himself from Delille and Chénier, Baudelaire started writing in the late 1830's, after the advent of modernism. Between him and Vigny lie not only some twenty-odd years but also the *genre romantique* as practiced by Gautier and the *bouzingos*. One might expect Baudelaire to have pruned his verses of the adjectives *beau, charmant, vaste, grand, immense*,[9] which we find everywhere in them. But he did not, and we must determine what charms eighteenth-century diction had for him.

For many of Baudelaire's contemporaries, of course, the *ancien régime* was coming to seem like an enchanted age. Traces of this can be found

[8]His verbs, furthermore, have been called colorless. See Peyre, *Connaissance de Baudelaire*, 117–18.

[9]These are Baudelaire's characteristic epithets. See Robert Vivier, *L'Originalité de Baudelaire* (Brussels, 1952), 50–51.

in Hugo, Gautier, and Nerval.[10] The Watteau revival was underway in the mid-century,[11] and, by the time of Verlaine and the Goncourts, nostalgia for the eighteenth century was widespread. Baudelaire seems to have felt a very particular identification with the days before 1789, witness this image:

> Je suis un vieux boudoir plein de roses fanées,
> Où gît tout un fouillis de modes surannées,
> Où les pastels plaintifs et les pâles Boucher,
> Seuls, respirent l'odeur d'un flacon débouché.

("Spleen")

Two reasons for this bond between the poet and the past come readily to mind: Baudelaire admired the idea of aristocracy—at least after 1848—and he associated his childhood with the eighteenth century.[12] But there are deeper, sounder reasons for Baudelaire's imitation of neoclassical diction.

Of all the nineteenth-century French poets, Baudelaire had probably the most delicate sense of tone; he realized more fully than any other what subtle effects could be obtained from deliberately faded and insipid language. "Les Petites Vieilles," from which we have earlier quoted, is probably the most audacious, lengthy, and brilliant example of conscious *fadeur* in *Les Fleurs du mal*, but elsewhere there are equally studied uses of old-fashioned poetic diction. The following lines, thought to be early Baudelaire, are especially relevant:

> Je t'adore à l'égal de la voûte nocturne,
> O vase de tristesse, ô grande taciturne,
> Et t'aime d'autant plus, belle, que tu me fuis,
> Et que tu me parais, ornement de mes nuits,
> Plus ironiquement accumuler les lieues
> Qui séparent mes bras des immensités bleues.

Voûte nocturne, belle, tu me fuis, and *ornement* suggest the language of the *fête galante,* the tradition of erotic pastoral. *Vase de tristesse* is probably modelled on *vas electionis* or the *vas spirituale* of the Litany of the

[10]See, for example, "La Fête chez Thérèse" (Hugo), "Pastel" (Gautier), and *Les Illuminés* (Nerval).

[11]See Jacques-Henry Bornecque, *Lumières sur les Fêtes galantes de Paul Verlaine* (Paris, 1959), 20–44, and Seymour O. Simches, *Le Romantisme et le Goût esthétique du XVIIIe Siècle* (Paris, 1964), 65–101.

[12]See the "Note autobiographique" in the *Journaux intimes.*

Holy Virgin; it has, in any case, a ceremonious solemnity of tone. Of course, these words and expressions are embedded in a far more intricate context than an eighteenth-century poet would have created: the identification of Jeanne Duval with the moon is both genuine and ironic, as Baudelaire expressly puts it. This first verse-paragraph is intended to build up a mood of *galanterie* which the second one will destroy:

> Je m'avance à l'attaque, et je grimpe aux assauts,
> Comme après un cadavre un choeur de vermisseaux . . .

The shift to the vocabulary of *bas-romantisme* produces an effect we are accustomed to in more recent ironic poets; Baudelaire seems to have been the first in France to have consciously juxtaposed dissimilar poetic styles.[13]

The second archaizing rhetorical device that we must consider is personification, and it also is more characteristic of the late eighteenth-century poets than of Racine or Corneille. Baudelaire had one curious bond with the eighteenth-century estheticians, which is generally overlooked: he was fascinated by the possibility of *painting pictures with words*,[14] just as the *ut pictura poesis* school could not resist philosophically rather dubious parallels between the plastic arts and literature. One of the more concrete *transpositions d'art* that emerged from the generally hazy theories of *ut pictura poesis* was the equivalence established between sculpture and personification. The kind of sculpture that could be "translated" by personification is necessarily quite iconographic in tendency: Michelangelo provides us with a handy example since he both sculpted Night and wrote lines for her to speak.[15] Baudelaire's sonnet "La Beauté" ("Je suis belle, ô mortels, comme un rêve de pierre") is conceived directly in this tradition of story-statues and statue-characters. Aside from poems like "La Beauté," which are built around one central abstract personage, so many passing personifications occur in Baudelaire's work that we must consider it an essential element of his style. When the personifications accumulate we are in the presence of one form

---

[13]For another kind of mingling of styles, see Erich Auerbach, *Scenes from the Drama of European Literature* (New York, 1959), 201–26.

[14]For conjectures about what works of art inspired Baudelaire, see Jean Prévost, *Baudelaire* (Paris, 1953), 239–84.

[15]"Caro m'è il sonno e più l'esser di sasso / Mentre che 'l danno e la vergogna dura. / Non veder, non sentir m'è gran fortuna; / Però non mi destar, deh! parla basso."

of allegory, as in the late sonnet "Recueillement." The initial personification is of *douleur* as a child:

> Sois sage, ô ma Douleur, et tiens-toi plus tranquille.
> Tu réclamais le Soir; il descend; le voici :
> Une atmosphère obscure enveloppe la ville,
> Aux uns portant la paix, aux autres le souci.
>
> Pendant que des mortels la multitude vile,
> Sous le fouet du Plaisir, ce bourreau sans merci,
> Va cueillir des remords dans la fête servile,
> Ma Douleur, donne-moi la main; viens par ici,
>
> Loin d'eux. Vois se pencher les défuntes Années,
> Sur les balcons du ciel, en robes surannées;
> Surgir du fond des eaux le Regret souriant;
>
> Le Soleil moribond s'endormir sous une arche,
> Et, comme un long linceul traînant à l'Orient,
> Entends, ma chère, entends la douce Nuit qui marche.

It is difficult to imagine that any other major nineteenth-century poet would have added personification to personification in this way. But again, we must consider Baudelaire's mastery of tone and mood: the theme of "Recueillement" is the contented acceptance of death on the part of one who is weary of life. At the same time, the speaker retains some nostalgia for his past: this mixed mood is epitomized by the oxymoron *Regret souriant*. It is as if in the face of approaching death, the distant past becomes more vivid and merges curiously with the future. The age of the speaker and his serenity are rhetorically rendered by the stately, grave, old-fashioned personifications. Their very insipidness conveys his waning vitality. Thoughts of the past are couched in a language which belongs, literally, to the past: Baudelaire's sense of memory, of psychological time, is supported by a historical sense of literary style. One feels that the *robes surannées* the speaker recalls are the elegant gowns of the *ancien régime*. When Baudelaire uses personification there is usually some element of mood which it supports: some part of the varied, but limited range of impressions that can be generated by a statue—coldness, gravity, age, immobility, purity, serenity, strength, hugeness—is usually implicit in Baudelaire's personifications. By his deliberate and sure handling of this rhetorical device, Baudelaire surpasses his neoclassical masters in the richness of effects derived from it.

There are other kinds of allegory than that based on personification. The classical distinction is between the practice of Guillaume de Lorris and that of Dante: the first part of the *Roman de la Rose* concerns figures named Liesse, Bel Accueil, Male Bouche, and so forth, while Dante's narrative is literal as well as symbolic. Baudelaire had a taste for all forms of symbolism: one can extract several theories of it from the sonnet "Correspondances," [16] and his critical essays are filled with references to the Book of Nature and Universal Analogy. Most writers tend, in my opinion, to ascribe to Baudelaire a far too coherent and detailed theory of symbolism, but, be that as it may, his poetic practice shows a great range of symbolic modes. To begin with the simplest example, traditional kinds of analogical poems, which we discussed earlier in reference to Gautier's work, abound in *Les Fleurs du mal;* "L'Albatros" follows this pattern.

More distinctive is what we may call the emblematic poem. An emblem is a pictorial representation which is presumed to contain elliptically a wealth of meaning; it is obtrusive, pregnant with significance and, as such, demands to be interpreted. *Emblem* is a word Baudelaire was fond of; summarizing the catalogue of infernal images with which "L'Irrémédiable" opens, he comments:

> — Emblèmes nets, tableau parfait
> D'une fortune irrémédiable,
> Qui donne à penser que le Diable
> Fait toujours bien tout ce qu'il fait!

The renaissance emblems were didactic or sententious and drew on a long iconological tradition. Baudelaire's, of course, are either private or belong to the common romantic iconology.

An emblem is presented with a kind of fascinating focus, which distinguishes it from the initial term of an ordinary analogical poem. The emblem is, as it were, the basic unit of a certain kind of allegory, urging solution of its enigma. "Le Masque" offers perhaps the most orthodox example of an emblem, but a poem like "Un Voyage à Cythère" is somewhat more characteristic of Baudelaire's practice. Here the corpse hanging from the gibbet stands out from the surrounding landscape, since it alone is fraught with meaning, and the poet perceives it as an intended object of contemplation:

[16]For a recent discussion of them see D. J. Mossop, *Baudelaire's Tragic Hero* (New York, 1961), 63–85.

> — Le ciel était charmant, la mer était unie;
> Pour moi tout était noir et sanglant désormais,
> Hélas! et j'avais, comme en un suaire épais,
> Le coeur enseveli dans cette allégorie.
>
> Dans ton île, ô Vénus! je n'ai trouvé debout
> Qu'un gibet symbolique où pendait mon image...
> — Ah! Seigneur! donnez-moi la force et le courage
> De contempler mon coeur et mon corps sans dégoût!

There is a frankly didactic note in this handling of the emblem, which we may consider another aspect of Baudelaire's fondness for the moods and conventions of earlier poetry. Furthermore, the allegorical gloss at the end of the poem, far from seeming mechanical, is the most intense and dramatic part of it.

When emblems combine to make more sustained allegories, the element of symbolic setting becomes particularly important. The opening lines of the *Inferno* provide a classic example of a landscape which prepares one for allegory, and Baudelaire was familiar with Dante.[17] Although there is no lengthy allegory in *Les Fleurs du mal*, "Les Sept Vieillards" has all the traditional aspects of one, including arithmosophy. Its beginning establishes a background suitable for an apparition:

> Fourmillante cité, cité pleine de rêves,
> Où le spectre en plein jour raccroche le passant!
> Les mystères partout coulent comme des sèves
> Dans les canaux étroits du colosse puissant.

The poetic word *cité* rather than *ville* serves to establish the particularity of this metropolis, and its canals are specifically mentioned in order to recall the elaborate fluvial system of Dante's hell. Prostitutes grabbing at the arm of passers-by (the special sense of *raccrocher*) were a characteristic sight of Paris streets, and here they are replaced by phantoms. Baudelaire's sense of the allegorical mode is seldom displayed so thoroughly, but we can conclude, I think, that he understood it intimately. Goethe's famous distinction between allegory, which is bad, and symbol, which is good,[18] would have meant little to Baudelaire.

---

[17]See Mark Musa and John Porter Houston, "Dante, 'La Béatrice,' and Baudelaire's Archaism," *Italica*, XLII (March, 1965), 169–74.
[18]See René Wellek, *A History of Modern Criticism* (New Haven, 1955), I, 210–12.

Although Baudelaire wrote a great deal—if somewhat vaguely—about symbolism, he was less inclined to discuss the concomitant matters of metaphor and simile. Yet the rhetorical virtuosity he displayed in handling the latter suggests that he must have had elaborate and complex theories about these stylistic details. First of all, we notice not only the great density of Baudelaire's imagery, but the extraordinary number of ways he found to convey analogies. Three short poems will illustrate this variety. The first is "La Cloche fêlée," which, while perhaps of no great weight in *Les Fleurs du mal,* is a fascinating piece of rhetoric.

Perhaps the first thing we should observe is that there is no cracked bell mentioned in the poem; the title draws together two different analogical patterns, which are not joined in the body of the sonnet:

> Il est amer et doux, pendant les nuits d'hiver,
> D'écouter, près du feu qui palpite et qui fume,
> Les souvenirs lointains lentement s'élever
> Au bruit des carillons qui chantent dans la brume,
>
> Bienheureuse la cloche au gosier vigoureux
> Qui, malgré sa vieillesse, alerte et bien portante,
> Jette fidèlement son cri religieux,
> Ainsi qu'un vieux soldat qui veille sous la tente!

The initial comparisons are clear, if not straightforward. The adjectives applied to the bell compare it to a man, an analogy which the soldier simile, introduced casually and as if by afterthought, strengthens. The relationship between the sound of the bell and memory is not underscored, yet it is essential to what will follow. At the beginning of the tercets the previous comparison of the sturdy bell to a healthy old soldier is complemented by the equation of the speaker to a cracked bell:

> Moi, mon âme est fêlée, et lorsqu'en ses ennuis
> Elle veut de ses chants peupler l'air froid des nuits,
> Il arrive souvent que sa voix affaiblie
>
> Semble le râle épais d'un blessé qu'on oublie
> Au bord d'un lac de sang, sous un grand tas de morts,
> Et qui meurt, sans bouger, dans d'immenses efforts.

The *semble* is one of Baudelaire's favorite ways of avoiding expressions such as *comme, être pareil à,* and so forth; the verb creates an analogy while avoiding the most commonplace grammatical signs of it. Here

Baudelaire is using a double comparison: when the speaker tries to sing like a bell, he sounds like a dying soldier. The military image, which initially appeared insignificant, ends by effacing the bell and swelling up to fill all the second tercet. The system of analogies is complex since there is a sound bell resembling a healthy soldier, and a speaker whose soul is cracked and gives forth the sounds of a dying soldier. The *cloche fêlée* of the title unites the two antithetical chains of similes.

Another, and very effective form of analogy, which Baudelaire imitated from *La Comédie de la Mort*, consists of a simple predicate nominative after *être*. "Causerie" uses this in conjunction with more traditional metaphors and similes:

> Vous êtes un beau ciel d'automne, clair et rose!
> Mais la tristesse en moi monte comme la mer,
> Et laisse, en refluant, sur ma lèvre morose
> Le souvenir cuisant de son limon amer.
>
> — Ta main se glisse en vain sur mon sein qui se pâme;
> Ce qu'elle cherche, amie, est un lieu saccagé
> Par la griffe et la dent féroce de la femme.
> Ne cherchez plus mon coeur; les bêtes l'ont mangé.
>
> Mon coeur est un palais flétri par la cohue;
> On s'y soûle, on s'y tue, on s'y prend aux cheveux!
> — Un parfum nage autour de votre gorge nue !...
>
> O Beauté, dur fléau des âmes, tu le veux!
> Avec tes yeux de feu, brillants comme des fêtes,
> Calcine ces lambeaux qu'ont épargnés les bêtes!

The sequence of images is notable for the sharpness of each one and their contrasting relations: the external sky and the inner sea are doubly antithetical, while the speaker's heart is at once a place and something devoured. The heart-place image dominates the first tercet, where, instead of its being empty, the implications of the adjective *saccagé* are developed: palaces are ransacked by crowds. The second tercet then works a change on the direction of the imagery: fire replaces pillage, the women-beasts are mentioned once more, and the heart has again become an organ. This fondness for sudden changes of metaphor accounts in part for Baudelaire's predilection for sonnets and quatrains: the stanzaic divisions provide convenient articulations for a series of images. In this respect, Baudelaire is often reproached with lack of *souffle*, as if all metaphors should be prolonged. There is, on the contrary, an admirable effect of density produced in poems like "Causerie."

One of Baudelaire's favorite comparisons is between a woman and a climate or landscape. In "Ciel brouillé" he uses four different verbs as equivalents of "is like" to build up to a climax in which a person *is* a climate:

> On dirait ton regard d'une vapeur couvert;
> Ton oeil mystérieux (est-il bleu, gris ou vert?)
> Alternativement tendre, rêveur, cruel,
> Réfléchit l'indolence et la pâleur du ciel.
>
> Tu rappelles ces jours blancs, tièdes et voilés,
> Qui font se fondre en pleurs les coeurs ensorcelés,
> Quand, agités d'un mal inconnu qui les tord,
> Les nerfs trop éveillés raillent l'esprit qui dort.
>
> Tu ressembles parfois à ces beaux horizons
> Qu'allument les soleils des brumeuses saisons...
> Comme tu resplendis, paysage mouillé
> Qu'enflamment les rayons tombant d'un ciel brouillé!
>
> O femme dangereuse, ô séduisants climats!
> Adorerai-je aussi ta neige et vos frimas,
> Et saurai-je tirer de l'implacable hiver
> Des plaisirs plus aigus que la glace et le fer?

With the apposition *paysage mouillé* the woman becomes a landscape. At this point the initial analogy is inverted: at first she merely reflects real weather; now she creates the weather, which reflects her. Rhetorically, the shift is very subtle; it might be represented schematically as follows: A is like B; A is B; B is part of A. Logical twists in the use of analogy are extremely important for the subsequent development of French poetry: Mallarmé and Rimbaud were to exploit causal inversions with great brilliance. One other type of logical shift consists of reversing the expected initial and secondary terms of a comparison. Here the concrete is compared with the abstract:

> — Je suis un cimetière abhorré de la lune,
> Où comme des remords se traînent de longs vers,
> Qui s'acharnent toujours sur mes morts les plus chers.
>
> ("Spleen")

Since worms usually crawl and remorse does not, the image is somewhat strange.

One of Baudelaire's greatest poems begins with an elaborate tangle of unexpected analogies; "Le Cygne" initially presents its theme in deceptive terms:

> Andromaque, je pense à vous! Ce petit fleuve,
> Pauvre et triste miroir où jadis resplendit
> L'immense majesté de vos douleurs de veuve,
> Ce Simoïs menteur qui par vos pleurs grandit,
>
> A fécondé soudain ma mémoire fertile,
> Comme je traversais le nouveau Carrousel.
> Le vieux Paris n'est plus (la forme d'une ville
> Change plus vite, hélas! que le coeur d'un mortel);
>
> Je ne vois qu'en esprit tout ce camp de baraques,
> Ces tas de chapiteaux ébauchés et de fûts,
> Les herbes, les gros blocs verdis par l'eau des flaques,
> Et, brillant aux carreaux, le bric-à-brac confus.

The initial statement appears to be contradicted by the following lines: the poet speaks not of Andromache but of the buildings which used to fill the Place du Carrousel before 1852. The analogy would seem to be between Andromache beside the "false" Simois, which was built in Epirus to console her for the destruction of Troy, and the poet, who sees the changing face of his own city. Her heart did not change with the fall of Troy, and the poet seems to feel some similar regret for the past. Yet there is a strange contradiction in the verb *féconder:* instead of the new look of the Place du Carrousel reminding him of Andromache, the classical legend has reminded him of what is before his eyes. The normal causality of association has been reversed: the more remote image suggests the more immediate one.

The system of analogies is both clarified and complicated by the next stanzas:

> Là s'étalait jadis une ménagerie;
> Là je vis, un matin, à l'heure où sous les cieux
> Froids et clairs le Travail s'éveille, où la voirie
> Pousse un sombre ouragan dans l'air silencieux,
>
> Un cygne qui s'était évadé de sa cage,

Et, de ses pieds palmés frottant le pavé sec,
Sur le sol raboteux traînait son blanc plumage,
Près d'un ruisseau sans eau la bête ouvrant le bec

Baignait nerveusement ses ailes dans la poudre,
Et disait, le coeur plein de son beau lac natal :
"Eau, quand donc pleuvras-tu? Quand tonneras-tu, foudre?"
Je vois ce malheureux, mythe étrange et fatal,

Vers le ciel quelquefois, comme l'homme d'Ovide,
Vers le ciel ironique et cruellement bleu,
Sur son cou convulsif tendant sa tête avide,
Comme s'il adressait des reproches à Dieu!

What appeared to be the initial comparison of Andromache and the speaker, sustained by the reference to destruction of buildings, has given way to an analogy between Andromache and the swan, the latter's native lake and Troy, the false Simois and the dry gutter. The chain of associations still remains logically peculiar, but poetically justified. The traditional image of Andromache is introduced first and the unusual one of the swan is slowly elaborated to a climax. The missing link in the associations is the present bare look of the Place du Carrousel which recalls the swan, which, in turn, recalls Andromache. But there persists the secondary association between Andromache's recollections of Troy and the poet's memories of the old Carrousel. The complexity of these relations depends on the order in which they are introduced. As if to show how much less vivid the logical order is, Baudelaire begins the second part of the poem by reintroducing all his images in a rational pattern:

Paris change! mais rien dans ma mélancolie
N'a bougé! palais neufs, échafaudages, blocs,
Vieux faubourgs, tout pour moi devient allégorie,
Et mes chers souvenirs sont plus lourds que des rocs.

Aussi devant ce Louvre une image m'opprime :
Je pense à mon grand cygne, avec ses gestes fous
Comme les exilés, ridicule et sublime,
Et rongé d'un désir sans trêve! et puis à vous,

Andromaque, des bras d'un grand époux tombée,
Vil bétail, sous la main du superbe Pyrrhus,
Auprès d'un tombeau vide en extase courbée;
Veuve d'Hector, hélas! et femme d'Hélénus!

From the new Paris to the old, from the swan to Andromache, the logic of association is intact. This permits Baudelaire then to add further a more distant analogy to the swan:

> Je pense à la négresse, amaigrie et phtisique,
> Piétinant dans la boue, et cherchant, l'oeil hagard,
> Les cocotiers absents de la superbe Afrique
> Derrière la muraille immense du brouillard . . .

The circle widens until the poet thinks

> A quiconque a perdu ce qui ne se retrouve
> Jamais, jamais! à ceux qui s'abreuvent de pleurs
> Et tettent la Douleur comme une bonne louve!
> Aux maigres orphelins séchant comme des fleurs!

But, to pursue the metaphor of the circle, all these images are peripheral. The center of the poet's preoccupation has not yet been stated:

> Ainsi dans la forêt où mon esprit s'exile
> Un vieux Souvenir sonne à plein souffle du cor!
> Je pense aux matelots oubliés dans une île,
> Aux captifs, aux vaincus !... à bien d'autres encor!

Souvenir is in the singular: the swan, Andromache, the Negress, the sailors, the captives, and the vanquished all drift into the poet's mind by association with the one unstated memory which is the nucleus of the poem.[19]

"The forest where my mind takes exile" is a kind of accessory image at the end of "Le Cygne"; it has no very clear thematic relation with the preceding imagery, yet it suggests a further direction of inquiry into Baudelaire's handling of metaphor. Things inside things are everywhere in his verse: images of the container and the contained are virtually obsessive.[20] And, what is equally important, these images frequently involve paradoxical inversions, like the cause-and-effect relations we have been examining. The sonnet "Le Mauvais Moine," which is generally considered to be very early Baudelaire, provides us with a fairly simple illustration:

[19]For further allusions see Lowry Nelson, Jr., "Baudelaire and Virgil: A Reading of 'Le Cygne,'" *Comparative Literature*, XIII (Fall, 1961), 332–45.

[20]See J. D. Hubert, *L'Esthétique des Fleurs du mal: Essai sur l'ambiguïté poétique* (Geneva, 1952), 115–48.

Les cloîtres anciens sur leurs grandes murailles
Etalaient en tableaux la sainte Vérité,
Dont l'effet, réchauffant les pieuses entrailles,
Tempérait la froideur de leur austérité.

En ce temps où du Christ florissaient les semailles,
Plus d'un illustre moine, aujourd'hui peu cité,
Prenant pour atelier le champ des funérailles,
Glorifiait la Mort avec simplicité.

The quatrains carefully describe real places—cloisters and a *campo santo*, for there is a covert allusion to Orcagna's frescoes in Pisa. In the tercets space becomes metaphoric:

— Mon âme est un tombeau que, mauvais cénobite,
Depuis l'éternité je parcours et j'habite;
Rien n'embellit les murs de ce cloître odieux.

The cloister-soul is not only metaphoric, it is paradoxical, for the speaker contains himself. Similar figures are frequent in *Les Fleurs du mal*. In the last "Spleen" poem ("Quand le ciel bas et lourd . . .") the initial image of the earth as a closed prison is replaced by that of processions occurring in the poet's soul, while Anguish stands on his head. At the end of "Obsession," when the poet has escaped from all light and movement, his eyes project the content of his memory onto the screen-like shadows. Baudelaire's fondness for the imagery of both closed rooms and open skies evidences his feeling for spatial symbolism. He juxtaposes the open and the closed, the inner and the outer, the container and the contained, real space and metaphoric space with great richness of effect.

Baudelaire's experiments with spatial ambiguities are abundant, but nowhere, perhaps, so elegantly elaborated as in "La Chevelure." The first stanza presents us with the image of a small object, the head of hair, enclosed in a dark bed alcove:

O toison, moutonnant jusque sur l'encolure!
O boucles! O parfum chargé de nonchaloir!
Extase! Pour peupler ce soir l'alcôve obscure
Des souvenirs dormant dans cette chevelure,
Je la veux agiter dans l'air comme un mouchoir!

The magnificent conceit of shaking memories out of the hair suggests expansion and growth, for, as the sea-sky analogy of the verb *moutonner* implies, the large is contained by the small. The hair next becomes a forest:

> La langoureuse Asie et la brûlante Afrique,
> Tout un monde lointain, absent, presque défunt,
> Vit dans tes profondeurs, forêt aromatique!
> Comme d'autres esprits voguent sur la musique,
> Le mien, ô mon amour! nage sur ton parfum.

Odor is, as it were, the catalyst which permits the hair to metamorphose into a whole world. The paradox of the container and contained is then expressly stated:

> J'irai là-bas où l'arbre et l'homme, pleins de sève,
> Se pâment longuement sous l'ardeur des climats;
> Fortes tresses, soyez la houle qui m'enlève!
> Tu contiens, mer d'ébène, un éblouissant rêve
> De voiles, de rameurs, de flammes et de mâts :
>
> Un port retentissant où mon âme peut boire
> A grands flots le parfum, le son et la couleur;
> Où les vaisseaux, glissant dans l'or et dans la moire,
> Ouvrent leurs vastes bras pour embrasser la gloire
> D'un ciel pur où frémit l'éternelle chaleur.
>
> Je plongerai ma tête amoureuse d'ivresse
> Dans ce noir océan où l'autre est enfermé;
> Et mon esprit subtil que le roulis caresse
> Saura vous retrouver, ô féconde paresse,
> Infinis bercements du loisir embaumé!

All of Baudelaire's customary ecstatic imagery is deployed in these lines: sea, sky, and light, and the correspondences between odor, sound, and color. The tropics become in these gorgeous lines the lost paradise of the past remembered in the night-bound hell of a European city. The merely exotic is transcended by the moral and esthetic force of Baudelaire's thought. Finally the hair becomes a tent, whose ceiling is the warm blue sky:

> Cheveux bleus, pavillon de ténèbres tendues,
> Vous me rendez l'azur du ciel immense et rond;
> Sur les bords duvetés de vos mèches tordues
> Je m'enivre ardemment des senteurs confondues
> De l'huile de coco, du musc et du goudron.

The tent which contains the infinity of the ether is the final point of evolution of Baudelaire's imagery, and is followed by a brief recollection of the exotic port mentioned earlier. This leads us back to the bed alcove and, for the first time, to the woman whose hair is the point of departure for the poem:

> Longtemps! toujours! ma main dans ta crinière lourde
> Sèmera le rubis, la perle et le saphir,
> Afin qu'à mon désir tu ne sois jamais sourde!
> N'es-tu pas l'oasis où je rêve, et la gourde
> Où je hume à longs traits le vin du souvenir?

The second-person pronoun has switched dramatically from *vous* to *tu*. The tent of hair has dwindled into a mane, and the woman, appearing as an oasis as opposed to a broad sky, and a gourd as opposed to the sea, represents a shrinking of the poet's mind from imaginative scope into the tiny elements of reality. The evocation of the past has recondensed, so to speak, into the well of the oasis and the contents of the drinking gourd. The supporting imagery of *parfums* throughout the poem has given coherence to the implied analogy between remembering and vaporization of liquids.

The spatial imagery of "La Chevelure," like that of "Le Mauvais Moine," and many other *Fleurs du mal* has a temporal aspect which is worth emphasizing. By an analogy with mind and body, memories are represented as being contained: sometimes it is within an object like the head of hair, sometimes within a kind of mental space like "la forêt où mon esprit s'exile." In one of the "Spleen" poems ("J'ai plus de souvenirs . . .") the speaker identifies himself with containers holding objects associated with remembrance:

> Un gros meuble à tiroirs encombré de bilans,
> De vers, de billets doux, de procès, de romances,
> Avec de lourds cheveux roulés dans des quittances,
> Cache moins de secrets que mon triste cerveau.
> C'est une pyramide, un immense caveau,
> Qui contient plus de morts que la fosse commune.

The past is thus being shut up in enclosed spaces, which, furthermore, are structures—chests, pyramids, and vaults—suggesting death or by-gone days. With a sudden dramatic shift, the speaker is now himself contained, as he looks out on the surrounding present:

> — Désormais tu n'es plus, ô matière vivante!
> Qu'un granit entouré d'une vague épouvante,
> Assoupi dans le fond d'un Sahara brumeux . . .

The present and future stretch out drearily to the horizon. The subject of the poem is not stated but must be inferred from the imagery: its theme is regret, the poisoning of the present by the past. This time pattern is characteristic of Baudelaire, for whom the categories of the future and potentiality seldom had imaginative relevance.

The spatial character of time is particularly well shown in "Mœsta et errabunda." The initial image of the poem is one of aspiration, of rising from a lower, viler sphere into one of spiritual perfection:

> Dis-moi, ton coeur parfois s'envole-t-il, Agathe,
> Loin du noir océan de l'immonde cité,
> Vers un autre océan où la splendeur éclate,
> Bleu, clair, profond, ainsi que la virginité?
> Dis-moi, ton coeur parfois s'envole-t-il, Agathe?

The movement upward seems at first to be sustained in a later stanza:

> Comme vous êtes loin, paradis parfumé,
> Où sous un clair azur tout n'est qu'amour et joie,
> Où tout ce que l'on aime est digne d'être aimé,
> Où dans la volupté pure le coeur se noie!
> Comme vous êtes loin, paradis parfumé!

However, *loin* is an important hinge-word in its ambiguity: we can place paradise in a distant place or in a distant time. Finally it is both meanings which are implied:

> — Mais le vert paradis des amours enfantines,
>
> L'innocent paradis, plein de plaisirs furtifs,
> Est-il déjà plus loin que l'Inde et que la Chine?
> Peut-on le rappeler avec des cris plaintifs,
> Et l'animer encor d'une voix argentine,
> L'innocent paradis, plein de plaisirs furtifs?

The aspiration upward has become an inspiration *backward:* what seemed attainable through soaring is out of reach. Vertical movement is replaced by horizontal rotation as the words China and India occur; they also suggest the progressive movement of the day westward, and consequently the hopelessness of ever capturing fugitive time.

Time patterns are in great evidence in *Les Fleurs du mal,* and one poem, "Le Balcon," tries to press the question of cyclic time. The tense usage suggests some ambiguity in temporal perspective:

> Mère des souvenirs, maîtresse des maîtresses,
> O toi, tous mes plaisirs! ô toi, tous mes devoirs!
> Tu te rappelleras la beauté des caresses,
> La douceur du foyer et le charme des soirs,
> Mère des souvenirs, maîtresse des maîtresses!
>
> Les soirs illuminés par l'ardeur du charbon,
> Et les soirs au balcon, voilés de vapeurs roses.
> Que ton sein m'était doux! que ton coeur m'était bon!
> Nous avons dit souvent d'impérissables choses
> Les soirs illuminés par l'ardeur du charbon.

At first the present seems to be the ecstatic moment, which will later be remembered. But in the second stanza this precious time is situated in a vague past: the imperfect tense and reference to both winter and summer imply that it constitutes a whole epoch. One wonders what the present means in this time-scheme. Baudelaire next introduces an ambiguous present tense, which could be taken as a general assertion:

> Que les soleils sont beaux dans les chaudes soirées!
> Que l'espace est profond! que le coeur est puissant!
> En me penchant vers toi, reine des adorées,
> Je croyais respirer le parfum de ton sang.
> Que les soleils sont beaux dans les chaudes soirées!

Somehow the vivid present tense relates the past and present: there is none of the usual contrast between them, to which we are accustomed in Baudelaire. After a further stanza in the imperfect ("La nuit s'épaississait ainsi qu'une cloison . . ."), we find another ambiguous fusion of past, present, and future:

> Je sais l'art d'évoquer les minutes heureuses,
> Et revis mon passé blotti dans tes genoux,
> Car à quoi bon chercher tes beautés langoureuses
> Ailleurs qu'en ton cher corps et qu'en ton coeur si doux?
> Je sais l'art d'évoquer les minutes heureuses!

Does *revis* mean "relive" or "saw again"? Is the poet *blotti* in the past or the present? Or is it his past which is *blotti*? Is he presently evoking the past, or will he evoke the present when it has become preterite? The affirmative "je sais l'art . . ." is qualified by the interrogative of the final stanza:

> Ces serments, ces parfums, ces baisers infinis,
> Renaîtront-ils d'un gouffre interdit à nos sondes,
> Comme montent au ciel les soleils rajeunis
> Après s'être lavés au fond des mers profondes?
> — O serments! ô parfums! ô baisers infinis!

Nor is the future *renaîtront* clear in any way: there remains the ambiguity of life and the afterlife. The juxtaposition of the three time planes nostalgically suggests, without completely affirming it, some possibility of recapturing the past. The cyclic theme of "Le Balcon" is sustained by its form: the lyric *quintil* with its repeated line has a circular movement, and the framing first and last tenses in the poem are futures. If "Le Balcon" has a somewhat exceptional pattern, it only demonstrates the great variety of structural elements in *Les Fleurs du mal.*

The dimensions of time and space are not the only ones which Baudelaire reinterprets and recreates in his verse. There is also in *Les Fleurs du mal* a sense of relationship between individual minds and souls which is unique in nineteenth-century French poetry. This system of bonds, identifications, and antipathies constitutes the dramatic aspect of Baudelaire's work: he is given neither to the solipsism of much lyric poetry nor to the conventionalized declamation before an audience of readers, such as we have seen in Hugo and Vigny. Laforgue spoke of Baudelaire's intimate, "confessional" tone, but the term is too narrow: what Baudelaire achieves through the persistent presence, overt or implied, of a second-person singular is a feeling of personality and situation which can only be compared with theater, where our chief concern is the interplay of idea and emotion among the dramatis personae.

The poetry of the second-person singular, which addresses itself to an individual and is merely overheard by the public, has taken so many forms in the history of literature that we can here suggest only its manifestations in France. The love poem and, to a lesser degree, the satire and devotional lyric, are the principal genres in which *you* is as important as *I* or *they.* But love poems, vituperations, and prayers tend strongly toward conventional patterns of image and idea, so that often they fall short of a truly dramatic effect. To take a simple illustration, "Mignonne, allons voir si la rose . . ." is so completely conceived in the tradition of *carpe diem* poems that we think no more of the person it is addressed to than we would meditate on Horace's Leuconoe, Lalage, Cinara, or similar shadowy recipients of ritual tribute. On the other hand, Maurice Scève's lady—and Catullus'—seem like the magnetic fields holding together their poets' work. The personalities of Délie and Lesbia are, of course, mere illusions wrought of poetic style: in Scève's case the strangeness of his language gives individuality to his mistress, while Catullus achieved the same effect through violent shifts of tone unexpected in a "classical" writer.

Baudelaire's great contribution to the poetry of *tu* and *vous* lies in his exploitation of dialogue. He was certainly not the first French poet to adapt the patterns of conversation to verse, for Musset's "Souvenir" shows expert manipulation of the colloquial, but he was, of all the romantic poets, the one who most consistently used the relationship between *I* and *you* for dramatic purposes. The last lines of "Au Lecteur" are exemplary:

> Tu le connais, lecteur, ce monstre délicat,
> — Hypocrite lecteur, — mon semblable, — mon frère!

The generalities of the previous stanzas prepare us in no way for so blunt a shift: the poet has been declaiming before an audience, as poets will; now the public disintegrates into a group of isolated individuals, each of whom becomes the specific object of the poet's words. Discourse yields to conversation and, appropriately enough, Baudelaire adapts to verse the dash, which in French anticipates dialogue.

The characteristic thing about Baudelaire's use of dialogue is that we hear only one side of it, without, for that, the poem becoming monologue: the sense of the *other person* remains acute, and we always feel that she, for it is usually a woman, is about to reply. We need not attempt to catalogue all of Baudelaire's uses of half-dialogue: they range from the vituperative love poems addressed to Jeanne Duval (for which we may find baroque antecedents in Sigogne) to prayers like "Réversibilité" and traditional eulogies. However, we can examine with some profit the poem beginning "La servante au grand coeur . . ." whose second person does not place it in the famous cycles of the Black, White, and Green-eyed Venuses, as critics persist in naming Baudelaire's muses. This poem contains not only an exquisite handling of dramatic situation, it will also permit us to refute certain commonplaces about Baudelaire's poetic limitations:

La servante au grand coeur dont vous étiez jalouse,
Et qui dort son sommeil sous une humble pelouse,
Nous devrions pourtant lui porter quelques fleurs.
Les morts, les pauvres morts, ont de grandes douleurs,
Et quand Octobre souffle, émondeur des vieux arbres,
Son vent mélancolique à l'entour de leurs marbres,
Certes, ils doivent trouver les vivants bien ingrats,
A dormir, comme ils font, chaudement dans leurs draps,
Tandis que, dévorés de noires songeries,
Sans compagnon de lit, sans bonnes causeries,
Vieux squelettes gelés travaillés par le ver,
Ils sentent s'égoutter les neiges de l'hiver
Et le siècle couler, sans qu'amis ni famille
Remplacent les lambeaux qui pendent à leur grille.

The source of these lines is patently Gautier's "Comédie de la mort," yet nothing better shows Baudelaire's originality in handling the conventional imagery of the morbid. Four words, "jealous," "ungrateful," "friends," "family," serve to establish the tense relations between the speaker and his listener: instead of violent recriminations, his remarks are inspired by guilt, which, in turn, detaches him from her. Though she is so intimate a part of his life as to have taken part in some sordid domestic clash, he addresses her with the formal *vous*, as is done in many stiff, hypercorrect French families. Attachment to her—her sex is elegantly revealed by the feminine ending of *jalouse*—and loathing of her cruelty are fused in an ambivalent mood. The occasion for the speaker's anguish is subtly implied: the time is October, All Soul's Day is approaching, and, with the advent of the time when Catholics think of their dead, he guiltily remembers some cowardice on his part and some pain on that of the old servant. The subdued tone of the speaker's words is rendered by the thoughtful, halting movement of the syntax. The first sentence is colloquial in structure; a noun, placed at the beginning, is caught up and syntactically ordered by the pronoun *lui* in the third line, a pattern common in speech and demonstrative of the devious way in which language follows thought. The rest of the verse-paragraph consists of one long complex sentence which shows Baudelaire rivaling Hugo in ability to write a cohesive series of alexandrine couplets. It is commonly said that Baudelaire lacked the capacity for elaborating sentence structure within the framework of verse. "La servante au grand coeur . . . ," which everyone ascribes to Baudelaire's early years, proves quite adequately that, had he not preferred stanzas to verse-paragraphs—for various effects of design—he could have excelled in the freer form.

The concluding portion of "La servante au grand coeur . . ." is likewise one long sentence-paragraph:

> Lorsque la bûche siffle et chante, si le soir,
> Calme, dans le fauteuil je la voyais s'asseoir,
> Si, par une nuit bleue et froide de décembre,
> Je la trouvais tapie en un coin de ma chambre,
> Grave, et venant du fond de son lit éternel
> Couver l'enfant grandi de son oeil maternel,
> Que pourrais-je répondre à cette âme pieuse,
> Voyant tomber des pleurs de sa paupière creuse?

The question mark at the end of the poem brings our attention back to the *vous* of the first line: the speaker delicately needles his listener, who, by implication, has contributed to the old servant's sorrowful death. The latter's gentleness has made her an easy object of undeserved persecution, and the tormentor is now being arraigned. The key word here is *maternel;* the servant was the speaker's true mother, and the listener is either an unnatural mother or a vicious mistress. That Baudelaire allows this ambiguity to remain is characteristic of the elegance and concision with which he builds up dramatic situations: it does not matter who the *you* is; we realize that she is an imperfect woman in contrast to the mother figure of the old servant.

With regard to the verse-paragraphs of "La servante au grand coeur . . . ," as with Baudelaire's use of time patterns and his distribution of metaphor, we can observe an unusually acute concern on his part for introducing clear divisions within poems. This is hardly a peculiarity of Baudelaire's, since any poem of several lines must consist of parts within the whole, but yet Baudelaire makes a much more obvious use of structuring devices than his contemporaries. His versification reflects this tendency. Judged by superficial textbook standards the prosody of *Les Fleurs du mal* is not more "modern" or "free" than that of other mid-nineteenth-century poets. In the domains of line-length, rime, enjambment, and caesura, Baudelaire innovated no more, no less than any French romantic poet.[21] At the same time, however, anyone who has carefully read the major nineteenth-century poets knows that there

[21]Genuine infractions of traditional rules are rare; see, however, "Ciel brouillé," which has only masculine rimes.

is something different about the prosodic patterns of *Les Fleurs du mal*, something that we do not find even in such expert versifiers as Gautier, Leconte de Lisle, or Hugo himself. What distinguishes Baudelaire's work, I think, is a delicate care for the poem as a visual object: Baudelaire, reluctant to publish, seems, along with Flaubert, to have been the first French writer to realize the importance of space and typography for the reader.[22] Blank separating spaces are essential to his style. Many simple illustrations come to mind: Baudelaire loved short stanzaic forms to order his inspiration; in particular he liked the *quintil*, often with a framing line, because of its look of fullness in comparison with the commonplace quatrain; he patiently elaborated more sonnet forms than any other French poet,[23] and, finally, Baudelaire indulged in numerous isolated experiments in prosodic patterns, none perhaps constituting a major discovery, but all of them fascinating. The common denominator of all Baudelaire's verse forms seems to be an attempt to make the poem look interesting or unusual on paper. From a purely phonetic standpoint he did little that was new, but the impact of his verse is served by typographic devices which are as powerful in their effect as more purely prosodic innovations.

The single detached alexandrine which stands at the beginning of the second "Spleen" poem is a fine example of the use Baudelaire made of blank space as a psychological and rhythmic entity. The almost banal words "J'ai plus de souvenirs que si j'avais mille ans" acquire a foreboding weight, which they would not have if joined to the following rime line. Even Hugo, the greatest nineteenth-century master of the alexandrine verse-paragraph, seldom achieved such dramatic results. Elsewhere spacing creates unusual effects within ordinary prosodic forms. The last line of the *quintil* in "Le Goût du néant" acquires a gnomic force by its typographical detachment:

> Esprit vaincu, fourbu! Pour toi, vieux maraudeur,
> L'amour n'a plus de goût, non plus que la dispute;
> Adieu donc, chants du cuivre et soupirs de la flûte,
> Plaisirs, ne tentez plus un coeur sombre et boudeur!
>
> Le Printemps adorable a perdu son odeur!

[22]All biographers tell of the concern Baudelaire had for the typography of *Les Fleurs du mal*.

[23]Cassagne claims (p. 95) that Baudelaire used thirty-one different sonnet patterns.

The brusqueness of the movement is accentuated by the blank. In "Abel et Caïn" the quatrain is broken up into two-line groups:

Race d'Abel, dors, bois et mange;
Dieu te sourit complaisamment.

Race de Caïn, dans la fange
Rampe et meurs misérablement.

The rhetorical pattern demands separation of the apostrophes to the two races, but *rimes plates* would have made the verse disintegrate. The form Baudelaire chose points up at once the parallelisms and antitheses between Cain's and Abel's descendants. Where the one group has food, the other has mud, and so forth: the rime serves an ironic purpose. Furthermore this odd form contains a delicate reminiscence, in rhythm and rime, of the old-fashioned French form of the Decalogue:

Un seul Dieu tu adoreras
Et aimeras parfaitement.

. . . .

Tes père et mère honoreras
Afin de vivre longuement.

Baudelaire is creating, in "Abel et Caïn" a demonic version of Scriptures, in which Abel's descendants are identified with an unjust God.

Baudelaire's prosodic inventions are small enough, but they are important insofar as they attest his care for all manner of detail in verse. Although he is the only major nineteenth-century French poet whose work is not central to the history of versification, it is nevertheless impossible to think of the richness of romantic stanzaic forms without poems like "Harmonie du soir" or "L'Irréparable" coming to mind.

Baudelaire's place in the history of French poetry is usually assessed —too hastily—as that of the symbolists' precursor. He was, of course, the poet whom Rimbaud and Mallarmé imitated as soon as they had finished their Hugolian phase, but Baudelaire was also a passing influence for them. Huysmans next mistook Baudelaire for Des Esseintes and popularized his own rather special vision of the poet. Finally, Laforgue, in some brilliant but rather one-sided notes, argued that with Baudelaire poetry had effectuated a clean break with the past.[24] Most criti-

²⁴See Warren Ramsey, *Jules Laforgue and the Ironic Inheritance* (New York, 1953), 106–107.

cism has done little else but echo Laforgue. These notions were largely formed before all the posthumous Baudelaire material was published and before many biographical problems had been solved. Certain corrections are necessary.

First of all his relation to literary life and the public was not essentially different from that of his contemporaries: Baudelaire remained a man of letters, a part-time journalist who stated his hatred for the public no more ferociously than other writers in similar circumstances. The notes he made for a preface to *Les Fleurs du mal* even show him trying to argue with his critics in the time-honored fashion. He belonged to no tight literary coteries, no *chapelle*, such as Mallarmé was to create, but lived in the journalistic Bohemia that was the normal society of French writers in the July Monarchy and Second Empire. With the symbolists under the Third Republic a very different situation was to prevail: a separation took place between an elite of poets and other writers; hermetic literature was formed.

Also we find in Baudelaire's verse none of that explosion of modernism which led Mallarmé through the late unpunctuated sonnets to *Un Coup de dés* and Rimbaud from *vers libérés* to the *Illuminations*. His rhythms remained those of Hugo and his contemporaries; his verse forms are unusual principally in his fondness for the *quintil* and irregular sonnets. Above all he showed no consciousness of that *crise de vers* which affected the next generation of poets; his verse was that of his day, and he apparently foresaw no change in its structure. We must remember that Baudelaire's world of esthetic conceptions was far more conventional and limited than that of later poets. For him Delacroix's canvasses of the 1820's were still modern art; music was no broader than the limits of *Tannhäuser*; and the forms of verse had been largely established by Victor Hugo. In respect to literature, Baudelaire's thought was not at all that of a modernist: he accepted unequivocally the traditional conception of the poem as having a meaning and a definable subject. The mode of being of poetry did not concern him as it did Rimbaud and Mallarmé, and therefore he was not tempted toward experimentation in order to see how far literature could be pushed. Above all Baudelaire did not substitute poetry for theology and ethics in the symbolist fashion.

Nor is the content of Baudelaire's symbolism radically different from that of the other romantics. In this respect, the influence of Gautier and the *bouzingo* vocabulary was enormous: all the romantic iconography of snakes, bats, ravens, cats, and female demons passed into *Les Fleurs du mal*. The drab urban landscape was, of course, Sainte-Beuve's before it became Baudelaire's. Even his ecstatic imagery—that of synesthesia and artifacts—which has often been considered his greatest innovation, has its origins in Hoffman's and Gautier's prose.[25] Yet in reading *La Comédie de la Mort*, although we recognize many good Baudelairean passages, we do not ultimately feel that satisfaction that *Les Fleurs du mal* gives us. With regard to the two poets' symbolism we can observe at least one new dimension that Baudelaire added to romantic iconography: an intense sense of heat, light, cold, and dampness—in short, the symbolism of weather and seasons.

It would perhaps be rash to claim that Baudelaire was the first French poet to exploit fully the seasons, and yet there is something in such a contention. Spring and autumn are everywhere in French poetry, but winter and summer were less favored in the early nineteenth century. Furthermore, the rain, characteristic of all seasons in the Ile-de-France, seems seldom to have received the literary attention it deserves. The sunny, conventionalized autumn of pre-romantic poetry or of Hugo's *Feuilles d'automne* is, in short, a literary myth. Even Gautier lacked imagination for weather. Here is the fresh kind of effect Baudelaire created by supporting the romantic iconography of death with an appropriate climate:

> O fins d'automne, hivers, printemps trempés de boue,
> Endormeuses saisons! je vous aime et vous loue
> D'envelopper ainsi mon coeur et mon cerveau
> D'un linceul vaporeux et d'un vague tombeau.
>
> Dans cette grande plaine où l'autan froid se joue,
> Où par les longues nuits la girouette s'enroue,
> Mon âme mieux qu'au temps du tiède renouveau
> Ouvrira largement ses ailes de corbeau.
> ("Brumes et pluies")

The urge toward immobility and a death-like state is similar to that we found in Gautier's "Thébaïde," but here the imagery has a delicate and sensuous realism. The seasons lose some of their traditional poetic associations: the autumn evoked is late and cold; spring brings not flowers but mud. Baudelaire can take a familiar demonic symbol like the raven

---

[25]See Enid Starkie, *Baudelaire* (New York, 1958), 234–36.

and surround it with such concrete, commonplace details that we tend to forget the filiation of his theme. With Baudelaire the demonic becomes part of everyday reality.

The symbolism of the seasons has always been most closely associated with elegiac verse, which compares or contrasts the cycle of man's life with that of nature. Baudelaire completely renovated the elegiac convention, and one of his greatest accomplishments is the new urgency and intensity the turn of the seasons conveys in his verse:

> Bientôt nous plongerons dans les froides ténèbres;
> Adieu, vive clarté de nos étés trop courts!
> J'entends déjà tomber avec des chocs funèbres
> Le bois retentissant sur le pavé des cours.
>
> Tout l'hiver va rentrer dans mon être : colère,
> Haine, frissons, horreur, labeur dur et forcé,
> Et, comme le soleil dans son enfer polaire,
> Mon coeur ne sera plus qu'un bloc rouge et glacé.
>
> J'écoute en frémissant chaque bûche qui tombe;
> L'échafaud qu'on bâtit n'a pas d'écho plus sourd.
> Mon esprit est pareil à la tour qui succombe
> Sous les coups du bélier infatigable et lourd.
>
> Il me semble, bercé par ce choc monotone,
> Qu'on cloue en grande hâte un cercueil quelque part,
> Pour qui?— C'était hier l'été; voici l'automne!
> Ce bruit mystérieux sonne comme un départ.
>
> ("Chant d'automne")

The web of associations between the season and the speaker is complex: summer is not simply the season of maturity, and winter that of death, for winter is also a moral state. The lurid red sun imprisoned in blackness, an astronomically verifiable phenomenon, adds an element of color symbolism (yellow and green will dominate the second part of the poem), yet by far the most important chain of analogies concerns sound: the wood being chopped for the winter suggests death and destruction, which, with great syntactic elegance, Baudelaire renders in four different grammatical ways: the adjective *funèbre*, the "no more than" comparison with the scaffold, the "is like" analogy of the besieged tower, and the fantasy "it seems to me," where the speaker drifts into daydreams of a coffin. The association between winter and the sound of tools has ramifications; tools destroy, but also build: the infernal city rings with the sound of "forced labor." The city belongs to winter as the sea and sky do to summer; the demonic, man-made contraptions have been evoked in order to contrast with a vision of light and space:

> J'aime de vos longs yeux la lumière verdâtre,
> Douce beauté, mais tout aujourd'hui m'est amer,
> Et rien, ni votre amour, ni le boudoir, ni l'âtre,
> Ne me vaut le soleil rayonnant sur la mer . . .

Despite Baudelaire's famous scorn for poets who grow sentimental over vegetables, he was himself something of a nature poet: the difference is that the sky meant more to him than the earth, weather more than plants.

The dimension of climate gives the symbolic universe of *Les Fleurs du mal* greater density than that of *Les Destinées*, although their demonic character is frequently similar. "Le Reniement de Saint Pierre," even if it is only a youthful blasphemy, is Baudelaire's version of Vigny's sinister gospel and is central to Baudelaire's vision of the world. If the demonic transformation of Christian myth in Baudelaire's verse seems much more complex than anything we find in the poets we have studied up to now, it is perhaps because he was alone among his contemporaries to have been seriously influenced in his sensibility by Catholicism. As a result we find in his work the traces of dialectic patterns reminiscent of theology. Indeed, we have only to turn to his notebooks to discover how fond Baudelaire was of theological propositions and arguments, such as the following: "Qu'est-ce que la chute? Si c'est l'unité devenue dualité, c'est Dieu qui a chuté. En d'autres termes, la création ne serait-elle pas la chute de Dieu?" [26] None of these hypotheses, however, constitutes a definitive belief, for Baudelaire's dualistic temperament demanded a double theology which could account for both the Tyrant God and the Merciful God. This again distinguishes him from Vigny, the simple pessimist. *Les Fleurs du mal* have been analyzed as a vast pattern of ambivalent symbols in which art, beauty, nature, sex, and mankind appear initially as divine only to turn into demonic forces.[27] Each aspect of life seems capable in Baudelaire of assuming antithetical symbolic values. It has been pointed out that whereas "Correspondances" seems to reflect the conventional Swedenborgian theory that

[26]"Mon coeur mis à nu" XXXIII.
[27]See Mossop, *Baudelaire's Tragic Hero*, 16–27.

nature reflects heaven, a later poem in *Les Fleurs du mal*, "Alchimie de la douleur," provides a theory of infernal *correspondances*: [28]

> Hermès inconnu qui m'assistes
> Et qui toujours m'intimidas,
> Tu me rends l'égal de Midas,
> Le plus triste des alchimistes;
>
> Par toi je change l'or en fer
> Et le paradis en enfer;
> Dans le suaire des nuages
>
> Je découvre un cadavre cher,
> Et sur les célestes rivages
> Je bâtis de grands sarcophages.

"Alchimie de la douleur" appears to have been placed toward the end of "Spleen et Idéal" to counterbalance the earlier sonnet. Instead of the ecstatic metamorphoses produced by synesthesia, it uses alchemical symbolism. The moral overtones of alchemy are numerous and contradictory: it was regarded with suspicion by the church, for Satan is traditionally the master of precious metals and other underground treasures. On the other hand, the pretentions of the art could be beneficent and noble, the literal resurrection of a Golden Age. Baudelaire inverts the traditional alchemical process to intensify its demonic character, and transforms the divine Hermes Trismegistes of occultist lore into a sinister figure presiding over debasement and death. The tercets contain an example—rare in Baudelaire—of clouds assuming a funereal look.

The whole pattern of *Les Fleurs du mal* would seem to reflect a dualism in which the forces of evil have the upper hand. The arrangement of the poems is partly autobiographical and partly dialectic. The demonic poems addressed to Jeanne Duval precede the loftier verse in honor of Mme Sabatier or Marie Daubrun; yet the whole section called "Spleen et Idéal" ends in darkness, with the vision of a sinister universe modifying the initial one of a comforting world. Paradise is remote in space or time. Christianity without redemption—or original sin without Christ—is the usual way of describing Baudelaire's metaphysic, and it

---

[28]See Lloyd James Austin, *L'Univers poétique de Baudelaire* (Paris, 1956), 92–97.

is not inaccurate, as regards his symbolism. Yet there are many intimations and recollections of paradise in Baudelaire's poetic universe, and they are important, for without them his volume would lack its rich patterns of antithesis and ambivalence. Reading the second quatrain of "Obsession,"

> Je te hais, Océan! tes bonds et tes tumultes,
> Mon esprit les retrouve en lui; ce rire amer
> De l'homme vaincu, plein de sanglots et d'insultes,
> Je l'entends dans le rire énorme de la mer.

we recall the earlier line "Homme libre, toujours tu chériras la mer," ("L'Homme et la mer"). This possibility of shift and inversion in symbolism makes the poems interact, as it were. Undoubtedly Baudelaire's feelings, changing over the years, account somewhat for the inner contradictions of *Les Fleurs du mal*, but beneath the diversity there seems to be some constant: a dualistic, antithetical play of sensibility which led Baudelaire to perceive both divine and Satanic facets in phenomena. "Il y a dans tout homme, à toute heure, deux postulations simultanées, l'une vers Dieu, l'autre vers Satan." [29] Baudelaire's flexible mind could see summer as the symbol of life or as a cruel mockery on the part of deity, the sky as heaven or a prison roof, motion as fulfillment or futility. Any reader can easily pick out countless antithetical symbols in *Les Fleurs du mal*. What is important is not the value of any one symbol in any one poem, but the anagogical intensity of his symbolism. Gautier's demonic iconography is not supported by an adequate framework of ideas, Vigny's lacks a sustained poetic immediacy. In Baudelaire the iconography of French romanticism is finally used with both intellectual acumen and stylistic brilliance.

Perhaps the most important nexus of symbols in *Les Fleurs du mal* concerns time, space, and movement, three interlocked concepts, which often seem to play a dominant role in symbologies of good and evil. One critic has noted that there seem to be two conceptions of time in *Les Fleurs du mal*: the paradisiacal *durée*, so often associated with infinite, richly colored reaches like the sunset, and the infernal ticking of clock-time which leads into nothingness or an abyss.[30] The symbolism of movement is likewise ambivalent. Baudelaire remarks that "dans tout changement il y a quelque chose d'infâme et d'agréable à la fois, quelque

---

[29]"Mon coeur mis a nu" XIX.
[30]See Georges Poulet, *Etudes sur le temps humain* (Paris, 1953), 336.

chose qui tient de l'infidélité et du déménagement." [31] Thus the lost paradise of the past pains as it recedes, but future death, on the other hand, is inviting.

This unresolved dualism of sensibility, which so irritates Sartre,[32] finds at least an artistic solution in *Les Fleurs du mal*. We have already seen how the past and approaching death seem strangely associated in "Recueillement": there is a hint that the antithesis of pleasure and pain will be relieved by a kind of cyclic or dialectic progression in which the beginning and the end will merge. The keystone in the architecture of *Les Fleurs du mal* is "Le Voyage," which is Baudelaire's most ambitious attempt to order his conflicting thoughts and symbols. The antithesis of innocence and experience is set forth at the beginning of the poem:

> Pour l'enfant, amoureux de cartes et d'estampes,
> L'univers est égal à son vaste appétit.
> Ah! que le monde est grand à la clarté des lampes!
> Aux yeux du souvenir que le monde est petit!

Later on the dialogue between the child and the old traveler will become explicit: here the former is introduced so as to suggest who the listener of the poem is. The narrative begins:

> Un matin nous partons, le cerveau plein de flamme,
> Le coeur gros de rancune et de désirs amers,
> Et nous allons, suivant le rythme de la lame,
> Berçant notre infini sur le fini des mers . . .

In "Le Voyage" Baudelaire draws together a great deal of his customary symbolism. Here the paradox of the container and contained achieves one of its fullest statements: whereas the nightbound room suggested by the lamp of the first quatrain stands in implicit contrast to the vastness of the world, the great stretches of ocean are reduced to a finite known quantity, while true infinity is contained within ourselves. But the inner space is unreachable. By his container images Baudelaire renews the meaning of the hackneyed word *infini*, which the nineteenth century used so abundantly.

---

[31]"Mon coeur mis à nu" VII.
[32]It is the principal theme of his *Baudelaire* (Paris, 1947).

The image of the ship in motion is an important one for Baudelaire, and he even comments on it in *Fusées:* a "complicated but eurythmic" pattern of movement suggests "all human sighs and ambitions." But regular movement can have other symbolic values as well, and at the beginning of Part II, futility characterizes the voyage:

> Nous imitons, horreur! la toupie et la boule
> Dans leur valse et leurs bonds; même dans nos sommeils
> La Curiosité nous tourmente et nous roule,
> Comme un Ange cruel qui fouette des soleils.
>
> Singuilière fortune où le but se déplace,
> Et, n'étant nulle part, peut être n'importe où!
> Où l'Homme, dont jamais l'espérance n'est lasse,
> Pour trouver le repos court toujours comme un fou!

It is characteristic of Baudelaire's mixed diction that one stanza ends with a strange simile, suggested perhaps by the earlier *cerveau plein de flamme,* while the next one culminates in a familiar cliché, *courir comme un fou.*

The paradox of movement—it leads toward an end or resting point—has always been a potent source of symbolism, for it is associated with man and nature, whereas the realm of godhead is immobile and eternal. Cyclic or unending movement, especially if aimless, can therefore represent dissatisfaction or frustration. The only respite for the tossed and battered spirit is to move out of the world:

> La gloire du soleil sur la mer violette,
> La gloire des cités dans le soleil couchant,
> Allumaient dans nos coeurs une ardeur inquiète
> De plonger dans un ciel au reflet alléchant.
>
> Les plus riches cités, les plus grands paysages,
> Jamais ne contenaient l'attrait mystérieux
> De ceux que le hasard fait avec les nuages,
> Et toujours le désir nous rendait soucieux!

Oceans, clouds, and sunset are Baudelaire's favorite images of paradisiacal infinity. The visible but intangible spectacle of light and color is the divine *correspondance* which is the reverse of the demonic lid-prison-sky. Appropriately the Tyrant God will not appear in "Le Voyage," and his evil role will be assumed by mankind. After a catalogue of exotic sights, the traveler, in answer to a question from the child, describes "Le spectacle ennuyeux de l'immortel péché":

> L'Humanité bavarde, ivre de son génie,
> Et, folle maintenant comme elle était jadis,
> Criant à Dieu, dans sa furibonde agonie :
> "O mon semblable, ô mon maître, je te maudis!"
>
> Et les moins sots, hardis amants de la Démence,
> Fuyant le grand troupeau parqué par le Destin,
> Et se réfugiant dans l'opium immense!
> — Tel est du globe entier l'éternel bulletin."

The world is presented as a kind of nether region presided over by Fate, and mankind as engaged in an endless cycle of blasphemy and self-love. The refuge of opium, itself symbolic of art, beauty, dreams, and the ideal, is called immense because it belongs to the divine infinity of the sky.

The spatial symbolism is further developed, and the idea of a *correspondance* between man's mind and his surroundings is made explicit:

> Amer savoir, celui qu'on tire du voyage!
> Le monde, monotone et petit, aujourd'hui,
> Hier, demain, toujours, nous fait voir notre image :
> Une oasis d'horreur dans un désert d'ennui!

The words "yesterday, tomorrow, always" prepare us for the symbol of infernal time: a desert emptiness. *Ennui* has particular connotations of vacuity in Baudelaire, for it is his translation of *acedia*, the indifference to good or evil, the absence of moral choice. Ennui is what all of life, pain or pleasure, resolves itself into, and by this dialectic turn, the antithesis of good and evil is abolished.

The second voyage, that of death, is a repetition, in Kierkegaard's sense, of the earlier one. The old traveler is rejuvenated, and the sunset-sky-infinity returns:

> Nous nous embarquerons sur la mer des Ténèbres
> Avec le coeur joyeux d'un jeune passager.
> Entendez-vous ces voix, charmantes et funèbres,
> Qui chantent: "Par ici! vous qui voulez manger
>
> Le Lotus parfumé! c'est ici qu'on vendange
> Les fruits miraculeux dont votre coeur a faim;

Venez vous enivrer de la douceur étrange
De cette après-midi qui n'a jamais de fin?"

A l'accent familier nous devinons le spectre;
Nos Pylades là-bas tendent leurs bras vers nous.
"Pour rafraîchir ton coeur nage vers ton Electre!"
Dit celle dont jadis nous baisions les genoux.

It is like the mature Baudelaire to use passing mythological ornaments at a time when they had largely been banished from poetry. The comparison between the speaker and the fury-driven Orestes has one curious romantic twist: Baudelaire, like Chateaubriand, found brother-sister incest to be the ideal erotic relation, and Electra here replaces the *soeur* so frequent in his love poetry.

The Stygian banks metamorphose back into the ocean shore in the following lines, in accordance with Baudelaire's customary practice of shifting metaphor with every quatrain. The funereal darkness of the landscape is now contrasted with contained light, promising a new sky:

O Mort, vieux capitaine, il est temps! levons l'ancre!
Ce pays nous ennuie, ô Mort! Appareillons!
Si le ciel et la mer sont noirs comme de l'encre,
Nos coeurs que tu connais sont remplis de rayons!

Verse-nous ton poison pour qu'il nous réconforte!
Nous voulons, tant ce feu nous brûle le cerveau,
Plonger au fond du gouffre, Enfer ou Ciel, qu'importe?
Au fond de l'Inconnu pour trouver du *nouveau!*

Death will replace time with eternity, which, like the infinite, has a positive meaning for Baudelaire. The antithesis of good and evil, resolved by ennui, will again spring into being, but the speaker accepts joyfully the renewed cycle of experience, for it will be of absolute good *or* evil, rather than an oscillation between the two.

By placing "Le Voyage" at the end of *Les Fleurs du mal*, Baudelaire succeeded in constructing a dialectic out of what would otherwise have been a mere thematic antithesis. We have seen how Baudelaire sharpened and gave depth of meaning to the romantic iconology of evil, through the rigorousness of his thought. But, unlike Vigny, whose moral thought was also precise, Baudelaire's mind was too subtle for him to emprison himself in any one dogma or intellectual system. His *journaux intimes* are remarkable both for their acuteness and their self-contradictions. In "Le Voyage," however, he managed artistically to do what he was incapable of in his life: to order his dualistic vision of the world and to move beyond it. By doing so, he gave his volume a dimension of meaning, which all the flaws in its structure cannot diminish.

VI

NERVAL AND *LES CHIMÈRES*

Nerval's career as a poet is a puzzling one. He belonged to the generation of Musset and Gautier, but produced no verse of any interest in the 1830's when they were establishing their reputations. His early poems are no more than colorless imitations of Sainte-Beuve and others. It was not until the 1840's that Nerval wrote anything—in any genre—that merits some attention, and even such works as the *Voyage en Orient* and the sonnet cycle *Le Christ aux Oliviers* are probably known today only because Nerval ultimately wrote *Les Chimères, Sylvie,* and *Aurélia.* The chronology of Nerval's *opera* cannot be determined precisely, but one has the general impression that for most of his life he was little more than another of the countless founding members of Bohemia, supporting himself by journalistic hackwork and remaining far more arresting as a person than a writer.

Nerval's attacks of schizophrenia have become closely associated with his major work, thanks to the relentless nineteenth-century tendency to confuse literature and life. It is true, of course, that the development of Nerval's poetic imagination seems so tardy and unprepared that it would be convenient to be able to attribute it to some clear-cut psychological factor. There is something disturbing about a mediocre writer who suddenly produces three or four great sonnets, two very original prose narratives, and then commits suicide. However, Nerval's unusual career simply cannot be explained by amateur psychoanalysis or anything else. The proof—if we can really speak of "proofs" in such matters—is that insanity does not seem, initially at least, to have affected Nerval's originality as a poet.

Nerval's first fit of madness occurred, so far as we know, in 1841. Three years later he published *Le Christ aux Oliviers* which preceded the appearance of Vigny's "Mont des Oliviers" by some two and a half months. I think there can be no question of influence here. Rather, I believe that Nerval's sonnet cycle demonstrates the extent to which he had absorbed not only the demonic vision common to so many of his contemporaries but also certain of their stylistic devices. Certainly it is not in his own style—as yet nonexistent—that the poems are written, but, ironically enough, in that of Vigny:

> Quand le Seigneur, levant au ciel ses maigres bras,
> Sous les arbres sacrés, comme font les poètes,
> Se fut longtemps perdu dans ses douleurs muettes,
> Et se jugea trahi par des amis ingrats,
>
> Il se tourna vers ceux qui l'attendaient en bas
> Rêvant d'être des rois, des sages, des prophètes...
> Mais engourdis, perdus dans le sommeil des bêtes,
> Et se prit à crier : "Non, Dieu n'existe pas!"

Vigny's "Moïse" appears to be the prototype for these lines: the poet-Moses has become the poet-Christ, and the style has the same heavy, adjective-laden movement. Also, Mount Sinai is a typological equivalent of the Mount of Olives. The tercets expound a demonic gospel or *bonne nouvelle:*

> Ils dormaient. "Mes amis, savez-vous la *nouvelle?*
> J'ai touché de mon front à la voûte éternelle;
> Je suis sanglant, brisé, souffrant pour bien des jours!
>
> Frères, je vous trompais. Abîme! abîme! abîme!
> Le dieu manque à l'autel où je suis la victime...
> Dieu n'est pas! Dieu n'est plus! Mais ils dormaient toujours!

The image of Christ's hitting the sky with his forehead suggests that the "eternal vault" is a prison roof, and the important theme of God's absence, of man's solitude, is also introduced. In short, *Le Christ aux Oliviers* is a *summa* of the usual demonic imagery: in later sonnets of the cycle the image of the black sun[1] is joined to the themes of "Destin," "Nécessité," and "Hasard." Judas has "du moins . . . la force du crime,"

---

[1]The black sun is a characteristic sinister image. It can be found in Gautier, Hugo, and Baudelaire, as well as elsewhere in Nerval. See Hélène Tuzet, "L'Image du soleil noir," *Revue des Sciences Humaines,* Nouvelle série, Fasc. 88 (October–December, 1957), 479–502.

and Christ is at the end placed in the perspective of comparative religion by a series of analogies with Icarus, Atys, and Phaeton. These parallels, in fact, are the only aspect of *Le Christ aux Oliviers* which differentiates it from Vigny's view of the world. Nerval had, from an early age, an extraordinary interest in the history of religions; his concern with deities other than the Christian one was to characterize his mature poetic imagination.

Syncretic identifications of religious figures is a part of pagan sensibility which survived even into medieval Christianity in the form of typological interpretations of the Bible. Nerval was to evolve a totally pagan mythology into which Judaic and Islamic elements are blended by syncretism. The last line of *Le Christ aux Oliviers* contains an allusion to one of the fundamental myths in this system: Jupiter is asked who created the new god, Christ, but he is unable to answer, for the only one capable of doing so is Jehovah, "Celui qui donna l'âme aux enfants du limon." The legend, told by Nerval in the *Voyage en Orient*, is that the Children of Clay descend from Adam (whose name means clay) while the Children of Fire have Cain as their ancestor.[2] Jehovah of course protects the former, who are identified with Christianity, whereas the Children of Fire worship the pagan gods. Recent research has made much of the pervasive theme of fire in Nerval's work,[3] and we shall frequently be obliged to recall his myth of the two races.

We can see further elements of Nerval's mythology in "Delfica," which the poet dated from 1843. This poem is the simplest of the *Chimères*, being a development of a line from Virgil's fourth eclogue ("Ultima Cumaei venit jam carminis aetas"):

> La connais-tu, Dafné, cette ancienne romance,
> Au pied du sycomore, ou sous les lauriers blancs,
> Sous l'olivier, le myrthe, ou les saules tremblants,
> Cette chanson d'amour qui toujours recommence ?...
>
> Reconnais-tu le TEMPLE au péristyle immense,
> Et les citrons amers où s'imprimaient tes dents?
> Et la grotte fatale aux hôtes imprudents
> Où du dragon vaincu dort l'antique semence ?...

[2]See "Les Conteurs" in the section "Les Nuits de Ramazan." According to this account Cain is the son of Eblis, not Adam.

[3]See, for example, Norma Rinsler, "Gérard de Nerval and the Divinities of Fire," *French Studies,* XVII (April, 1963), 136–47.

The title of the sonnet "Delfica" can be interpreted as a Latin neuter: "matters Delphic"; it is evident we are dealing with prophecy. The great oracles of antiquity were feminine, and here Nerval associates the Delphic Pythia and the Cumaean Sybil (later mentioned) with Daphne, beloved of Apollo. Godhead is female for Nerval; the figure of Apollo vanishes behind these feminine ones: one can sense an implied contrast with the overwhelmingly masculine deity of the Judaeo-Christian tradition. Female gods are usually associated with nature and fertility, whence the plant imagery and also that of the seed in the cave. Despite the fact that the Children of Fire are opposed to those of Clay, the former possess the fecund depths of the earth and the subterranean regions of grottoes and caverns. They have an emblematic beast—the fire-breathing and cave-dwelling dragon, who, as in the myth of Cadmus, will be the author of their reborn race. The nexus of analogies present in the quatrains of "Delfica" seems to imply that the rite of Fire has gone underground during the Christian era and has drawn new strength from its chthonic, female origins. Daphne, like some centuried sleeper, is awakened by the poet, and visions of places swim in her mind. Above all, that of the "TEMPLE" with its peristyle is important for the final lines of the sonnet.

The first tercet announces the return of the Age of Gold:

> Ils reviendront, ces Dieux que tu pleures toujours!
> Le temps va ramener l'ordre des anciens jours;
> La terre a tressailli d'un souffle prophétique...

The second tercet adds, however, a seemingly cryptic proviso to the above lines:

> Cependant la sibylle au visage latin
> Est endormie encor sous l'arc de Constantin
> — Et rien n'a dérangé le sévère Portique.

This modification, so contrary to the usual prophetic style, creates an intense feeling of suspense and malaise. The long adverb *cependant* placed in an accentuated position sharply contradicts the three preceding iterative verbs beginning in *re-*; the return of the old gods is not a mechanical matter, but will be the realization of some burst of unforeseen energy in which both the speaker and Dafné of the poem are involved. The allusions become more recondite at the same time: Constantine the Great's triumphal arch betokens his victory over Maxentius (A.D. 312) and, by extension, the victory of Christianity over Paganism. Thus the Cumaean Sybil—the greatest of the pagan Roman prophets —is figuratively buried beneath. The "Portique" is probably not the Porch or Stoa of Greek philosophy but simply the elaborate columns of the Arcus Constantini. The final image, then, is one of an imposing structure whose ruin will come from beneath: the Children of Fire will await underground their moment of triumph.

The idea of the earth's inner fire is delicately suggested in "Myrtho," one of the later and more hermetic *Chimères*. The figure the poet addresses is a more clearly defined one than the Dafné of "Delfica"; Myrtho is a fertility goddess, an amalgam of Venus, Ceres, Demeter, and Cybele. Opulence and warmth surround her:

> Je pense à toi, Myrtho, divine enchanteresse,
> Au Pausilippe altier, de mille feux brillant,
> A ton front inondé des clartés d'Orient,
> Aux raisins noirs mêlés avec l'or de ta tresse.

In Nerval's private symbolism, Naples, the nearby promontory called the Posillipo, the Italian volcanoes, and Sicily are "Greek" and pagan; grapevines and flowers constitute their flora. The second quatrain is devoted to the speaker, who is an initiate of the Eleusinian mysteries ("Iacchus"—synonym of Bacchus or Dionysus—apparently derives from an invocation used in their ceremonies):

> C'est dans ta coupe aussi que j'avais bu l'ivresse,
> Et dans l'éclair furtif de ton oeil souriant,
> Quand aux pieds d'Iacchus on me voyait priant,
> Car la Muse m'a fait l'un des fils de la Grèce.

These quatrains have a solemn enumeratory character; the asyndetic phrases of the first and the oddly expressive *aussi* and *et* of the second produce almost a ritual movement. The mood is the timeless one of prayer. The tercets suddenly interrupt this:

> Je sais pourquoi, là-bas, le volcan s'est ouvert...
> C'est qu'hier tu l'avais touché d'un pied agile,
> Et de cendres soudain l'horizon s'est couvert.

Hypotaxis suddenly introduces odd notions of causality: the eruption of Vesuvius or Etna is a sign that the old gods will return, in their fiery element. The *hier* and the present perfect *s'est ouvert* suggest the beginning of a chain of events which will end the current phase of history, described in the last tercet:

> Depuis qu'un duc normand brisa tes dieux d'argile,
> Toujours, sous les rameaux du laurier de Virgile,
> Le pâle Hortensia s'unit au Myrthe vert!

The Norman invasion of Sicily is taken to mark the end of antiquity, and the old gods have since been obliged to exist alongside the new one. The botanical symbolism at first seems in part strange: the hydrangea had been cultivated in Europe for only two or three centuries and naturally has no place in the traditional language of flowers. I think, however, that the difficulty is resolved if we consider the epithets attached to both plants: green suggests life and vigor, while the pallid hydrangea, the new flower, represents the sickly morbid aspects of Christianity, the new religion. Furthermore, hydrangea is frequently dried as a winter ornament: it would thus contrast with a living plant which, moreover, remains green all winter.

At this point we might interrupt our discussion of individual poems in order to résumé and synthesize certain patterns in Nerval's imagination. The initial distinction between the Children of Fire and those of Clay needs further refining: the Children of Fire belong to a restricted geographical area, Southern Italy, Greece, and the Orient, and, their element, far from being opposed to earth, is inseparable from it. Nerval avoids the classical division of elements into the pairs air-fire and earth-water: "purumque relinquit aetherium atque aurai simplicis ignem" (*Aeneid* VI, 746–47); "I am fire and air; my other elements I give to baser life." The Children of Fire not only dwell within the earth, lurking in caves and volcanoes, but the fertility of the land—colored flowers and Mediterranean foliage—betokens their presence. Water, likewise, signifies fecundity in Nerval's universe. The element which seems to be neglected is air, for it is the domain of the usurping god. The changing cycle of the gods is usually represented as a bursting forth on the earth's surface rather than an ascension into the sky. Thus in the tercets of "Antéros," where the successive generations of the gods are fertility deities as opposed to Jehovah, the return of the former is being prepared in Hades:

Jéhovah! le dernier, vaincu par ton génie,
Qui, du fond des enfers, criait : "O tyrannie!"
C'est mon aïeul *Bélus* ou mon père *Dagon*...

Ils m'ont plongé trois fois dans les eaux du Cocyte,
Et, protégeant tout seul ma mère Amalécyte,
Je ressème à ses pieds les dents du vieux dragon.

By now we can see how tightly related the *Chimères* are: Baal, Dagon, and the fertility-worshipping Amalekites correspond to the classic gods and the Children of Fire, while the dragon's posterity has already been mentioned in "Delfica." Yet it would be rash to maintain that Nerval's later poems contain an absolutely fixed system of symbols. The universe of fire, earth, and water which we have been investigating admits of exceptions. In "Horus," which follows the same prophetic pattern as the other *Chimères*, Egyptian mythology is used, and the volcano ceases to symbolize life and the return of the true gods. Isis is speaking of Set, whom Nerval oddly calls Kneph, who has been conquered by Horus, her son by the slain Osiris:

"Le voyez-vous, dit-elle, il meurt, ce vieux pervers,
Tous les frimas du monde ont passé par sa bouche,
Attachez son pied tors, éteignez son oeil louche,
C'est le dieu des volcans et le roi des hivers!

The commonplace identification of Isis and Aphrodite has suggested that of Set and Hephaestus. Nerval's imagination seems unimpeded by any rigid system and inclined rather to make quite free associations within his usual thematic pattern of the cycle of the gods.

The tangentiality of Nerval's symbols and their sometimes reversible values are most evident when we approach "Artémis" and "El Desdichado"; these sonnets are the most famous and most complex of the *Chimères*, and we cannot entirely rely for their interpretation on analogies with the simpler poems of the cycle. They are more intricate not only in symbolism but also in syntax: "Artémis" and "El Desdichado" are problematic pieces above all because they are constructed in a gnomic parataxis which makes it difficult to interpret the relations of the various parts to each other. All sorts of autobiographical material may well be alluded to, but in so elliptical a fashion that biography remains irrelevant, and we must first study these poems as symbolic patterns of words. A private anguish is apparent without our needing to elicit any precise references to people or events; the pathos of Nerval's poems transcends any personal misfortune.

The title of "Artémis" need not bother us, the huntress and patroness of chastity, familiar from simplifications of Greek mythology, was in origin a fertility goddess and always retained some of her early attributes. Nerval's lore was sufficient for him to have been aware of this fact. Female fertility gods usually have a double role: representing both mother and wife, they symbolize permanence, while the male, the king, is associated with the transitory, the cycle of birth and death. While the hero's origins and fate provide the dramatic center of epic literature, the spouse and mother figures—without origins or ends—have the timeless character of, say, Penelope. The female survives the death of the male and ensures the continuity of the race, and it is perhaps through just such reasoning that Goethe, whose *Faust* Nerval translated, evolved the notion of the *Ewig-Weibliche*.

In "Artémis" we find a development of this particular aspect of sexual symbolism combined with another, more idiosyncratic theme: the cycle of the poet's life and that of the generations of the gods suddenly correspond; the magic time-point of the poet's death seems to coincide with the vanishing of Christianity. The quatrains deal with the poet's life:

> La treizième revient... C'est encor la première;
> Et c'est toujours la seule, — ou c'est le seul moment :
> Car es-tu reine, ô toi! la première ou dernière?
> Es-tu roi, toi le seul ou le dernier amant ?...

The cycle of life is symbolized by the face of a clock, on which one and thirteen are the same: birth and death are both the mysterious, absolute moment when time ceases to tick on monotonously and becomes a revelation. (We might compare this with Baudelaire's "ecstatic" time.) The king and queen are the gods of fertility and so are the speaker and the feminine figure he addresses. The theme of the life cycle and the mother-wife are further developed in the second quatrain, where the female figure and death are associated, in keeping with the equivalence of one and thirteen, the beginning and the end:

> Aimez qui vous aima du berceau dans la bière;
> Celle que j'aimai seul m'aime encor tendrement :
> C'est la mort — ou la morte ... O délice! ô tourment!
> La rose qu'elle tient, c'est la rose *trémière*.

The hollyhock (the first root of which in English comes from "holy") unquestionably had a symbolic value for Nerval, because *rose trémière* supposedly means *rose d'outre-mer* (from the Holy Land), and was indeed so called in some regions. Thus the hollyhock would be a flower from the distant Kingdom of Fire. The female figure now undergoes a metamorphosis in the first tercet, for shifts of identity are fundamental to Nerval's imagination. Here she has become a saint, but a somewhat unorthodox one, whose attributes are enumerated in a litany-like style:

> Sainte napolitaine aux mains pleines de feux,
> Rose au coeur violet, fleur de sainte Gudule,
> As-tu trouvé ta croix dans le désert des cieux?

The adjective "Neapolitan" discreetly recalls Vesuvius and the Kingdom of Fire, while the rose is often associated with flames, and, of course, can be identified with the hollyhock, which indeed can have a dark red or purple center. Although the hollyhock is not Saint Gudula's flower, she does have one among her attributes. The emptiness of the heavens indicates the non-existence of Jehovah, the sky god: the sterile *cieux* are shortly to be contrasted with a fertile *abîme*. In short, the saint is a Child of Fire without realizing it, and in death has discovered her error.

The final tercet celebrates the end of Christianity, which, as in "Myrtho," is symbolized by white flowers:

> Roses blanches, tombez! vous insultez nos dieux;
> Tombez, fantômes blancs, de votre ciel qui brûle;
> — La sainte de l'abîme est plus sainte à mes yeux!

Here we come up against a typical problem in Nerval's symbolism: there are two saints—that of heaven and that of the abyss—as well as two roses—white and red—and between these pairs there are elements both of similarity and of contrast. We might describe the similarities as cases of mistaken identity, since the antitheses between the roses and the saints seem more fundamental, and so read these lines as follows: fire has overcome Jehovah's heaven, and its inhabitants fade into pale spectres. It is uncertain whether "la sainte de l'abîme" is a general expression equivalent to a plural or whether Nerval is referring to the saint already mentioned. However the two seem associated. Thus the fire saint appears to be a "sainte de l'abîme" whether she also belongs to the church or not. Nerval noted the names of three saints on different manuscripts but it is unlikely, given his syncretism, that he had one exclusively in mind. As is often the case, Nerval's recondite allusions, once tracked down, are neither univalent nor really helpful. The reader is hardly expected to know them or to investigate them in more than a superficial manner: the poet is moving toward a kind of hermetic rather than erudite style. His learning is not displayed for its own sake or even handled with great accuracy: it is not of one saint he speaks but of many who struck his imagination. What we must look for are not innumerable sources of his learned inspiration, but the patterns we can observe in the poems themselves.

The interpretation of "Artémis" depends on a complicated dialectic of ambivalence: the opposite and the same are continually paired. I do not think we can read the sonnet with any assurance unless we can accept certain mythopoeic notions: that mother and wife, birth and death, white flower and red, Jehovah and Cain, heaven and hell, are complementary symbols, at once antithetical and identical. Nerval's universe is, like Baudelaire's, a dualistic one, with the difference that for Nerval the future tense signifies regeneration rather than decay. Baudelaire and Nerval thus represent two contrary visions of common origin, but differentiated by their feeling for time. Whereas Baudelaire feels good and evil to be in eternal opposition, Nerval presages a cyclic end to one of them. The question of time-points, changes, and endings is in fact the major problem in interpreting Nerval's best-known sonnet, "El Desdichado."

The first quatrain of "El Desdichado" presents a contrast between the radiant past and the dark present; the theme of widowhood dominates:

> Je suis le ténébreux, — le veuf, — l'inconsolé,
> Le prince d'Aquitaine à la tour abolie :
> Ma seule *étoile* est morte, — et mon luth constellé
> Porte le *soleil noir* de la *Mélancolie*.

There is an odd interplay of images created by the juxtaposition of *soleil, étoile,* and *constellé* (the latter two both derive from *stella*), but I think incoherence can be avoided if we think of the lute as covered with the signs of the zodiac, thus identifying the poet's song and his destiny in astrological terms. That the lute "bears" a "black sun" means apparently that this sonnet will irradiate melancholy as a solar center does rays of light. As for the second line of the quatrain, it seems that the theme of disinheritance is secondary and is generated by that of widowhood. The title, incidentally, meant "disinherited" to Nerval: his mistake (the word means "unhappy") can be traced to his source, *Ivanhoe*, where Scott mistranslates. The second quatrain is thematically linked with the first by the use of *consolé* in the first rime, which corresponds to the earlier *inconsolé*, but, in contrast, offers a vision of light, the south, and a cyclic future (*rendre* implies a return to an earlier situation):

> Dans la nuit du tombeau, toi qui m'as consolé,
> Rends-moi le Pausilippe et la mer d'Italie,
> La *fleur* qui plaisait tant à mon coeur désolé,
> Et la treille où le pampre à la rose s'allie.

The prepositional phrase at the beginning of the quatrain is ambiguous: it at first seems that the woman addressed is obviously the person in the tomb, but, as it will appear later, a case can be made for placing the speaker there. The flower, like other plants in Nerval, is associated with the female figure, and the concluding image is one of union in contrast to widowhood just as the Mediterranean proper names contrast with that of Aquitaine. The patterns of analogy and antithesis evident in the quatrains of "El Desdichado" now become denser in the tercets:

> Suis-je Amour ou Phébus, Lusignan ou Biron?

Obviously there is a system of parallelisms and contrasts at work here, and the first problem is to discover what it is. *Amour* and *Lusignan* seem to be parallel, as do *Phébus* and *Biron*. *Amour* is less opaque if we translate it back into Latin and recall the story of Cupid and Psyche.[4] The important thing about the myth is that it deals with a love-affair ended by the breaking of an interdiction. The story of Lusignan contains similar material. The sire of the ancient and noble Lusignan family is lost in the obscurity of medieval history, but the family maintained that he founded the house by marrying the fairy Mélusine "Mère-Lusignan") The crucial stipulation in their marriage was that he should not try to see her on Saturdays since, unbeknownst to him, her body metamorphosed into a serpent's on that day. He violated this agreement and she fled away forever. Both tales, that of Cupid and that of Lusignan, contain taboos against *looking* at someone. The contrast between the Cupid of the

---

[4] See John W. Kneller, "The Poet and his Moira: 'El Desdichado,' " *PMLA*, LXXV (September, 1960), 402–409. I am indebted to this study for several details.

Psyche myth and Phoebus can readily be explained; there is, to begin
with, the obvious distinction between a god appearing at night and one
identified with the sun. Next, we might consider the order of the names
Cupid and Phoebus as a chronological one: the poet is now in the tomb
or underworld and is uncertain whether he shall be resurrected. One
might even maintain, like Professor John Kneller, that some opposition
exists here between love and glory, although such an interpretation involves many autobiographical hypotheses. The possible meaning of "Lusignan ou Biron" becomes simpler, if we consider these proper nouns to
correspond, however idiosyncratically, to "Amour ou Phébus." This
antithetical pair of names belongs to classical mythology, the other to
French history and legend. The two great Maréchaux de Biron were
famous figures in the late sixteenth and early seventeenth centuries, but
it is probably the son who is alluded to here.[5] Nerval writes of his fame
in folklore,[6] and he so impressed his age that Shakespeare used him as
the leading figure in *Love's Labours Lost*. Again, however, the contrast
between him and Lusignan is not a perfect antithesis: of Biron's traits
the most famous are heroism and heartiness. We must assume sorrow on
Lusignan's part: such are the interactions of even proper nouns in a poetic
context.

The poet has asked himself essentially whether his end will be tragic
or triumphant. The next two lines offer evidence for his doubts:

> Mon front est rouge encor du baiser de la reine;
> J'ai rêvé dans la grotte où nage la sirène...

Here occurs one of those strange shifts in symbolic value, which make
Nerval's verse so hard to interpret. Up to now the subterranean has been
represented by the tomb and associated with present sorrow and separation. Now a grotto is linked with a precious part of the past. This ambiguity of the underground is one of the most curious aspects of Nerval's
cosmology: he perceives subterranean cavities partly as the Christian
place of punishment, yet partly as a holy spot, like that of the abode of
the Children of Fire or that of the home of Virgil's dwellers in Elysium.
Furthermore, the parataxis of the above lines makes a conjectural reading
necessary: he tries to determine whether the past presages the future, in

[5]For a different view, see Norma Rinsler, "Nerval et Biron," *Revue d'Histoire
Littéraire de la France*, XLI (July–September, 1961), 405–10.
[6]See the *Chansons et légendes du Valois*.

cyclical fashion, or whether it is irremediably lost: the plea of the second quatrain ("Rends-moi le Pausilippe . . .") is replaced by wonder at his memories. It is not important, at this point, to decide whether the queen and the siren are identical or antithetical. Let us note simply the possible influence of *Tannhäuser*, with which Nerval was acquainted.[7] The two female figures of Venus and Elizabeth, who appear in an A-B-A cyclic order in Acts I, II, and III, embody the ancient theme of sacred and profane love—the fairy and saint—while a grotto is the setting of both the Venusberg episodes and Nerval's memories of a siren and of a "queen"— the *Königin* of Wagner's libretto. (It might not be out of place, in discussing this sonnet, with its insistence on changes of state, to recollect that at the height of the Venusberg scene Tannhäuser cries, "O Königin, lass mich gehen.")

The final tercet—and the most subtle passage in the poem—depends on number symbolism:

> Et j'ai deux fois vainqueur traversé l'Achéron,
> Modulant tour à tour sur la lyre d'Orphée
> Les soupirs de la sainte et les cris de la fée.

"Twice" has been taken by some to refer to Nerval's fits of insanity, but since he had more than two, this interpretation can hardly be considered incontestable. (Actually, the crossing of the Acheron, because of reminiscences not only of the story of Theseus but principally of the Orpheus myth, might best be considered with reference to the female figure who dominates the sonnet.) There is an implied question in these lines: two times is an imperfect number; three in most forms of Western symbolism represents perfection and resolution. On the simple level of rhetoric the number three is important: Virgil and others use the formula "thrice . . . thrice . . ." (*Aeneid* II, 792–93; VI, 700–701). And three seems to crop up everywhere from Christian theology to Hegelian dialectic. It is particularly significant to my mind that in Virgil's account of Orpheus and Eurydice the adverbs "thrice" and "a second time" occur at a crucial moment. When Orpheus, near the end of their journey, looks back at Eurydice, "ter . . . fragor stagnis auditus Averni," and she laments, "En iterum crudelia retro fata vocant . . . ." The speaker of "El Desdichado" is not in the exact situation of either Orpheus or Eurydice, but there are analogies between his uncertain return from death and theirs (as well as

[7]See "Lettres d'Allemagne" IV in *Notes de voyage*.

an analogy between Orpheus, forbidden to look at his beloved, and Cupid and Lusignan). I think, therefore, that the poet asks whether he shall not make a third crossing—perhaps that into a pagan beyond, the land of Isis and Dionysus. The *toi* he addresses in the second quatrain apparently presides over this farther country, and here we see how polyvalent the tomb image is: if the poet is in the grave, the latter is a metaphor for life's black side; if it is she who is entombed, a paradise beyond death is implied. Life and death are symbolically reversible states. It does not really matter whether we think of the third crossing as physical death or not: Nerval's imagination was more concerned with immortal longings and perfect cycles than with the decay of matter.

One principal question remains: Are the saint and the fairy antithetical? Does each one account for one of the two previous passages over the Acheron? It would be simplistic to completely accept our earlier analogy between these figures and the Elizabeth and Venus of *Tannhäuser* for, although *Tannhäuser* offers some suggestive parallels, its fundamental theme is different. A very delicate problem is involved here: Nerval has not provided in the course of the poem any pronounced distinction between the two figures. Indeed, we simply find four nouns ("queen," "siren," "saint," "fairy") put forth in such a way that only the last two seem to be distinct. And even at that, the poet sings of the saint and fairy "in turn," implying no rejection of one or the other. I have already mentioned the problem of identity in Nerval's work: his imagination seems to move in a dim world where there exist avatars, supernatural genealogies, and reconciliations of two souls into one. The saint and the fairy may be no more than two aspects of the same concrete, mortal, yet deified figure, whose traits are at once those of Artemis, Cybele, Mélusine, and the actress Jenny Colon, whose life and death, according to his biographers, so deeply affected Nerval.

"El Desdichado" is almost the perfect example of a symbolic *schema*, and, because of its evocativeness and diversity of sources, much the finest of Nerval's experiments, to my mind. The sonnet can be read only in terms of a pattern of parallelism and antithesis, yet both designs tend to melt together into sheer ambiguity. The one small key to its interpretation lies, I think, in the symbolism of the numbers two and three. The implied contrast between them creates the dramatic tension of the last tercet. Such recourse to the idea of a universe in movement, as opposed to a statal, dualistic one, stands in contrast to the perpetual antitheses we have found in Baudelaire and Vigny.

Gérard de Nerval's *Chimères* are perhaps the first exercise in French in pure symbolism. But his complicated patterns of words must be distinguished from those of Mallarmé or Verlaine: his are grounded in ancient mythologies and centuries-old *Weltanschauungen*. In this respect he resembles more productive great romantics such as Blake, Goethe, and, most relevantly, Victor Hugo. The *Chimères* contain in miniature the vast cyclic patterns which obsessed Hugo in his later years, and to which we shall now turn our attention.

VII

HUGO'S LATER POETRY

We have already seen the breadth of Victor Hugo's imagination in the early period of his verse. Between the poems written before 1840 and those first published during his exile from France it appears that he wrote less and less verse but extended his interest in occultism and religious philosophy. The peculiar strains of private vision that we remarked on in Chapter II now swell to occupy the whole foreground of his poetry, and his range of vocabulary greatly increases. Finally, when he went into exile, Hugo ceased to be the court-poet figure we have commented on and began a unique poetic career as estranged prophet of God and of the conscience of his country. The late poems are shot through with meditations on God and evil, the fate of France, the nature of the universe and its ultimate destiny. Our principal concern will be with *Châtiments, La Fin de Satan, Dieu,* and *La Légende des siècles,* for these are the most characteristic works of Hugo's great burst of creative energy in the 1850's.

Since all these books are remarkable in their detail and dissimilar—and often weak—in overall structure, I propose to examine them in the following manner: first, general comments on each (with the exception of *La Légende*), especially with reference to style; then a summing up of high points of innovation in Hugo's later diction; next comes a further examination of *Châtiments, La Fin de Satan,* and *Dieu* as large-scale poetic schemes and Hugo's failure to sustain them. Finally, we must probe the reasons of sensibility which prevented Hugo from creating the theodicy he aspired to. We shall conclude with some observations on *La Légende des siècles.*

Shortly after his exile, Hugo published his first volume of verse in over ten years, and all of it recent. It consists of diatribes, lyrics, and prophetic utterances against the government of Louis Napoleon, which had ostensibly exiled him.[1] Furthermore, *Châtiments* (1853) is unlike its earlier companion works both in having a general theme and in being structured into a series of separate but linked parts; before *Les Fleurs du mal*, Hugo thought of arranging shorter poems into a large design. The first six sections have for titles such Bonapartist political slogans as "La Société est sauvée," "L'Ordre est rétabli," "La Stabilité est assurée," and contain an intermittent poetic history of various aspects of the Coup d'Etat and the establishment of the Second Empire. "L'Autorité est sacrée," the center of the work, deals with Napoleon the First and the contrast between the two regimes. The seventh and ironically titled concluding book, "Les Sauvers se sauveront," foresees, in prophetic tones, the fall of Louis Napoleon. Thus *Châtiments* embodies an imaginative pattern of history.

The opening sections are dominated by images of night and urban filth, as Hugo scourges not only Louis Napoleon and his henchmen, but all Frenchmen who passively accepted the Coup d'Etat. The following lines concern the President of the Assembly, "colui che fece per viltà il gran rifiuto," having abdicated his authority to the usurper:

> Si par hasard, la nuit, dans les carrefours mornes,
> Fouillant du croc l'ordure où dort plus d'un secret,
> Un chiffonnier trouvait cette âme au coin des bornes,
>   Il la dédaignerait!
>
> (IV, 8)

Night is personified in an unusual image:

> Le jour parut. La nuit, complice des bandits,
> Prit la fuite, et, traînant à la hâte ses voiles,
> Dans les plis de sa robe emporta les étoiles
> Et les mille soleils dans l'ombre étincelant,
> Comme les sequins d'or qu'emporte en s'en allant
> Une fille, aux baisers du crime habituée,
> Qui se rhabille après s'être prostituée!
>
> (I, 5)

Dawn has apocalyptic associations and will mark the end of the Empire:

> Et le monde, éveillé par cette âpre fanfare,
>   Est pareil

---

[1] Hugo seems to have deliberately brought on his exile. See Pierre de Lacretelle, *La Vie Politique de Victor Hugo* (Paris, 1928), 53-209.

Aux ivrognes de nuit qu'en se levant effare
Le soleil.

(VII, 15)

The spiritual low point of the work occurs perhaps in a description of the sewers of ancient Rome, but the theme of regeneration emerges at the end, where the Tree of Life becomes a major image:

L'arbre saint du Progrès, autrefois chimérique
Croîtra, couvrant l'Europe et couvrant l'Amérique,
    Sur le passé détruit.
Et, laissant l'éther pur luire à travers ses branches,
Le jour apparaîtra plein de colombes blanches,
    Plein d'étoiles la nuit.

Et nous qui serons morts, morts dans l'exil peut-être,
Martyrs saignants, pendant que les hommes, sans maître,
    Vivront, plus fiers, plus beaux,
Sous ce grand arbre, amour des cieux qu'il avoisine,
Nous nous réveillerons pour baiser sa racine,
    Au fond de nos tombeaux.

("Lux," V)

Châtiments is, clearly, a cyclic work in which night yields to dawn, urban ugliness to a vision of nature, decadence to rebirth. The thematic material is a variation on the return of the Golden Age and not basically very different from the pattern of certain *Chimères*.

Whatever we think of the success of this verse, it is obvious that Hugo is doing something quite new; the work is ordered around archetypal symbols of good and evil, and its meaning transcends that of any single piece of verse in the volume. Despite many references to Second Empire notables, *Châtiments* tends to break loose from its historical context and, like biblical poetry, to strive toward the condition of prophetic myth. Although the work was hastily written and thus stylistically uneven, it is clear that, with it, Hugo was moving in a new poetic direction.

If *Châtiments* is remarkable, the posthumous *Fin de Satan* (written 1854, 1859–60), is even more so; in it Hugo tried to cope with the Christian concept of evil. The book is one of those odd nineteenth-century works, like *Faust* or *La Tentation de Saint Antoine*, whose form seems to owe a good deal to the idea of drama, without really achieving theatrical viability.[2] Rather than the traditional sequence of epic books, it consists of an alternance between Satan's scenes, whose rubric is "Hors de la Terre," and earthly ones; both shift between narrative and dialogue or soliloquy. We are struck equally by the particular terrestrial episodes in which Hugo depicts the moral history of man, and by his Satan, whose eloquence and theological capacities match the gifts of Milton's Prince of Darkness. Hugo's selection of episodes is curious, especially if we compare it with Milton's orthodoxy: he depicts Satan's plummeting into hell, Nimrod's attack on heaven (a tale derived from the medieval Persian poet Firdausi), Christ crucified, and Satan's change from an absolute devil to a fallen angel susceptible of redemption.

The crux of this poem lies in "Hors de la Terre" III, a lengthy monologue in which Satan, after expressing his ambivalent feelings toward God and creation, makes the discovery that he loves God. The greatest poetic difficulties are involved here: Satan's emotions must have some analogy to human ones, while, at the same time, he can be rendered neither as an insignificant inferior spirit nor as the hero of a stoic tragedy, in the manner of Milton; Hugo had to avoid motive and psychology in his presentation of Satan in order to make of him the expression of the universe's longing to be reintegrated into godhead. Hugo solved this problem by making Satan experience not pride, but spite, and suffer not Miltonic fires, which burn without scathing, but the absence of repose. The underlying theme of "Hors de la Terre" III is Satan's constant awareness and painful vigil, his incapacity for sleep:

> Encor si je pouvais dormir!
>
>   Si seulement
> Une heure, une minute, un soupir, un moment,
> Le temps qu'une onde passe au fond du lac sonore,
> Fût-ce pour m'éveiller plus lamentable encore,
> Sur n'importe quels durs et funèbres chevets,
> Si je pouvais poser mon front! si je pouvais,
> Nu, sur un bloc de bronze ou sur un tas de pierres,
> L'une de l'autre, hélas! rapprocher mes paupières,
> Et m'étendre, et sentir quelque chose de frais,
> De doux et de serein, comme si je mourais!
> Si je pouvais me perdre un moment dans un songe,

[2]For the theatrical origins of *La Fin de Satan*, see Jean Gaudon, *Victor Hugo dramaturge* (Paris, 1955), 38.

> Apaiser dans mon flanc ce qui remue et ronge,
> Aspirer un fluide étrange, aérien,
> Impalpable, et flotter, et n'entendre plus rien,
> Ni mon aile frémir, ni battre mon artère,
> Ni ces cris dont je suis la cause sur la terre . . .
> ("Hors de la Terre" III, ix)

The marvelous richness of Hugo's syntax and rhythms is evident here: the periodic sentence form is not in the least imprisoned by the alexandrine couplet, while its grammatical elaboration can equal any long passage in French verse. The last line of the quotation suggests another extraordinary aspect of the "Hors de la Terre" sections in *La Fin de Satan:* faced with representing hell after Virgil, Dante, and Milton, Hugo chose to represent it, not as a subterranean compartment with its own geography and inhabitants, but as sheer solitary darkness and emptiness, peopled only by Satan's own sensations, his insomnia, his all-seeing, and the sounds that continuously reach him. In short, Satan is no longer Milton's earth-wanderer seeking mischief to work, but the nadir of the world-soul:

> Je suis sous cette voûte,
> Je regarde l'horreur profonde, et je l'écoute.
> Pas un être ne peut souffrir sans que j'en sois.
> Je suis l'affreux milieu des douleurs. Je perçois
> Chaque pulsation de la fièvre du monde.
> Mon ouïe est le centre où se répète et gronde
> Tout le bruit ténébreux dans l'étendue épars;
> J'entends l'ombre. O tourment! le mal de toutes parts
> M'apporte en mon cachot sa triste joie aiguë;
> J'entends glisser l'aspic et croître la ciguë;
> Le mal pèse sur moi du zénith au nadir;
> La mer a beau hurler, l'avalanche bondir,
> L'orage entre-heurter les foudres qu'il secoue,
> L'éclatant zodiaque a beau tourner sa roue
> De constellations, sombre meule des cieux,
> A travers le fracas vaste et prodigieux
> Des astres dont parfois le groupe énorme penche,
> A travers l'océan, la foudre et l'avalanche
> Roulant du haut des monts parmi les sapins verts,
> J'entends le pas d'un crime au bout de l'univers.
> ("Hors de la Terre" III, ix)

The spatial imagery is especially remarkable in this passage. Satan occupies the earth's core, and, by analogy with the principle of gravity, the geocentric universe presses on him with the weight of its evil. (The equating of weight with evil is not, for Hugo, merely a constant metaphor but a real theological concept.) Once Satan's position as the object of all gravity is established, Hugo then evokes the surface of the earth (asp, hemlock, and ocean) and finally the spectacle of the night sky, pushing Satan's perceptions farther and farther out from a center. Circles and circular movement dominate (zenith, wheel, sliding stars, rolling avalanche), for Hugo is trying to convey the feeling that concentric rings of matter spin about the fixed point that is Satan. The sky he paints is therefore not serene but full of portentous objects and savage motion. As is so often the case, Hugo's spatial imagination strikes us as far more complex than that of most poets; he envisions not merely a flat earth domed with sky, but huge cosmological configurations—something especially rare in an age which had not yet known the experience of airplanes, much less of spacecraft.

Just as Hugo used a sophisticated cosmology in which there is no fixed point where heaven is located, he correspondingly abandoned the traditional myth in which Satan is King of the Damned and God is that of the Angels and the Elect. All the trappings of the divine and demonic kingdoms are eliminated, which permits Hugo to face squarely what was for him the essential problem of Christian theology: How can Satan endure eternally "cast into the lake of fire and brimstone . . . for ever and ever," as St. John affirms (20:10)? Such a doctrine denies, above all, God's omnipotence:

> Oui, c'est l'énigme, ô nuit, de tes millions d'yeux :
> Le grand souffrant fait face au grand mystérieux.
> Grâce, ô Dieu! Pour toi-même il faut que je l'obtienne.
> Ma perpétuité fait ombre sur la tienne.
> Devant ton oeil flambeau rien ne doit demeurer,
> Tout doit changer, vieillir et se transfigurer.
> Toi seul es. Devant toi tout doit avoir un âge.
> Et c'est pour ta splendeur un importun nuage
> Qu'on voie un spectre assis au fond de ton ciel bleu,
> Et l'éternel Satan devant l'éternel Dieu!
>   ("Hors de la Terre" III, vi)

This argument is the crux of *La Fin de Satan:* Can evil be eternal? Satan finally wills his own redemption and, as Lucifer, is rejoined with God. The problem of dualism, which, as we have seen, haunted Baudelaire, was likewise fundamental to Hugo's imagination, but he tried to overcome this obsessive vision by creating the myth of Satan's reunion with god-head, which, in turn, is symbolic of mankind and the universe's absorption into divinity.

Dieu is a further attempt to order Hugo's thoughts on good and evil, but this time patterned after biblical prophecy rather than epic or drama. The opening vision of a strange creature from which voices emerge owes something to Ezekiel, while scriptural reminiscences are not infrequent. "Les Voix" [3] is a remarkable series of poetic fragments; they express in bitter, somber, or ironical tones the remoteness or absence of God, Job being the obvious prototype. Frequently they are constructed around a striking image:

> Quelle pensée as-tu d'allumer ton esprit
> Au bord du noir problème où la raison périt?
> Pourquoi ne pas laisser les grandes ailes d'ombre,
> Songeur, se déployer sur cet univers sombre?
> Pourquoi vouloir leurrer d'un feu follet qui fuit
> L'antique Adam, errant dans l'insondable nuit?
> . . . .
> La blanche aurore est morte, et l'homme est dans la nuit.
> Il lui restait encor, dans le temple où Dieu luit,
> L'effrayant chandelier dont la flamme constante
> Pendant qu'ils écrivaient, éclaira les Septante;
> Mais il n'a même plus ce foyer du vrai jour;
> Les sept vices de l'homme ont, chacun à leur tour,
> Eteint un des flambeaux de la lampe à sept branches;
> Maintenant c'est fini. L'abîme où tu te penches,
> L'obscurité lugubre aux vagues épaisseurs,
> Le firmament formé de toutes les noirceurs,
> Cet océan de nuit où l'esprit flotte et sombre,
> Rit de te voir risquer ta lanterne en cette ombre
> Où dans la main de Dieu s'est éteint le soleil.
>
> (Quinzième fragment)

We have seen precedents for this somber deity, whose hand is the world's prison and whose dead sun sheds night. The importance of "Les Voix,"

[3] In referring to the parts of *Dieu* I have used the titles traditionally given to them by editors and in particular by Jacques Truchet in the Pléiade edition (Paris, 1955). René Journet and Guy Robert, the editors of the remarkable two-volume critical edition of the poem (Paris, 1960–61), reject some of these titles on the grounds that they do not represent the poet's definitive intentions. Because of the greater availability of the Pléiade edition I quote from it, but all passages have been checked against the Journet-Robert edition.

however, lies not in any dialectic of theology, but in its stylistic brilliance; unordered and incomplete as it is, the density and inventiveness of the language is compelling. In the passage quoted above, metaphor and comparison in the traditional sense have vanished, to be replaced by the literalness of mythopoeia. Hugo does not attempt to create an imaginary scene based on the ordinary elements of vision and enriched by metaphor; instead, all the images must be taken at face value. The "wings of shadow" are not part of an analogy between night and a bird; they are the sinister living presence of darkness. In the same way, the "ocean of night" which "laughs" is a truly mythic conception. Furthermore, the chaotic spatial relations must be understood literally: underlying the whole passage is an inverted cosmology in which the reaches of heaven are replaced by an abyss; up and down have become interchangeable.

"Ascension dans les Ténèbres," the second part of *Dieu*, consists of a series of visions, based on a biblical pattern. The poet first contemplates a symbolic object (cf. the beginning of Amos), which then utters prophecy or dogma. The objects belong largely to the romantic bestiary: a bat, an owl, a raven, a vulture, an eagle, a griffon, an angel, and Light personified. These correspond, furthermore, to stages (pseudo-logical or historical) in the development of religion: atheism is followed by skepticism, dualism, polytheism, Judaism, Christianity, and nineteenth-century occultism, in that order.

The language of certain passages demonstrates perhaps a greater audacity of metaphor than any other work of Hugo's. In "La Chauve-souris" a fantastic, evil spring is compared to a wet-dream, an analogy hardly to be expected in a nineteenth-century poet:

Le printemps, le soleil, les bêtes en chaleur,
Sont une chimérique et monstrueuse fleur;
A travers son sommeil ce monde effaré souffre;
Avril n'est que le rêve érotique du gouffre,
Une pollution nocturne de ruisseaux,
De rameaux, de parfums, d'aube et de chants d'oiseaux.
L'horreur seule survit, par tout continuée.
Et, par moments, un vent qui sort de la nuée
Dessine des contours, des rayons et des yeux
Dans ce noir tourbillon d'atomes furieux.

Discreet reference is made to the atheist Lucretius' doctrine of atoms, which is presented as a pattern of ceaseless, infernal movement. It is not farfetched to see in Hugo's evocation of spring the demonic version of the Latin poet's invocation to Venus Genitrix, for a passage in his critical writings shows how sinister Hugo felt *De Rerum Natura* to be.[4] The ancient theory of atomic motion becomes, in "La Chauve-souris," an image of idle swirling, and this is accompanied by a demonic vision of the Great Chain of Being:

> Les cailloux sont broyés par la bête de somme,
> L'âne paît le chardon, l'homme dévore l'homme,
> L'agneau broute la fleur, le loup broute l'agneau.
> Sombre chaîne éternelle où l'anneau mord l'anneau!

The chain does not lead upward but becomes a closed circle—the infernal counterpart to the perfect circle which traditionally symbolizes godhead.

"La Chauve-souris," which has as its theme the inexistence of God, is dominated by images of destruction, dissolution of appearances, and nothingness. In the following section, "Le Hibou," the theme changes to doubt and fear about the nature of God, and here the very meaning of the universe is questioned. "Le Hibou" contains some of the most splendid mythopoeic verse in French: poetry in which the animate and inanimate are one, in which landscape is penetrated with life. The following lines offer a fine example:

> On a peur quand l'aube qui s'éveille
> Fait une plaie au bas des cieux, rouge et vermeille;
> On a peur quand la bise épand son long frisson;
> On a peur quand on voit, vague, à fleur d'horizon,
> Montrant, dans l'étendue au crépuscule ouverte,
> Ramper le scarabée effroyable du soir;
> On a peur quand minuit sur les monts vient s'asseoir!

Here the cosmos is not a flickering illusion as in "La Chauve-souris," but a dreadful manifestation of life and will. The sequence of images is especially masterful: the "wound" inflicted by dawn complements the personification of midnight later on; dawn and night, like the breeze, are impalpable but shifting and present. On the other hand, the most developed image, that of the beetle, has a horrifying concreteness; Hugo was one of the first of those modern writers such as Dostoievsky or Sartre to feel that insects represent life in its most inhuman and repellent form. Of the highly organized creatures they seem the most blindly and most

[4] See Victor Hugo, *William Shakespeare*, Pt. 1, Book II, 6.

mechanically intent on survival, and blown-up representations of them thus occupy so large a place in the sinister iconography of recent art and literature. In these lines the scarab symbolizes the huge, destructive powers of sundown.

As we progress to the later sections of "Ascension dans les Ténèbres," and as Hugo speaks of established religious doctrines, his language changes in character: rather than the awesome visions of "La Chauve-souris" and "Le Hibou," he gives us odd, complicated metaphors in which the attempt to poetize theology is apparent:

> C'est le vivant, le vaste épanoui!
> Ce que contemple au loin le soleil ébloui,
> C'est lui. Les cieux, vous, nous, les étoiles, poussière!
> Il est l'oeil gouffre, ouvert au fond la lumière,
> Vu par tous les flambeaux, senti par tous les nids,
> D'où l'univers jaillit en rayons infinis.
> Il regarde, et c'est tout. Voir suffit au sublime.
> Il crée un monde rien qu'en voyant un abîme.
> Et cet être qui voit, ayant toujours été,
> A toujours tout créé de toute éternité.
>
> ("La Lumière")

Hugo construes godhead as a cone reaching upward to an eternal eye, from which creation radiates along the Great Chain of Being. The metaphor is the old one of God as light, supported by the occultist theory of the universe as emanation. This, however, is a *schema*, a rhetorical figure, for we know that not even for Hugo was God literally an eye. In short, *Dieu* concludes with demonstrations of godhead rather than intuitions of deity, unlike the earlier sections.

In our cursory examination of passages from *La Fin de Satan* and *Dieu* we have seen gorgeous elaborations on a number of themes, but it remains now to attempt a summary of Hugo's later stylistic practices, a discussion of his notions about language, and, finally, a comparison of Hugo's poetic style with others we have been considering.

Certain tendencies in Hugo's later style can readily be seen in the examples of it we have quoted. With the exception of the passage on insomnia from "Satan dans la nuit," all are characterized by parataxis, by the juxtaposition of relatively simple sentence structures. At most an occasional relative clause relieves their syntactic identity. (Differences in length and rhythm, however, compensate for grammatical sameness.)

Although adjectives and participles abound, it would be difficult to call this style phrasal in the same way as Vigny's or Baudelaire's: it breaks with the rhetorical principle that verse-paragraphs, like prose, need the variety created by frequent subordination. While short relative clauses are common enough in his late style, Hugo's peculiar and characteristic grammatical device is to build up his sentences by reduplication of subject or object and by apposition, in short, to create a primarily nominal syntax. One is especially struck by the scarceness of adverbial clauses, which express logical and temporal relationships, as they do in certain *Chimères*. Instead we find abundant examples of identification and parallel action, the patterns of meaning most associated with parataxis and enumeration of nouns. An especially good example of the lengths to which Hugo would go in lengthening an otherwise simple sentence by mere accumulation of nouns occurs in "Les Voix":

> L'espace, ici flot vague et là cratère ardent,
> Le grand fond immobile et sourd, la violence
> Des visions mêlées à l'éternel silence,
> Rien et Tout, le roulis gigantesque des cieux
> Dans on ne sait quel vent lugubre et monstrueux,
> Des tours d'ombre dont l'oeil ne peut compter les marches,
> Des déluges roulant d'inexprimables arches,
> La pluie immense au loin rayant les infinis,
> Des lueurs blanchissant des masques d'Erynnis,
> Des passages subits de méduses, frappées
> D'une clarté pareille à des reflets d'épées,
> Des ponts difformes, noirs, allants hors du réel,
> Sinistres, bleuissant vaguement près du ciel,
> L'ascension sans but et la chute sans bornes;
> Voilà ce que voyaient ces contemplateurs mornes...
>
> ("Les Voix," Cinquième fragment)

The range of verbal resources is remarkable, both in the way of individual words and their combinations: there are proper nouns (*Erynnis*), concrete ones frequently coupled with blurring modifiers (*tours d'ombre dont l'oeil ne peut compter les marches*), semi-abstract nouns (*fond immobile*), and completely abstract ones (*Rien et Tout*). Above all, Hugo uses verbal nouns (*roulis, passages, chute, ascension*) along with present participles to suggest hazy forms of motion, bare outlines of the immaterial. This preference for verbal nouns and participles, with their sometimes peculiar inchoative or frequentative aspects (*bleuissant, pas-*

sages) is a stylistic trouvaille which was to be a mannerism in later poets and prose writers, but in Hugo it serves the special function of creating a dense fusion of impressions. Image adjoins image with no connective words of sequence or relation.

Frequently, Hugo resorts to two other devices in order to confront nouns with one another. One is a radically antithetical use of the copula and predicate nominative: "la fange est cristal" (*Dieu*, "La Lumière"). Expressions like this one are not simply ultra-concise analogies like "Vous êtes un beau ciel d'automne . . ." (Baudelaire, "Causerie"), but have a metaphysical, incantatory character. "Mire is crystal" attempts to make a philosophical assertion or prophecy. Hugo's other idiosyncratic handling of nouns lies on the extreme confines of French syntax. He often yoked two nouns together as a single unit: the "oeil gouffre" in the passage quoted from "La Lumière" is an example, and a particularly good one, since eyes and depths have similar and dissimilar connotations. Elsewhere we find more normally affective linkings, such as "la fosse silence," but, in any case, this construction rarely occurs in ordinary French except for commercial expressions like *fermeture éclair*. It is significant that Hugo, whose grammar is on the whole conservative, should depart so much from normal usage. This device confirms the implications to be drawn from his fondness for the predicate nominative: Hugo's deepest tendency is toward a syntax of nouns, the magic, naming part of speech.

Hugo's feelings about language were rarely set down, yet, with the few indications of them we have, it seems safe to say that after 1850 he moved beyond his fellow romantics into an evocative theory of language which anticipates that of certain symbolists. The *verbe*, which is St. John's *logos* in French, is seen as an entity, above and beyond the reality of things in a poem from *Les Contemplations*, "Suite." A further curious text about words, which was published only posthumously, maintains that letters have implicit connotations of color and emotion—all this long before the corresponding affirmations of Rimbaud and Mallarmé.[5] Like these poets, Hugo seems to have arrived at the idea that words, *logoi*, generate a transcendent world, superior to the normal one we flounder in. However extreme the theory may be as a general view of language, it still commands respect because of the great poetry which was written in conjunction with it. And, as a matter of fact, when we examine certain manipulations of words in Hugo's later verse, it becomes

[5]See Victor Hugo, *Post-Scriptum de ma vie*, ed. Henri Guillemin (Neuchâtel, 1961), 99–100.

clear that this theory of language is not divorced from certain semantic effects.

The peculiar relationships which Hugo establishes among substantives invite some analysis of his use of specific words. The words which most obviously take on new values in Hugo's later verse are those which are primarily visual in sense. The largest number of them refer to darkness or the abyss: *abîme, gouffre, obscurité, sombre, ombre,* and *noir.* It is not just in overtly visionary poems like *Dieu* that those words obtrude; they are the constants of Hugo's imagination. In his earlier poetry they retain their customary connotations and use and are contrasted with light imagery in the tradition of Dante and Milton. However, *Dieu* and *La Légende des siècles* present us with a new and peculiar handling of the imagery of darkness: it is constantly used in a figurative way which defies visualization. A character in the *Légende* is called "ce noir rêveur," although he has a "front de neige" ("Le Comte Félibien"). In *Dieu,* which contains numerous visions of the world as godless or governed by an evil god, Hugo creates an arsenal of ambiguous symbols suggesting at once the divine and the demonic. "Sombre azur" is an example of this; it occurs in a passage which describes the destruction of him who seeks God:

> Aveugle de trop voir et sourd de trop entendre,
> Dans l'éblouissement du ciel toujours plus blanc,
> Effaré, désormais plus emporté qu'allant,
> Ivre de tout ce sombre azur qui le pénètre,
> Sentant l'écrasement de l'abîme sous l'être,
> Respirant mal l'air vierge et fatal du zénith,
> Il avance, et blanchit, et s'efface; et finit
> Par se dissoudre, avec son doute ou sa prière,
> Dans une énormité de foudre et de lumière.
>
> ("Les Voix," Sixième fragment)

These lines are a remarkable demonstration of spatial imagery and demonic symbolism in Hugo's later poetry: the godseeker ascends toward godhead as in traditional cosmology, but sound and sight create a feeling of pressure rather than one of weightlessness—heaven is chaos rather than illumination, despite the white light—and, later, the air "penetrates" him with its deadly weight. All this could symbolize a trial, were it not for the seeker's being sucked up *(emporté),* without so willing, into the *sombre azur.* This oxymoron either expresses the sinister quality of the inviting blue sky or else represents a sudden darkening of it in its threatening upper regions. We are confronted with a problem of the metaphoric or literal value of a word; one suspects here that in this kind of phantasmagoria of language Hugo hardly distinguished the two. "L'écrasement de l'abîme sous l'être" has contradictory implications: an "abyss" beneath one cannot "crush"; however, right from the beginning of *Dieu*, the poet speaks of an abyss stretching upward, a demonic vision of the sky. If *l'être* designates here, as it does elsewhere in *Dieu*, all visible creation, the line would seem to contain a paradox about up and down, lightness and weight. Finally, the bright light which traditionally symbolizes godhead is presented in a demonic modality: it becomes destructive lightning, and union with God is equated with death. Sinister white light thus becomes a symbolic equivalent to Hugo's "affreux soleil noir d'où rayonne la nuit" (*Les Contemplations*, "Ce que dit la bouche d'ombre").

Hugo's abundant use of substantives assures a richness of visual detail, but when they are coupled in such expressions as *azur noir* we cannot compare this poetry to the physical act of seeing. Indeed, if poetry wishes to be an act of creation totally divorced from mimesis, it should not allow comparison with the experience of the senses; one *sees* the world about one, but the visions of poetry are seen only in a metaphorical sense. Thus Hugo's visionary poems are paradoxically unsusceptible of complete visualization. His poetry escapes plastic definition; the images conflict with one another, vanish, or are blurred by abstract words and adjectives:

> Le fantôme géant se répandit en voix
> Qui sous ses flancs confus murmuraient à la fois,
> Et, comme d'un brasier tombent des étincelles,
> Comme on voit des oiseaux épars, pigeons, sarcelles,
> D'un grand essaim passant s'écarter quelquefois,
> Comme un vert tourbillon de feuilles sort d'un bois,
> Comme, dans les hauteurs par les vents remuées,
> En avant d'un orage il vole des nuées,
> Toutes ces voix, mêlant le cri, l'appel, le chant,
> De l'immense être informe et noir se détachant,
> Me montrant vaguement des masques et des bouches,
> Vinrent sur moi bruire avec des bruits farouches,
> Parfois en même temps et souvent tour à tour,
> Comme des monts, à l'heure où se lève le jour,
> L'un après l'autre, au fond de l'horizon s'éclairent.
> Et des formes, sortant du monstre, me parlèrent.
>   (*Dieu*, "L'Esprit humain")

The five similes attempt to give outline to the apparition, but adjectives like *informe* and *confus* dispel their effect. The voices which emanate from the phantom are of uncertain materiality; they appear *vaguement*. Finally, they are called *formes*, a word which implies visibility without describing. The poet is glimpsing something, but the object will not remain still long enough to be really contemplated. It continually recedes into the blackness, which, as the typical background of Hugo's visionary poetry, always defeats the attempt to see. As Georges Poulet puts it:

Such is . . . the Hugolian universe. The mass of forms which constitutes it does not stop the glance like a curtain. The eye, uneasy at what lies beyond, can pierce the labyrinth of things in all directions. There is always, farther than what one sees, something that one glimpses, and, beyond what one glimpses, there are still holes where there is nothing more, it seems, openings onto emptiness, where one's glance loses itself.[6]

Thus Hugo's poetry turns away from the ordinary realities of sight to erect a flickering, crepuscular vision, which tantalizes because one cannot quite seize it. It plays with one's sense of the visual by offering dense and massive imagery, but always cheats the eye in the end.

At the same time, however, we should qualify Poulet's very evocative description of Hugo's visionary cosmos. Against the dark background and amidst the flickering images we can distinguish certain recurrent geometrical forms: the circle, point of irradiation of light or gravity, cone of vision, and closed-in space. There is a continual conflict between chaos and pattern. Often these geometric designs break down into architectural elements, among which towers, walls, and arches are frequent. A keen sense of line seems to be dictating these images projected onto nothingness. Furthermore, the feeling of position in space is curious and original in Hugo's visionary poems: the angle of vision ranges from looking up from a low central point to the dizzying glance from on high of *survol*. The relativity of spatial relations is acutely rendered in this poetry, and one feels in it a more real conception of the cosmos than in Dante or Milton, whose pictures of hell and heaven are essentially, if not theoretically, derived from a flat, layered picture of the universe. At the same time, Hugo is not a poet whose vision is earth grounded, like that of Baudelaire or other contemporaries; his imagination soars, veers, plunges, but never confines itself to simple geocentric notions of up and down, high and low. Hugo's capacities for visualizing are, in short, totally ex-

[6]Georges Poulet, *La Distance intérieure* (Paris, 1952), 496.

ceptional insofar as he invented a personal morphology of the cosmos which symbolizes his conceptions of good and evil.

When we compare the style of *La Fin de Satan* and *Dieu* to that of *Les Chimères*, *Les Fleurs du mal*, or *Les Destinées*, the most essential difference seems to be that the authors of the latter works were stanzaic poets, while Hugo was not. By this I do not mean that Hugo never wrote stanzas, far from it, but that the characteristic verse forms of Nerval, Baudelaire, and Vigny, unlike those of Hugo, imply a great concern with regular metric units: Nerval's sonnet, Vigny's *septain*, and Baudelaire's great gamut of *quintils*, refrains, and false sonnets demand a kind of prosodic thought which is foreign to Hugo's inspiration. The comparison with Baudelaire is especially instructive, since he and Hugo were the most abundantly gifted of the French romantic poets. Baudelaire loved the sonnet in all its possible variations, while Hugo wrote but three of them, and those late in life; Baudelaire most often used quatrains, constructed so as to make of them distinct metaphoric structures, whereas Hugo's stanzas, varied as they are, show no signs of any esthetic peculiar to them. Finally, after 1830 Hugo generally ignored important stanzaic discoveries of the nineteenth century, such as terza rima and other old or exotic forms: none of his great poems are so metrically unusual as Baudelaire's "Harmonie du soir" or "Litanies de Satan." The conclusion seems to be that, while Hugo was the greatest innovator in displacing accents in the alexandrine line, his prosodic imagination was otherwise conservative.

Where Hugo's style was quite unconservative is in the domain of analogy and vocabulary. There are, of course, certain Hugolian mannerisms—such as the abundant use of words like *ombre*, *sombre*, and *abîme*—which anyone can recognize and which make it easy to parody his later style. However, the range of analogy of which Hugo was capable thoroughly surpasses that of any other French romantic poet. It frequently happens that a passage in which Hugo's habitual vocabulary dominates is made memorable by some rare expression or image; the following lines from *Dieu*, which contain a pantheist's diatribe against medieval theology, demonstrate this:

> Jette de la logique à sa grève déserte,
> Mais sans finir par donc ni commencer par certe.
> L'ombre est un grand hymen, l'abîme est un grand lit;
> L'Etre emplit l'étendue et l'emplit et l'emplit;
> . . . .

> L'air frémit, l'arbre croît, l'oiseau chante, l'eau fuit,
> Et des lumières vont jusqu'au fond de la nuit;
> L'illusion serait étrange, que t'en semble,
> De voir dans ce splendide et redoutable ensemble,
> Dans ce flot de la vie et dans ce noir torrent,
> Un docteur de Sorbonne énorme pérorant.
>
> ("Les Voix," Vingt-deuxième fragment)

The nature imagery is not very interesting in terms of vocabulary, except perhaps for the rather erotic connotations of the concrete bed; otherwise Hugo reiterates, without any great freshness, such constants of his imagination as the word *être*, taken in the rather vague sense of godhead and substance, and the spatial conception of light radiating. But what makes the passage extraordinary is the completely original image of God as a medieval professor and the attendant use of *donc* and *certe*. Balancing Hugo's almost ritual use of *hymen, flot, abîme*, is a kind of inventive power which no other French romantic had except Baudelaire, and he, because his production was small, devised only in a limited number of cases such unusual comparisons.

Sometimes Hugo draws marvelous effects from a relatively ordinary word, placed in a peculiar context. Such is the case of *l'être* in the following lines:

> Le fond de l'être est clos par un nuage obscur,
> Traversé de lueurs, aux prodiges semblable,
> Voile de l'insondable et de l'incalculable,
> Sans limite, sans fin, sans contour, sans milieu;
> C'est ce nuage noir que l'homme appelle Dieu.
>
> ("Les Voix," Neuvième fragment)

As we have seen, *l'être* is a frequent and vague term in Hugo's later poetry; its very imprecision gives it remarkable auras of connotation. While sometimes, as in an earlier quoted passage, *l'être* seems to be identifiable with divine presence, here it designates creation. (This ambiguity stems from the usage of articles in French and might be compared with the English expressions "Supreme Being" and "Being," the latter indicating quite a variety of concepts.) The notion of matter being closed off at one end, as expressed in the above lines, is an extraordinary variant of the image we have in Vigny and Baudelaire of the world as prison cell or box, but here the contours of the cell are dimmed, and the universe takes on the amorphous shape of a container with a blurred center of focus.

Nothing in the way of vocabulary is particularly arresting here, but the spatial concept created is eerie.

If Hugo's late visionary style has no analogue in the works of other French romantics, they share with him an essential concern for religious philosophy; none of the French romantic poets seems to have been without a private theology, and the interlocking theme of their verse is the existence and nature of God, as well as the problem of the very notion of godhead in a post-Christian world.

We have already alluded to Hugo's professed occultist ideas—they closely resemble the philosophy expressed in *Aeneid* VI, which is the locus classicus of esoteric belief: along the Great Chain of Being souls are gradually rising, through metempsychosis, toward an eventual reunion with godhead. Christianity's seemingly eternal hell is rejected as a denial of God's omnipotence and perfection, for Hugo espouses the cabalistic notion that creation is a flaw in God, an area from which his omnipresence receded. Briefly, Hugo's theology rejects dualism in favor of the idea of a cycle: creation begins with necessary imperfection, for it is not part of godhead, but eventually will lose its materiality and be reintegrated into deity.

There are perhaps practical reasons why this philosophy should be difficult to represent in an epic or dramatic poem, but we need not explore them, since any great poet might at any time show that our preconceived notions of suitability of subject are purely theoretical. The fact remains, however, that Hugo finished neither *Dieu* nor *La Fin de Satan*, which seems to indicate some conflict between his poetic capacities and his avowed beliefs. I have already tried to show the stylistic magnificence evident in large portions of these poems; now, it seems to me, with some closer analysis of the shape and theme of each poem, we may be able to determine the imaginative check which prevented either from being completed.

The opening of *La Fin de Satan* is a selective reworking of themes from Genesis, legend, and paleontology: the fable of Lucifer precedes the creation of a universe of monsters, the world of the pre-adamites, which, in turn, is covered by the Flood. (Hugo's narrative style here is less effective than elsewhere.) The Adam and Eve myth is omitted, but Cain is alluded to at the point where Isis saves the three instruments of his crime: a nail, a stick, and a stone. These three provide the origins for the episodes of Nimrod and his sword, the Cross, and the Prison. Hugo evidently wishes to represent the world as beginning in pure evil, not in Eden. The first episode is thus that of Nimrod, who constructs a flying machine in order to wage war on God. Up to this point, the poem seems rather static in theme; there is little variation in the uniform mood of despair and horror.

The second "Hors de la Terre" section announces the birth, from a feather of the fallen Lucifer, of the Angel Liberty. The allegory appears to have been suggested by Vigny and seems to belong to another poetic order than what precedes and follows, for as we shall see, there is an odd mixture of conventions in *La Fin de Satan*. This second interlude has no bearing on what follows, which is an account of the Crucifixion. "Le Gibet" is Hugo's equivalent of the demonic gospel we have encountered in Vigny, Baudelaire, and Nerval. Yet the sinister implication in Hugo's poem is not that God is absent, but that the Passion and Christ are meaningless; for Hugo, Christ is merely a noble man victimized by judicial murder: the fact that Christ's death was necessary, according to orthodox theology, does not occur to him, since he did not believe in salvation through Christ or in the importance of the Resurrection. As a result, the whole episode takes on a lurid color, quite absent from the Gospel where the story of Jesus ends on a serene, Paschal note. Hugo sees the Crucifixion purely in physical, human terms as a kind of ancient version of the horrors of the Inquisition. The almost bombastic tone of the style is suggested by the following passage in which Barabbas contemplates the Cross:

> Tout en marchant, il heurte un obstacle; il le touche.
> — Quel est cet arbre? où donc suis-je? dit Barabbas.
> Le long de l'arbre obscur il lève ses deux bras
> Si longtemps enchaînés qu'il les dresse avec peine.
> — Cet arbe est un poteau, dit-il. Il y promène
> Ses doigts par la torture atroce estropiés;
> Et tout à coup, hagard, pâle, il tâte des pieds,
> Comme un hibou surpris rentre sous la feuillée,
> Il retire sa main; elle est toute mouillée.
> Ces pieds sont froids, un clou les traverse, et de sang
> Et de fange et de fiel tout le bois est glissant.
> Barabbas éperdu recule; son oeil s'ouvre,
> Et, par degrés, un blême et noir linéament
> S'ébauche à son regard sous l'obscur firmament;
> C'est une croix.

("Le Gibet," xxi)

While "Le Gibet" is not, by and large, one of the best composed or subtly written parts of *La Fin de Satan*, it tells us a good deal about Hugo's religious sensibility: he could no more understand Christ as a redeemer than he could accept the Pope as Christ's Vicar. The metaphysical superstructures of orthodoxy had no immediacy for him; Hugo had to feel the forces of good and evil more directly, in concrete examples of suffering and joy.

The long third "Hors de la Terre" section I have already quoted from; in it Hugo is free from the requirements of narration and can indulge in rich cascades of imagery as Satan surveys his attitudes toward God and the world. This is the true turning point of the poem, and it would perhaps have been better if Hugo had omitted all the terrestrial episodes to focus on Satan; he might have, working on the plane of pure myth, written a very eloquent poem based on his occultist philosophy. But unfortunately Hugo did not feel his Satan was an adequate exponent of the balance of Good and Evil; he introduced the Angel Liberty and Lilith (previously Isis in the poem) to struggle over him. Liberty wins and here Hugo faced a problem which he never solved: how, once Liberty has rescued Satan, can the final reconciliation with God be represented.

Other epic poets have managed to depict man's regeneration under God or the approach of a Golden Age in various ways. For example, through Anchises' prophecy in *Aeneid* VI, Virgil convincingly suggested that, with the Pax Romana, his contemporaries stood at the threshold of a great era. Such prophecies are more commonly conveyed, however, in symbolic terms: Shelley, at the end of *Prometheus Unbound*, and the biblical apocalyptist both suggest an end to man's tribulations. Hugo chose, on the other hand, to balance the Crucifixion by mankind's redemption during the French Revolution, an event neither situated in the future nor in the mythic past. Here one's sense of recent history will allow no suspension of disbelief; nor did it for Hugo, since he never wrote more than a few lines of the episode. This inability or unwillingness to finish "La Prison" suggests one observation; it seems impossible to confer mythic dimensions on recent events, unless it is demonic myth which is being created, for decline and fall are more readily imagined than regeneration. (In regard to the unfinished French Revolution episode in *La Fin de Satan*, it might do to recall the thematic structure of *Châtiments:* there Louis Napoleon's Coup d'Etat is treated as God's punishment visited on Napoleon the First for his own arrogation of power. This is, of course, a myth of decadence following a Golden Age—a tenuous parallel to Solomon and his descendants—and might seem to work out poetically, but a careful reading of the central poem, "L'Expiation," reveals considerable ambivalence about the role of Napoleon: his epoch is not an unqualified Golden Age.)

In *Dieu* we are no longer dealing with mythic narrative but with a series of prophecies, revelations. They are juxtaposed with no principle of continuity save the beginning formula of each: "Et je vis au-dessus de ma tête un point noir." It strikes us immediately that Hugo has two ways of writing about godhead. The first involves much description of Nature's awesomeness: the creator is intuited through his creation, just as in the book of Job. The poet does not simply reflect on his own feelings and thus arrive at the idea of God by subjective means as, say, Pascal did; he can only understand God in terms of the spectacle of the universe. The difference from Job, however, is that he finds the monstrosity of the universe ("Canst thou draw out leviathan with a hook?") to be a sign not only of God's power but of his malevolence as well. The biblical voice out of the whirlwind is refuted by its own device of rhetorical questions:

> Vision! la mer triste entrechoque en grondant,
> Sous les nuages lourds que les souffles assemblent,
> Ses monstrueux airains en fusion, qui tremblent;
> Les flots font un fracas de boucliers affreux
> Se heurtant, et l'éclair sépulcral est sur eux.
> Quelle est la foi, le dogme et la philosophie
> Que cette impénétrable horreur nous signifie?
>
> ("Le Hibou")

The implied answer is that the universe is the work of an evil deity, and the image we have so frequently encountered of the sky as shroud or weighty ceiling confirms this implication. Hugo's representation of the world as the kingdom of a sadistic tyrant is superbly rich in poetry; the sense of terror before the manifestations of nature is conveyed in the above lines by battle imagery, which, however, does not degenerate into simple personifications of the sky and earth.

The other way in which Hugo writes about God, toward the end of *Dieu*, belongs to the domain of pure verbal affirmation; God is not here deduced to be evil, but declared to be light, good, and the point to which the whole universe aspires. This is apocalyptic, not mystical or devotional poetry, such as the following:

All manner of thing shall be well
When the tongues of flame are in-folded
Into the crowned knot of fire
And the fire and rose are one.
(T. S. Eliot, "Little Gidding")

Instead of having a basic body of Christian symbols to draw on like T. S. Eliot, Hugo must invent a language to reveal his own conception of God. Here, for example, is a grandiose passage on the Great Chain of Being and the movement of souls upward along it toward God:

Rien n'existe que lui, le flamboiement profond,
Et les âmes, — les grains de lumière, les mythes,
Le moi mystérieux, atomes sans limites,
Qui vont vers le grand moi, leur centre et leur aimant; —
Point touchant au zénith par le rayonnement,
Ainsi qu'un vêtement subissant la matière,
Traversant tour à tour dans l'étendue entière
La formule de chair propre à chaque milieu;
Ici la sève, ici le sang, ici le feu;
Blocs, arbres, griffes, dents, fronts pensants, auréoles;
Retournant aux cercueils comme à des alvéoles;
Mourant pour s'épurer, tombant pour s'élever,
Sans fin, ne se perdant que pour se retrouver,
Chaîne d'êtres qu'en haut l'échelle d'or réclame,
Vers l'éternel foyer volant de flamme en flamme,
Juste éclos du pervers, bon sorti du méchant,
Montant, montant, montant sans cesse, et le cherchant,
Et l'approchant toujours, mais sans jamais atteindre,
Lui, l'être qu'on ne peut toucher, ternir, éteindre,
Le voyant, le vivant, sans mort, sans nuit, sans mal,
L'idée énorme au fond de l'immense idéal!
("La Lumière")

What is particularly noticeable here is a depersonalization of the notions of both God and the soul: the former is an "idea," the latter an "atom" or "myth." The whole process of redemption—if that be the proper term for Hugo's theology—assumes the aspect of a play of beams of light in movement, a mechanical spectacle. In this attempt to avoid representing God in anthropomorphic terms, Hugo offers us a conception of Him as abstract as that of the exploding universe. By contrast, we might compare, in terms of poetic effect, a passage from the *Purgatorio* on the relation of God and the soul:

> Esce di mano a lui che la vagheggia
> Prima che sia, — a guisa di fanciulla
> Che piangendo e ridendo pargoleggia, —
> L'anima semplicetta, che sa nulla,
> Salvo che, mossa da lieto fattore,
> Volentier torna a ciò che la trastulla.
>
> (XVI, 85–90)

The homely comparison and the strongly anthropomorphic Creator suggest immediately a certain feeling about God, although Dante knew, of course, that this is poetic metaphor and not theology. But it connects God with human life in a way the passage from Hugo does not. On the other hand, when Dante must represent a vision of God at the end of the *Paradiso*, he simply resorts to the highly symbolic description of three rings of light, which is very evocative in the context of Christian tradition. Hugo's *flamboiement profond* is an equally rich, almost mystical symbol of God, but he is not satisfied with it and adds epithet after epithet until God is merely abstracted into an "idea."

The difficulty Hugo experienced in finishing *Dieu* seems to have lain in his inability to reach a final statement or evocation of God. He heaps image upon image, as if never feeling that he has definitively expressed his thoughts. The poem breaks off with the speaker's death, but continuations were sketched out. The most thorough editors of *Dieu* have suggested not only that doubt does not really yield to faith in the course of the poem, but even that the somber "Voix" may have at one time been intended as a conclusion, to follow the visions of God as light.[7] In that case, the cyclic structure of *Dieu* would have risen from the atheistic "La Chauve-souris" to an intimation of God, only to fall back into somber intuitions of deity's indifference. In any event, Hugo's manuscripts and notes do not seem to indicate any final point of certainty about godhead or its nature.

If we contrast the last part of *Dieu*, however, with the earlier suggestions of a tyrannical God, we realize that only the latter hold together poetically; they are not empty affirmations about an "idea," but visions of man in his universe attempting to pierce the mystery of it. In short, Hugo's gifts are at their fullest when his imagination is at its most demonic. We can better understand this cleavage in Hugo's prophetic poetry if we recall that from an early point in his career the

---

[7] *Dieu* ("Le Seuil du gouffre"), ed. Journet and Robert, 144–45.

sinister fascinated him, while his occultist theology developed only later. Furthermore, his particular form of occultism is rationalistic, as befits its roots in late antique thought, rather than oriented toward myth and symbol. It is difficult to imagine how this theology could be reconciled with demonic myth in an extended poem, and the proof is that neither *Dieu* nor *La Fin de Satan* seems to be informed by a dialectic pattern. In *La Fin de Satan,* the universe is first evil and, then, after Satan's change of heart, good. This is simple antithesis. Similarly, *Dieu* is made up of visions of the world under the sway of evil or nonexistent gods, which are simply juxtaposed to affirmations of God's goodness. There is no dialectic progression from one view to the other, no synthesis arrived at in stages. Vigny failed to write his projected *Fin de Satan* through perhaps similar incapacities, and Baudelaire escaped from dualism, as a poet at least, only when he wrote "Le Voyage" for the second edition of *Les Fleurs du mal.* But Hugo's poetic imagination could not bridge his gap of faith. Probably the only nineteenth-century French poet who succeeded in working out a perfectly articulated mythic poem on good and evil was Rimbaud, in *Une Saison en enfer.*

Despite his failure to bring *Dieu* and *La Fin de Satan* to conclusion, however, no other French romantic wrote such hallucinatory poems on the intimation of evil as Hugo; this achievement is unrelated to his inability to complete his long prophetic poems and confirms our contention that the demonic cast of imagination, in one form or another, dominates much of the best of French romantic verse. Hugo tried harder than any other to believe in an omnipotent God of goodness and justice, but his poetic powers never allowed him completely to express this. Nevertheless, in his last work, *La Légende des siècles,* he managed to suggest at least that God is an avenger, and, thereby, of course, the more primitive Judaeo-Christian conceptions of Him.

La Légende des siècles is largely a series of romances and myths with, here and there, a piece of prophetic poetry or apocalyptics inserted. The work promises, for the most part, no ultimate revelation of godhead, but consists of "little epics" or epic fragments, in which the conflict of good and evil is represented in heroic and legendary terms. Here Hugo is working in conventions which, if they do not produce such brilliant poetry as the best parts of *La Fin de Satan* and *Dieu,* allowed him at least to complete his task. Both God and Satan appear in *La Légende* in traditional mythic forms. In "Puissance égale bonté," for example, God and Eblis, the Islamic devil, make a wager over the extent of their creative powers (one recalls the beginning of Job); Eblis creates the spider, which he then offers to God as raw material:

> Et Dieu prit l'araignée et la mit au milieu
> Du gouffre qui n'était pas encor le ciel bleu;
> Et l'Esprit regarda la bête; sa prunelle,
> Formidable, versait la lueur éternelle;
> Le monstre, si petit qu'il semblait un point noir,
> Grossit alors, et fut soudain énorme à voir;
> Et Dieu le regardait de son regard tranquille;
> Une aube étrange erra sur cette forme vile;
> L'affreux ventre devint un globe lumineux;
> Et les pattes, changeant en sphères d'or leurs noeuds,
> S'allongèrent dans l'ombre en grands rayons de flamme;
> Iblis leva les yeux, et tout à coup l'infâme,
> Ebloui, se courba sous l'abîme vermeil;
> Car Dieu, de l'araignée, avait fait le soleil.

The metamorphosis, a common enough mythic pattern in Hugo's later poetry, is particularly successful here: the strange association between spider and sun is of the sort critics are wont to call pre-surrealist, although it is typical of the sinister high romantic imagination. God's creative powers, we must also note, do not lie in His hands, in accordance with the Psalmist's notion of His handiwork, but in His eye. God is the eye which peers into the darkest corner: "L'oeil était dans la tombe et regardait Caïn" ("La Conscience"). In "Le Titan," when the Titan has broken the bonds imposed on him by the Olympians, he crawls through the earth to the other side, where he contemplates infinity:

> Il sent en lui la joie obscure de l'abîme;
> Il subit, accablé de soleils et de cieux,
> L'inexprimable horreur des lieux prodigieux.
> Il regarde, éperdu, le vrai, ce précipice.
> Evidence sans borne, ou fatale, ou propice!
> O stupeur! il finit par distinguer, au fond
> De ce gouffre où le jour avec la nuit se fond,
> A travers l'épaisseur d'une brume éternelle,
> Dans on ne sait quelle ombre énorme, une prunelle!

The counterpart to God's all-seeing is His power to make Himself invisible. In "Suprématie," God appears before the lesser deities of the Hindu pantheon, and, in answer to the claims of Indra, the sky god, to seeing all creation, asks:

> — Vois-tu ce brin de paille?"
> Dit l'étrange clarté d'où sortait une voix.
> Indra baissa la tête et cria : "Je le vois.
> Lumière, je te dis que j'embrasse tout l'être;
> Toi-même, entends-tu bien, tu ne peux disparaître
> De mon regard, jamais éclipsé ni décru!
>
> A peine eut-il parlé qu'elle avait disparu.

Invisibility is, of course, merely a variant on the theme of darkness. It is useful to compare the God of *La Légende*, who appears as an eye or else withdraws from sight, with the symbolism of the earlier part of *Dieu*. There, God's refusal to be contemplated or to be figured in any stable way implies His sinister character, His enmity to mankind. But in *La Légende*, God's inaccessibility represents His omnipotence with no sinister overtones. Darkness is a sign of His majesty: in the closing line of the last poem He declares, "Je n'aurais qu'à souffler et tout serait de l'ombre" ("Abîme"). This does not imply that God is a menacing figure but simply bespeaks His power, as set above that of natural forces and inferior deities.

The Satan of *La Légende des siècles* is not the supreme deity of the early parts of *Dieu* nor God's antagonist as in *La Fin de Satan*. He now appears on earth, lurking behind evil-doers or identified with false gods. His presence is especially felt in the lurid medieval tales whose very landscape suggests demonic conspiracy. "Les Conseillers probes et libres" will serve as an example. A warlord of some vague medieval epoch has summoned his vassals:

> Sont présents cent barons et chevaliers, la fleur
> Du grand arbre héraldique et généalogique
> Que ce sol noir nourrit de sa sève tragique.
> . . . .
> Dans ce réseau de chefs qui couvrait l'Italie,
> Je passe Théodat, prince de Trente; Elie,
> Despote d'Avenzo, qu'a réclamé l'oubli;
> Ce borgne Ordelafo, le bourreau de Forli;
> Lascaris, que sa tante Alberte fit eunuque;
> Othobon, sieur d'Assise, et Tibalt, sieur de Lucque;

The rich interplay of proper names and epithets gives a condensed feeling of the darker ages and their brutal, picturesque history. These personages, and many others, assemble before the cathedral:

> Derrière eux, sur la pierre auguste d'un portail,
> Est sculpté Satan, roi, forçat, épouvantail,
> L'effrayant ramasseur de haillons de l'abîme,
> Ayant sa hotte au dos, pleine d'âmes, son crime
> Sur son aile qui ploie, et son roc noir qui luit
> Dans son poing formidable, et, dans ses yeux, la nuit.

The council has been convoked to divide up spoils and plan further rapine. The city in which it is held is itself an occupied one:

> Dans Ancône, est-ce deuil, terreur, indifférence?
> Tout se tait; les maisons, les bouges, les palais,
> Ont bouché leur lucarne ou fermé leurs volets;
> Le cadran qui dit l'heure a l'air triste et funeste.
>
> Le soleil luit aux cieux comme dans une peste . . .

After the sycophantic speeches by which the Holy Roman Emperor is greeted, each lord present is meted out a fief to plunder and terrorize, while churchmen condone the proceedings and receive their own sinecures. Finally,

> Pendant que le conseil se tenait de la sorte,
> Et qu'ils parlaient ainsi dans cette ville morte,
> Et que le maître avait sous ses pieds ces prélats,
> Ces femmes, ces barons en habits de galas,
> Et l'Italie au loin comme une solitude,
> Quelques seigneurs, ainsi qu'ils en ont l'habitude,
> Regardant derrière eux d'un regard inquiet,
> Virent que le Satan de pierre souriait.

"Les Conseillers probes et libres" suggests rather well the peculiar coloring of so many poems of *La Légende*. These are emphatically not "historical" poems, such as Leconte de Lisle was writing; they do not give the impression of highly researched attempts to recreate any specific period of history. Instead, they evoke a fantastic past, whose meaning is more anagogical than sociological. Hugo did not really care about sound historiography, and the proof is that, living in the first great age of historical study, he principally relied for inspiration on the already quaint, outmoded seventeenth-century encyclopedic dictionary of Moréri. Hugo merely needed a certain amount of information or lore about which his imagination could then play freely.

The epic fragments of *La Légende des siècles* tend to follow certain patterns. They present the conflict of good and evil in political terms: kings, knights, tyrants, and new gods rising to overthrow the old ones are typical figures. The central theme of the collection might be defined as the revelation of power, since the tales are commonly built around the appearance of an avenging hero or deity come to mete out justice. The world of *La Légende* is thus seen to stand between the domain of realism and the absolute, anagogical realm of God and Satan presented in *Dieu* and in parts of *La Fin de Satan*, thereby lessening the poetic problems. In the latter poems, the difficulty lies partly in the fact that deity is more a presence than an actor; here Hugo could depict men and gods in action. While Hugo failed to complete his equivalents of the *Commedia* or *Paradise Lost*, the less ambitious genre of the legend proved to be an excellent vehicle for his need to express both visions of evil and the intimation of a benevolent supreme being. Furthermore, *La Légende* finally provided Hugo with a new and appropriate thematic use for the fantastic architectural imagery, which, as we have already seen, obsessed him from a very early point in his career. The introductory poem of the collection sets the tone:

> Et qu'est-ce maintenant que ce livre, traduit
> Du passé, du tombeau, du gouffre et de la nuit?
> C'est la tradition tombée à la secousse
> Des révolutions que Dieu déchaîne et pousse;
> Ce qui demeure après que la terre a tremblé;
> Décombre où l'avenir, vague aurore, est mêlé;
> C'est la construction des hommes, la masure
> Des siècles, qu'emplit l'ombre et que l'idée azure,
> L'affreux charnier-palais en ruine, habité
> Par la mort et bâti par la fatalité,
>
> . . . .
> Ce livre, c'est le reste effrayant de Babel;
> C'est la lugubre Tour des Choses, l'édifice
> Du bien, du mal, des pleurs, du deuil, du sacrifice,
> Fier jadis, dominant les lointains horizons,
> Aujourd'hui n'ayant plus que de hideux tronçons,
> Epars, couchés, perdus dans l'obscure vallée;
> C'est l'épopée humaine, âpre, immense, — écroulée.
>
> ("La Vision d'où est sorti ce livre")

The imagery of sinister ruined buildings becomes a suitable symbol of the past; labyrinthine convolutions represent not only the concrete rem-

nants of the ages but also the mysterious complexity of fate and freedom, good and evil. With *La Légende* a number of Hugo's favorite
themes and images converge in a harmonious whole: the eye of heaven,
night, strange architecture, God's remoteness, vengeance, and revelation
all combine to create an atmosphere heavy with suggestions of evil but
illuminated here and there with apocalyptic warnings.

In discussing Hugo's later poetry I have not gone further than *La
Fin de Satan, Dieu*, and *La Légende des siècles*, although there is much
of poetic interest to explore, because none of it would add a great deal
to the questions of theme and symbolism which we have been investigating. These three works are without doubt Hugo's most ambitious
poetic projects in the sense that they were conceived of as great wholes,
whereas a book like *Les Contemplations* is simply a series of poems of
varying inspiration put together with some semblance of thematic
order. (The same charge of miscellany might be brought against the
later additions to *La Légende* but, by and large, they reinforce the tone
of the original series.) Furthermore, as Hugo pointed out in the 1859
preface to *La Légende*, he thought of it as forming with *Dieu* and *La Fin
de Satan* an even greater whole which would give a comprehensive account of the Great Chain of Being: evil or the sub-human, mankind in
its diversity, and God or the concept of the infinite. Of course, these
three books, as they stand, are related only insofar as they are the work
of one powerful imagination. Anyone who has examined Hugo's notes
and worksheets knows that he strove constantly to arrive at syntheses
without ever working out the necessary articulations.[8] The failure to
achieve a dialectic in *Dieu* or *La Fin de Satan* is merely a particular case
of his incapacity for putting an entire building behind his peristyle, to
borrow a metaphor from the preface to *La Légende*, in which Hugo
argues desperately that his mythic poems are not fragments but will
eventually be seen as a coherent whole. Whatever we may think of the
unity of Hugo's thought and poetic practice, however, *La Fin de Satan,
Dieu*, and *La Légende* still remain the most persistent and successful attempt in nineteenth-century French poetry to see, in epic scope, the
universe, past, present, and future.

We have seen that much French romantic poetry can be interpreted
as a series of questions or propositions about good and evil, with the

---

[8]Hugo's notes are reproduced by his more thorough editors, such as Journet
and Robert, or Paul Berret in his edition of *La Légende des siècles* (Paris, 1920).

awareness of evil becoming especially dominant. The poets speak of God and Satan with varying degrees of literalness: for Vigny or Petrus Borel, God is merely a figure to designate Christianity or the bourgeois mentality, while for Baudelaire and Hugo, God and Satan have genuine theological meaning. These last two poets were consequently the most obsessed by dualism. Nerval is another matter: his conception of godhead is completely cyclic, with Christianity as a temporary eclipse of the true gods. All these writers share, moreover, a post-Christian view of the world, for even Baudelaire uses only fragments of traditional religion, and Hugo's God coincides but now and then with that of Christianity. The feeling that the cycle of history is at an end can be found in Gautier and even Musset (as in the beginning of "Rolla"), while in other poets, especially Nerval and Hugo, the themes of apocalypse and regeneration occur.

The symbolism which supports theological themes in French romantic poetry grows out of traditional archetypes, but it is frequently given realistic, contemporary reference or even constitutes a demonic mode of the familiar symbolism of godhead. For example, the nineteenth-century city is sinister, as in Sainte-Beuve or Vigny, while the very notion of architecture is associated for Hugo with the labyrinths of hell: Satan's Pandemonium rather than the New Jerusalem is the relevant archetype. Baudelaire carries perhaps farthest, with his rich use of commonplace detail, the identification of a real contemporary metropolis with the demonic citadel of tradition. At the same time, he created a new version of the terrestrial paradise: in his verse the tropics have intense emotive connotations which are without analogue in other French romantic poets. They rarely conceived of an earthly form of heaven, with the possible exception of Nerval, whose Mediterranean landscapes fulfill much the same function.

Complementing the symbolism of place is that of motion: movement and immobility are recurrent themes, and either may express serenity or despair. There is a demonic circular movement in "Les Destinées" and demonic aimless movement in *Dieu*. At the same time, Hugo's Great Chain of Being is a variant of the divine circle, its fixity suggesting lack of change, while the immobility of Satan in *La Fin de Satan* implies imprisonment and suffering.

But the most persistent image is doubtless the sky, which can represent paradisiacal light, as often in Baudelaire, or the dividing and indifferent blue which torments the godseeker of *Dieu*. The converse of the bright sky is a dark prison-like lid, with the attendant image of a black sun pouring forth shadow. The dark sky, which shuts man off from the God who traditionally lies behind it, provides the characteristic backdrop for a demonic gospel, in which the good news is ironically that God has withdrawn from mankind.

Many changes can, of course, be wrought within these patterns. In Vigny, nature is no longer opposed to the city but becomes equally hostile, and in Hugo, the landscape inspires panic. Nerval opposed the consoling bowels of the earth, the traditional hell, to the evil sky, while considering nature as belonging to the former. Baudelaire, finally, could use almost any symbol—sky, ocean, city, wildwood—in either a divine or demonic sense. But it is perhaps Hugo who carried farthest the principle of the anagogical ambiguity of any image: in the early part of *Dieu*, Satan's and God's traditional attributes are inextricably mingled, while in *La Légende des siècles* both, though remaining distinct, are vested with the power of darkness.

Regardless, therefore, of the comparative merits of each poet or poem, it appears that demonic symbolism reached its most complex form with Hugo—and to a lesser extent, with Baudelaire—about the middle of the century. Leconte de Lisle, who was almost Baudelaire's contemporary, attempted in "Qaïn" and "La Fin de l'Homme" to rework the demonic interpretation of Genesis which goes back to Byron, but his pessimism was more literary than theological.[9] It is only with Rimbaud and *Une Saison en enfer* that the dialectics of God and Satan received a final statement and solution in French poetry, for Rimbaud drew together the various strands of divine and demonic imagery that had run through the French romantics and devised an issue from their dualism: he equated Christian good and evil and thereby rejected both of them.

Although the history of the demonic imagination in nineteenth-century French poetry ends, for our purposes, with Hugo, certain dominant themes of the symbolists consist of further variations on the Satanic: the rejection of life for the artifact, the worship of sterility as opposed to nature, and the obsession with nothingness all derive clearly, however altered in context, from romantic concerns. The symbolists, insofar as they were "decadents," took a rather perverse delight in elaborating, without any theological *inquiétude*, the anti-natural visions

[9]See Irving Putter, *The Pessimism of Leconte de Lisle: The Work and the Time* (Berkeley, 1961), 389.

of the romantics in which minerals replaced trees, death reproduction, imagination reality. Finally, the wheel came full swing, and in Proust the true life of art, as opposed to the vile everyday one, leads again to resurrection and salvation: estheticism has become a new Way of the Cross, replacing the old Christian one. Satan's attributes become redemptory. But that is the subject of another book.

INDEX

173